ALASKA
A CLIMBING GUIDE

MICHAEL WOOD & COLBY COOMBS

THE MOUNTAINEERS BOOKS

Published by

The Mountaineers Books

1001 SW Klickitat Way, Suite 201

Seattle, WA 98134

First edition, 2001

Published simultaneously in Great Britain by Cordee, 3a DeMontfort Street, Leicester, England, LE1 7HD

Manufactured in the United States of America

Project Editor: Julie Van Pelt

Copy Editor: Steve Mackay

Cover and Book Design: Ani Rucki

Layout: Ani Rucki

Mapmaker: Caitlin Palmer, Moore Creative Designs

Topos: Gray Mouse Graphics

Photographers: Richard Baranow, John Bauman, Mark Bebie, Jeff Benowitz, Thomas Bol, Greg Collins, Colby Coombs,
Roman Dial, Chris Flowers, James Garret, Kennan Harvey, Ruedi Homberger, Mikey K, Dieter Klose, John Krakauer,
Danny Kost, Philip Marshall, Brian McCullough, Brian Okonek, Raina Panarese, Michael Pennings, Bill Pilling, Joe Reichert,
Paul Roderick, Charlie Sassara, Georgie Stanley, Carl Tobin, Randy Waitman, Bradford Washburn, Mike Wood

Cover photograph: *Mount Saint Elias (Photo: Paul Roderick)*

Library of Congress Cataloging-in-Publication Data

Wood, Michael, 1968–

　　Alaska : a climbing guide / by Mike Wood and Colby Coombs—1st ed.

　　　　p.　　　cm.

　　　ISBN 0-89886-724-X (pbk.)

　　　1. Mountaineering—Alaska—Guidebooks. 2. Trails—Alaska—Guidebooks. 3. Alaska—Guidebooks. I. Coombs, Colby. II. Title

　　GV199.42.A4W66 2001

　　796.52'2'09798—dc　　　　　　　　　　　　　　　　　　　2001007259

This book is dedicated to the spirit of Matt Porter,

who fully embodied the adventure and apprenticeship,

attitude and desire that this book is all about.

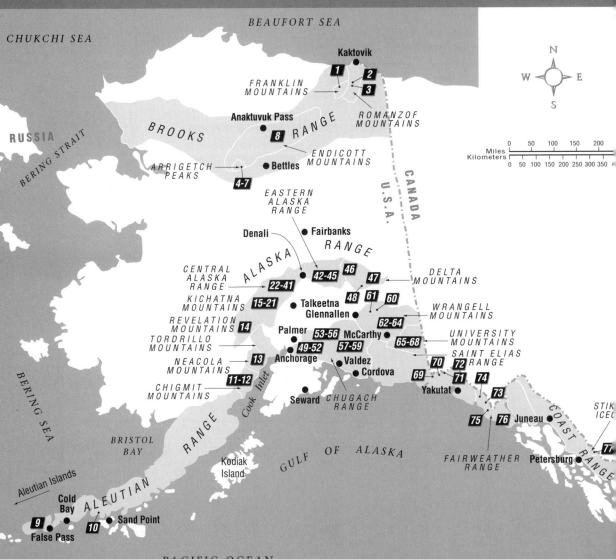

CHUKCHI SEA

BEAUFORT SEA

RUSSIA

BERING STRAIT

Kaktovik

1 **2** **3**

FRANKLIN
MOUNTAINS

ROMANZOF
MOUNTAINS

Anaktuvuk Pass

BROOKS **8** RANGE

ENDICOTT
MOUNTAINS

ARRIGETCH
PEAKS

Bettles

4-7

EASTERN
ALASKA
RANGE

Denali

Fairbanks

RANGE

CENTRAL
ALASKA
RANGE

ALASKA

42-45 **46**

47

DELTA
MOUNTAINS

22-41

KICHATNA
MOUNTAINS **15-21**

Talkeetna

48 **61** **60**

REVELATION
MOUNTAINS **14**

Glennallen

WRANGELL
MOUNTAINS

Palmer

62-64

TORDRILLO
MOUNTAINS

53-56 McCarthy

UNIVERSITY
MOUNTAINS

49-52

57-59

65-68

NEACOLA
MOUNTAINS **13** Anchorage

Valdez

SAINT ELIAS
RANGE

CHIGMIT
MOUNTAINS **11-12**

Cook Inlet

Cordova

69 **70**

71 **74**

BERING
SEA

Seward CHUGACH
RANGE

Yakutat

73

COAST RANGE

STIK
ICEC

BRISTOL
BAY

RANGE

75 **76** Juneau

FAIRWEATHER
RANGE

Petersburg

77

Kodiak
Island

GULF OF ALASKA

Aleutian Islands

Cold
Bay

9 ALEUTIAN **10** Sand Point

False Pass

PACIFIC OCEAN

N
W E
S

Miles
Kilometers

0 50 100 150 200
0 50 100 150 200 250 300 350

CANADA
U.S.A.

CONTENTS

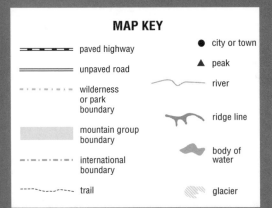

MAP KEY

▬▬▬▬ paved highway	● city or town
═══════ unpaved road	▲ peak
─·─·─·─ wilderness or park boundary	∿ river
▭ mountain group boundary	⋎ ridge line
─··─··─ international boundary	◟ body of water
─ ─ ─ ─ trail	▨ glacier

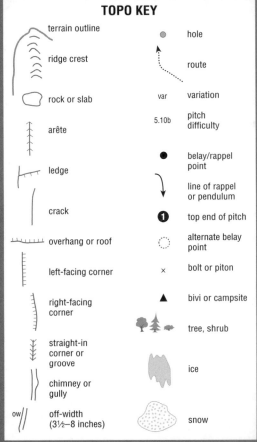

TOPO KEY

terrain outline	● hole
ridge crest	⇗ route
rock or slab	var variation
arête	5.10b pitch difficulty
ledge	● belay/rappel point
crack	↴ line of rappel or pendulum
overhang or roof	❶ top end of pitch
left-facing corner	⭕ alternate belay point
right-facing corner	× bolt or piton
straight-in corner or groove	▲ bivi or campsite
chimney or gully	🌲 tree, shrub
ow off-width (3½–8 inches)	❄ ice
	snow

ACKNOWLEDGEMENTS

A huge amount of gratitude and respect is extended to the list of people below for their assistance and contributions to this project. All of the route information was written or proofread by ascentionists of the route. Like so many guidebooks, this would not have worked without them:

Mike Alkaitis, Dave Anderson, Richard Baranow, John Bauman, Kelly Bay, Christian Beckwith, Jeff Benowitz, Barry Blanchard, Tom Bol, Josh Borof, Tyson Bradley, Doug Byerly, Greg Collins, Kelly Cordes, Roman Dial, Keith Eckelmeyer, Chip Faurot, Chris Flowers, James Garrett, Josie Garton, Kurt Gloyer, Kennan Harvey, Vaughn Hauffler, Peter Haussler, Gardner Heaton, Jeff Hollenbaugh, Ruedi Homberger, Steve House, Donna Jefferson, Mark Jonas, Stan Justice, Dieter Klose, Danny Kost, Jon Krakauer, Mike Litzow, Keli Mahoney, Arthur Mannix, Christopher Mannix, Phillip Marshall, Brian McCullough, David McGivern, Mike Meekin, Daryl Miller, Brian Okonek, Andi Orgler, Caitlin Palmer, Nick Parker, Meg Perdue, Mike Pennings, Nancy Phfeiffer, Bill Pilling, Matt Porter, Joe Reichert, David Roberts, Roger Robinson, Paul Roderick, Charlie Sassara, Andy Selters, Peter Sennhauser, Jay Smith, Kirby Spangler, Georgie Stanley, Karl Swanson, Jack Tackle, Brian Teale, Carl Tobin, John Tuckey, Mark Twight, Randy Waitman, and Bradford Washburn.

On Mount Eldridge in the Central Alaska Range (Photo: Brian Okonek)

FOREWORD

by Brian Okonek

Mike Wood and Colby Coombs, as with many climbers, don't quite fit society's traditional molds. In their rebellion they found satisfaction, contentment, and purpose among the rugged mountains of Alaska.

With tireless energy these two have attempted and climbed an enviable number of Alaskan routes. Not all these climbs were pure fun. Tragically, the lives of close friends and belay partners have been ripped from them by uncaring mountains. Hard lessons have been learned, their lives' meanings probed. Yet the mountains continue to pull them back.

Their experiences with these cloud-shrouded sentinels piqued their curiosity about those who had climbed before them. What stories were unfolded pitch by pitch on routes throughout the ranges of Alaska? What peaks beckoned in ranges beyond the horizon? What impacts are climbers having on the wild mountains of Alaska?

Most of Mike and Colby's professional careers have been spent instructing and leading novice mountaineers in the way of the mountains and fostering an attitude of sensitivity for the alpine environment, while passing on techniques for safe climbing. Their love of Alaska's mountains, the fascination they have with their beauty, the interest they have in their history, their concerns for the future, and their desire to share information with fellow climbers led to this book.

Since the first mountaineers ventured to the remote peaks of Alaska, the rest of us have benefitted from the trails they broke. Exploratory, lengthy overland approaches to the mountains gave way to maps, aerial photos, and a mind-numbing transition from civilization to base camp in airplanes. Crude equipment has evolved into today's stronger, lighter, warmer, and more efficient gear.

Looking out my window I can trace the routes of early explorers and mountaineers who struggled just to get to the base of Denali less then 100 years ago. Along the way they faced fast-moving rivers; tangled alders; deep winter snow; and intricate, glacier-filled valleys with nothing but common sense and hearsay as their guides. Now nearly every peak has a name, official or unofficial. Most have been climbed and each has its story.

Mountaineering lore has long been an important part of the climbing tradition. Before I ever climbed I had read with barely containable excitement of climbers' exploits. Dave Johnston's vivid accounts of traversing the entire Alaska Range from Wonder Lake to Talkeetna, with side trips to both summits of Denali and all three summits of Mount Hunter, and later returning to do the first winter ascent of Denali sent shivers down my spine. I read Johnston's worn mountaineering books from split-log shelves with gusto and I was hooked on climbing before I even had an ice ax.

While I was still in high school, an extensive collection of mountaineering literature bequeathed to the Mountaineering Club of Alaska by the indomitable climber Vin Hoeman was housed in my bedroom. Among those pages was a treasure chest of exhilaration, camaraderie, struggle, and fear of challenging the splendors of the mountains. Club members would stop by to check out a book and would always share the memories of a trip. Even Fred Beckey visited while on yet another Alaskan odyssey and would dig for information, flashing photos of peaks that he had his eye on. Finally, one magical spring day I stepped out of the pages and photos into real mountains with my mentor. This book will give you the dreams to begin such a journey.

As much as I love mountaineering history, I have always resisted guidebooks. Mountaineering, like everything else, advances with the accumulated knowledge passed along by those who came before. It makes sense to take advantage of lessons learned and mistakes made and to use the most advanced equipment available. With guidebooks, there is danger that too many people will be attracted to a given peak, resulting in overcrowding and degradation. Climbers might also choose to rely solely on a guidebook, not searching out valuable information from other sources. Ultimately, my fear is that there will no longer be places for future generations to experience the unknown, to be explorers themselves.

With that in mind, use the climbs in this book not as a checklist, but as a springboard for your imagination; and take the environmental ethics within the pages of this book to heart. It is your responsibility to keep the mountains of Alaska wild.

There are many hundreds of climbs to be done and you should not let a book inhibit your exploratory spirit. Mountaineering is a free-spirited activity that can be enjoyed at many levels of difficulty and style. Whether you prefer the long approaches and the security of a pioneer-type expedition or are pushing the cutting edge of today's techniques and equipment on committing alpine climbs, you will find inspiration in Alaska's peaks.

PREFACE

We have all had moments in the mountains when we have made decisions, especially at altitude where the lack of oxygen clouds the brain, and have asked, "Was that the most prudent decision?" In the spring of 1998, Colby and I made one such decision after waiting 7 days hunkered down at 17,000 feet on Denali's West Buttress. With climbing ropes holding the tents down, we shared a three-person tent with our future wives, Meg Perdue and Caitlin Palmer. Colby was thinking about writing a guidebook that captured the essence of climbing in Alaska, and I had long dreamed of creating a resource to inspire the imaginations of aspiring Alaska mountaineers. Two more days of storms were spent daydreaming about the countless routes that best represent Alaskan mountaineering. The first of many lists was made, and our destinies to climb them all were paved. We aborted the West Buttress, but we turned around at base camp to make use of a 3-day window and climbed the Cassin—a shoe-in route for "the book."

The Mountaineers Books would not wait the lifetime it would take us to climb all the routes, so we have relied heavily on a core group of committed Alaskan mountaineers to provide first ascent photos and route descriptions. All descriptions have been edited or rewritten by climbers who know the routes firsthand, a monumental task due to the intricacies of alpine routes. The quality of this project is tied to these individuals. The reader should beware that, due to the ever-changing nature of alpine routes, inaccuracies should be expected.

The Alaskan landscape has long inspired and stimulated the imaginations of explorers. Of particular concern to the authors is the potential impact this book will have on pristine wilderness. It is our belief that modern, educated, and ethical backcountry users will leave no lasting trace of their passage. It is our greatest hope that visiting climbers will recognize the need for impeccable minimum-impact practices and care enough to follow through. *Alaska: A Climbing Guide* skims the surface of the vast amount of climbing opportunities available in the Great State. It is a small resource to help direct climbers to mountaineering objectives that suit their abilities and interests. We hope you enjoy the read as much as we have enjoyed putting it together.

Tom Walter descending Hydra in the Revelation Mountains (Photo: Greg Collins)

INTRODUCTION

Alaska is a place of myth and legend, particularly for the climber. Stories abound of seemingly perpetual winter and storms in the midst of vast, impenetrable wilderness. Most notably, we hear about the "Alaska Factor," an affectionate term climbers use to describe the uniqueness that makes climbs in Alaska seem harder, longer, and then longer still than they first appear. This mythic quality can be distilled down to the basic ingredients that make Alaska what it is, and that make the climbing so all-encompassing.

NORTHERN LATITUDE

Alaska's vast amount of land starts at 54 degrees north latitude and goes to 73 degrees north latitude. The Alaska Range is centered at 62 degrees latitude. Alaska's proximity to the Arctic Circle, North Pole, and Bering Sea affects the weather, available sunlight, and atmospheric pressure. Cold air descends from the north, big storm systems roll in off the Pacific, and the thinning of the atmosphere due to "atmospheric squash" makes the effects of any given elevation equivalent to those 2,000–3,000 feet higher than at the equator.

SUNLIGHT

There is a remarkable rhythm in Alaska that coincides with the number of daylight hours. In the dead of winter, a month or two on either side of the winter solstice (December 21), the sun is so low on the horizon that in the northern part of the state it fails to make an appearance at all. A blanket of cold and darkness stifles outside activity and locals' thoughts of climbing are all but quelled. Conversely, during the

months before and after summer solstice (June 21), the sun barely sets and the pulse rate is rapid across the state. By May, the increased buzz of outdoor activity signals the arrival of summer and the seasonal migration of climbers. In jumping-off towns like Talkeetna, the Gore-Tex literally blooms on Main Street with climbers from all over the world dressed in their fashion wear.

TEMPERATURE AND ALTITUDE

Except for reflected heat from glaciers during the day, Alaska can rarely be considered a balmy place. Average temperatures in the summer lie between 55 and 65 degrees Farenheit and seldom rise above 70 degrees. On the glaciers, it can be freezing in the shade throughout the summer. Alaska has sixteen mountains over 14,000 feet, so when you reach the higher elevations it is always cold. With the wind, temperatures of minus 20 to minus 30 degrees Farenheit are not uncommon above 17,000 feet. Experienced climbers of 8000-meter peaks have commented on the extreme cold at the higher elevations during the summer not found in equatorial mountain ranges like the Himalayas.

It is important to note that the extreme cold puts the body under stress, often complicating altitude related illness. The cold makes climbers more susceptible to both high-altitude pulmonary edema (HAPE) and high-altitude cerebral edema (HACE).

REMOTENESS

Alaska's enormous size, lack of roads, and small population brings true definition to the term "remote." In

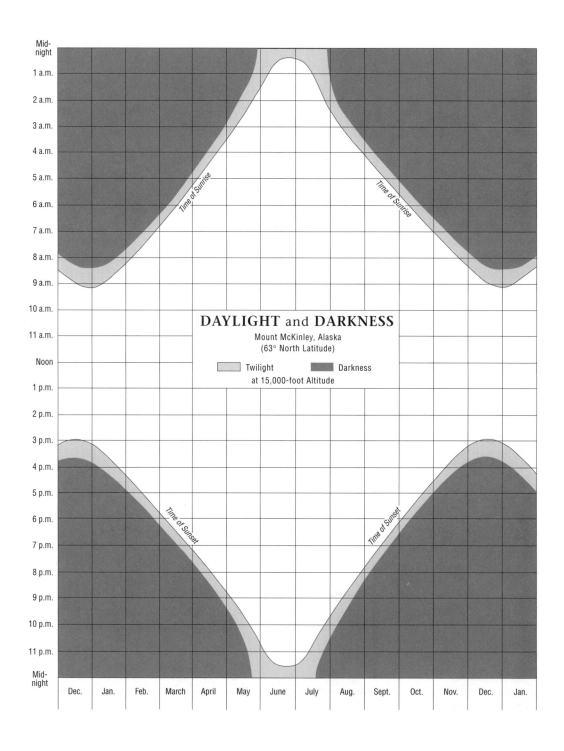

DAYLIGHT and DARKNESS

Mount McKinley, Alaska
(63° North Latitude)

Twilight   Darkness

at 15,000-foot Altitude

the early part of the century, just the approaches to climbs took months of careful navigation, treacherous river crossings, and serious bushwhacking. With the advent of small, fixed-wing airplanes equipped with ski/wheels, tundra tires, or floats, climbers gained access to almost anywhere in the entire state.

Present-day Alaska is more oriented toward accessing remote areas than are Pakistan, Patagonia, or Baffin Island. The aircraft, communication, and rescue support is unparalleled. This relative ease of getting into truly remote areas can give a false sense of security, false because access depends entirely on the weather. Parties should prepare for being marooned for days—even weeks—in some areas. If the weather is unflyable, the grocery store or hospital might as well be in another country.

HAZARDS:
Objective and Subjective

Weather

The weather defines the character of the mountains and climbing in Alaska. The mountains are incredibly glaciated due to constant precipitation and generally low seasonal temperatures.

The prevailing flow of weather is from the west, which carries huge amounts of moisture from the Arctic Ocean, Chukchi Sea, Bering Sea, and Pacific Ocean. When this moisture is carried inland it is elevated by the mountain ranges that border the vast majority of this state, cooling and leaving enormous amounts of precipitation on the mountain flanks. Patterns are evident in the summer and winter, and forecasters in Anchorage and Fairbanks do an admirable job of trying to predict what is coming our way. Nevertheless, elevation and temperature compound the variability of mountain weather.

It is important for climbers to get a sense of the weather pattern in their intended destination, prior to arriving in the mountains. Good websites for Alaska can be found at the National Weather Service, Alaska Region (listed in appendix B). Once in the mountains

it is possible to receive weather channel frequencies at the higher elevations. The safest bet, however, is to stick your head out of the tent and make your decision based on current observations and a pattern that may become obvious.

Bushwhacking

Hiking trails are a rare luxury in Alaska, and tales of struggling through Alaska's "bush" can rival the difficulty of any climb. Alder and willow bushes thrive along valleys and rivers and create an impregnable web. Patches of devil's club wound the unwary with infection-causing thorns. Thankfully, bush line gives way to tundra at about the 1,500–3,000-foot elevation statewide.

Other vegetation to be wary of includes the thick black spruce forests and the large amounts of deadfall in the coastal ranges. Picture clambering on top of the brush and not touching ground for hours or crawling on your knees along bear trails hoping you don't run into one. Add to that picture a large pack, sled, and skis and you are in for the Alaska experience!

River Crossings

Considered the most dangerous part of a mountaineering approach, Alaska rivers are of the classic, glacier fed, braided, and full-of-silt variety. The volume of water and the amount of silt fluctuate through spring and summer depending on temperatures at the glacial source. As the rivers flow to the lowlands and eventually the ocean, they accumulate runoff from other glaciers and rainwater and create braided channels up to a mile or more in width.

Glacial rivers are diurnal; the lowest water volume for safe crossing is dependent on the temperature at higher elevations and, to a lesser degree, on the amount of cloud cover. In the evenings, glacier temperatures at higher elevations dip below freezing, thus lowering the water volume by morning. The sun has the greatest effect on glacial melt during the months of April through August. Typically the rivers are at their lowest volumes in the morning after the previous day's melt has run out the toe of the glacier and the next day's melt has yet to begin. The rain does not significantly affect the amount of volume in a glacial river near its source.

The level of silt or "glacial flour" can make it difficult to judge the depth and the nature of the river bottom. River bottoms vary greatly. Some rivers are obvious because you can hear the boulders thundering down the river under the water.

Winter can be the opportune time to travel across rivers. Some rivers freeze solid and provide highways for travel into the backcountry. There are exceptions, as when the surface freezes, but glacial water generally still flows below. As the winter progresses the water level drops, creating a widening gap between the surface ice and the water below. In canyons, this gap can reach staggering distances—up to 20 to 30 feet—and pose a significant risk to the unfortunate victim who breaks through.

Glaciers

Alaska receives an abundant amount of annual snowfall, resulting in heavy glaciation in most of its mountain ranges. Some areas hold the largest mountain glaciers in the world. Active glaciers present endless obstacles that demand constant vigilance. Crevasses are the obvious hazard, but surface rivers, moulins, and loose moraine detritus below the snow line are equally hazardous. Just getting on and off a glacier with a raging river flowing along its flank can be an ordeal.

Above the snow line, the snowpack, wind, and fluctuating temperatures cause a huge variability in the strength and size of snow bridges spanning crevasses that can reach more than a 100 feet deep. Sudden changes in the terrain under a glacier can make the ice surface so jumbled it becomes impassible. Frequent whiteouts can make safe travel impossible, even with a GPS and compass. The firn zone, the area advancing up and down the glacier between the ablation zone (the part of the glacier where more snow melts or evaporates than falls) and the accumulation zone (the part where more snow falls than can melt or evaporate), is notorious for shallow snowpack and weak snow bridges. The thin snowpack can make it difficult to self-arrest in the event of a crevasse fall.

Proper education in the art of crevasse rescue is a prerequisite in Alaska. Standard glacier travel techniques in the lower 48, Europe, or South America may not be adequate in Alaska, where one must be prepared for a large fall while encumbered with a heavy pack and sled. It is not uncommon for three or four persons on a rope team, travelling perpendicular to a crevasse, to be on the same snow bridge simultaneously. The amount of gear you carry to sustain a 20- or 30-day expedition will break your back if you fall into a crevasse with your pack and sled unless you wear a chest harness.

Do not expect a glacial use-trail like that found on Denali's popular West Buttress route. The routes in this book more accurately represent the norm and require you to navigate your own trail.

Icefall

Abundant glaciation is perhaps most noticeable with the frequency of hanging glaciers on near-vertical faces. Most people who climb in Alaska will eventually have to expose themselves to an icefall. With no rhyme or reason for when they will next burp an iceberg, it is basically Russian Roulette for the climber exposed underneath. Scientists have tried to predict the random nature of icefalls using temperature gradient, snowfall, sunlight, shade, time of day, and even tidal fluctuation of the ocean to no avail. The existence of a debris pile at the base of a climb gives a clue to recent activity, but it is best to avoid or minimize your time exposed to icefall altogether.

Avalanches

This is by far the most dangerous factor when travelling and climbing on snowy mountains in Alaska. Avalanche hazard exists at one elevation or another year-round in Alaska. A strong background in ava-

Ice and snow slab avalanche on Mount Foraker (Photo: Brian Okonek)

lanche awareness cannot be emphasized enough. As with most avalanche hazard, it may not be the large terrain that catches you unaware, but the much smaller, less obvious terrain traps that are present on most routes. It can be easy to let one's guard down after leading the last hard pitch of ice and topping out on the easier, yet more dangerous, 40-degree slope.

Alaska is so immense in scale that it is difficult to calculate the terrain 4,000–6,000 feet above you. Vigilance and awareness of snow conditions, weather pat-

terns, and wind direction will help give you a clearer understanding of current and developing potential hazards.

Cornices

The large amount of snowfall combined with wind results in extensive cornicing on most of Alaska's snow peaks. On sharp-edged ridges it is not uncommon to see double cornices forming on both sides and leaving the climber no safe travel option. Stories of cornices collapsing under a climber's weight and re-quiring the partner to dive off the opposite side are not uncommon.

A cousin of the cornice is the "snow pod," which is a buildup of wind-blown snow under a rock roof. During the day, when the rock heats up, these bombs release and can be lethal.

Animals

The grizzly bear is sacred in Alaska and habituates nearly every climbing environment. While there is an obvious concern about bear attacks, the greater risk is that bears will learn to associate humans with food and end up getting shot. Responsible climbers will read up on techniques for travelling and camping in bear country to avoid unwanted confrontations (see appendix C).

The cunning, mischievous, and playful ravens have exploited ecological niches throughout Alaska. They have learned how to take advantage of unwary climbers and venture into camps when no one is around. Known to dig up poorly cached food supplies and enter tent vestibules or kitchens for a meal or just to wreak havoc, the raven is not to be underestimated.

Mosquitoes

Alaska's state bird is the willow ptarmigan and not the mosquito, but you may wonder why as you lie awake trying to ignore their deafening drone outside your tent. Mosquitoes have driven herds of caribou off cliffs and brought the strongest humans to the edge of sanity. If you anticipate travelling in the lowlands, pre-pare to cover all exposed flesh.

Alaskans

People in Alaska, especially those who live in the bush, like their sovereignty and personal space and are well-prepared to protect it. While it is less of a concern for the approaches in this book, research the legal rights-of-way if you choose to explore elsewhere. State and federal land managers are usually the best resources.

LOGISTICS

Radios

As we've emphasized, remoteness defines Alaska, and communication, or lack thereof, is a main contribu-tor. Remoteness is a quality to be preserved, but it translates quickly into a life-threatening situation if an accident occurs. The current availability of light-weight and portable communication technology is an asset to the mountaineer. Radios, cell phones, and emergency locator transmitters (ELTs) can provide the vital survival link in an emergency situation.

Depending on which part of the state you are in, a radio that broadcasts on Citizens' Band (CB), Ma-rine Band VHF, or Aircraft Band VHF frequencies should be required equipment. The CB radio was pre-viously used extensively by bush pilots in air-to-air and air-to-ground communication. Currently, apart from Denali National Park and Preserve, the CB radio has been replaced by the VHF. Federal regulations re-strict nonlicense holders (i.e., nonpilots) to life-and-limb use only. Many areas in Alaska use a set frequency that the air service monitors when flying in those mountains. It is important to know which frequen-cies the local air taxis monitor.

For coastal mountains the standard radio is the Ma-rine Band VHF, which broadcasts on frequencies used by boats. If you ask nicely, the boat captain should relay a message to the air taxi service. Again, it is im-portant to know which frequencies are monitored. Your air taxi operator should be able to tell you.

Cell phones have increased in popularity, but their range is limited to locales where repeaters have been installed. It is best to inquire locally.

An ELT is a one-way communication device that transmits on 121.50, a reserved emergency frequency. All planes are required to monitor this frequency, but nothing is foolproof.

The epic story related by Andrew Politz and Walter Gove is a case in point. During the pair's first ascent of the South Face of Mount Saint Elias, Walter Gove developed high altitude cerebral and pulmonary edema and became hypothermic and frostbitten. When they finally reached base camp, Politz turned on the ELT and put it in his parka pocket. The ELT transmitted for 24 hours before the batteries died. Politz waited in camp another 24 hours to make sure that a rescue wasn't underway. When certain that no help was coming, he began a harrowing trip to the coast to signal a boat with a flare gun. After a 44-hour walk, a crab boat confirmed seeing his flare and Gove was rescued by the Coast Guard.

"Line of sight" transmission is necessary for all but the ELT. This may require the party to travel to the highest point of elevation possible in order to reach a distant party.

Permits

Less than 1 percent of the land in Alaska is privately owned. The majority of the land is managed as national forests, national parks and wildlife refuges, Bureau of Land Management lands, and state parks. Native lands complete the makeup.

The relevant land management agency is discussed in the introduction to each mountain range. To date the only agency that regulates user groups is the National Park Service in Denali National Park and Preserve. Preregistration and a special use fee are required of climbers undertaking expeditions to Mount Foraker or Denali. In addition, park rangers request that climbing parties register for all areas they are visiting, and that they check in after the expedition has returned. This is a common courtesy that all national parks appreciate. It is very beneficial to climbers in the event of an accident because the national and state agencies will be called upon to assist in an emergency. The Forest Service and the Bureau of Land Management lack the ability at present to monitor private parties in Alaska.

HOW TO USE THIS BOOK

Hopefully, this book will be useful to the beginner as well as the experienced alpinist. We have described a variety of climbs to suit all abilities and provide inspiration for further ventures into the mountains of Alaska.

We have arranged the guide with the hope that the reader will pay attention to the introductory chapters in order to gain a true sense of what Alaska may hold in store. The book consists of seven mountain regions, described in a generally north-to-south order. Geography is not an exact science, and throughout the writing of this book we have tried to determine the difference between "ranges" and "mountains." The United States Geological Survey (USGS) has not established a definition used consistently to distinguish the difference. We use local names to distinguish mountain areas. We use "range" to signify a massive grouping of mountains, and "mountains" to specify a subgroup within the range. For example the Kichatna Mountains are within the Alaska Range. This standard of nomenclature has been used with some consistency throughout the state—with the great exceptions of the Chugach Range, the Wrangell Mountains, and the Saint Elias Range.

The introduction to each mountain range provides general information about the area, weather, and approaches. Specific information on the climb itself appears within each route chapter.

Route. This names the feature climbed on any given peak or lists the actual name of the climb.

Difficulty. This rating most often consists of an Alaska Grade (see Difficulty Ratings Explained below). Common climbing ratings are used in addition to the Alaska Grade. These ratings indicate grade or commitment, class, aid required, and ice ratings (see Difficulty Ratings Explained). Rock routes do not have an Alaska Grade. Pay attention to the description and definition of difficulty grades as they appear in this book.

Elevation gain. The elevation gain of the route is given here. The vertical gain on routes is given subjectively from the point on the map where the terrain appears to become steep enough to require attention to position.

Average time. Here we give the amount of time required to approach and complete the route. A listing that says "2–3 weeks, 1 day on route," means that overall, completing this route will take 2 to 3 weeks, including the actual time spent on the route. The length usually depends on whether or not you fly in or walk in. If you choose walk-in approaches, you will discover that most of your time will be spent approaching and walking out from the route itself.

Maps. The map or maps necessary for approaches and routes are listed here. The United States Geological Survey (USGS) provides standard topographical maps of Alaska; maps listed are USGS unless otherwise noted. They can be purchased at climbing stores in Anchorage, or directly from the USGS (see appendix C).

Resources. Here we reference valuable previously published information about the route. Use it! For years the impression in Alaska has been that people climb mountains in the vast wilderness and do not bother to record their ascents. Although this statement may be true for a small percentage of climbers, it has been our experience that the records have been posted, but are sometimes difficult to find. The *American Alpine Journal (AAJ)* has been recording ascents for decades, a tribute to all who have ventured before and a springboard for future generations attracted to the mountains of Alaska. Other magazine articles and books are cited as well. Appendix C provides additional selected references. The more you know about a route's history, the better prepared you will be for any eventuality you might encounter.

History. The dates and parties of first and subsequent ascents are given, and sometimes we relate a good story or two.

Approach. The approach to the base of many a remote Alaskan climb often requires as much effort as the climb itself, and sometimes more. Historically, the approach to the mountain was an expedition in and of itself requiring months to complete or even years for some ill-fated parties.

Where **fly-in** approaches are possible, we give information pertaining to the most common landing areas. Sometimes we suggest air services (see appendix B for a complete list). Today, glacier landings are the standard method of access, as they eliminate the length and hazards of an overland approach.

There are some considerations when flying that will help you and your pilot. Pilots have a wealth of information concerning the area and where they are able or permitted to land. They can suggest the best communication to use in case of emergency and often have radios for rent. Bush planes do have load limits, so it is best to leave behind any extras. Most bush planes are small and need to be packed like a sardine can. It is best to have your gear arranged in small bags and divided into "light," "heavy," "sharp," and "stove fuel." If you anticipate more than one flight to get everything in, be sure you have the basic essentials with you in case the plane cannot return on the second run.

On the pick up, the pilot needs more than 100 yards of packed runway marked with sleds or plastic bags and an improvised wind sock. Be sure to leave enough survival gear if anyone is left for a second flight. The four common bush planes in order of size are the Piper Super Cub, Cessna 185, Cessna 206, and De Havilland Beaver. Depending on flying conditions, the Super Cub carries one climber and gear, the 185 and 206 carry three climbers and gear, and the Beaver carries five climbers and gear. All four can be equipped with floats, tundra tires, and skis.

Note that flying is a luxury that comes with a price, both in the pocketbook and if the plane doesn't show and you have to hike out.

Where possible, we give **walk-in** information. Overland approaches are coveted by the few who wish to experience connecting the mountain climb with its surroundings. Overland approaches are in fact mandatory in some areas where terrain features or designated wilderness areas prohibit plane landings.

Overland approaches vary greatly depending on the climb. A rock climb in the Arrigetch requires very little glacier travel to reach the base of the route. Some climbs can be accessed from the road in a

Mike Meekin taking off from the Nelchina Glacier in his Super Cub (Photo: Colby Coombs)

couple of hours, while others require 2 weeks to reach. On average, walk-in approaches take 2–7 days and involve river crossings, bushwhacking, mosquitoes, and bears. When does the approach end and the climbing begin? We have started route descriptions based on where the climbing looks steep enough on the map to require special attention to your position.

Route description. This section of each chapter describes the climb beginning from where your fly-in or walk-in approach has put you. Some climbs are fairly straightforward snow walk-ups with few features, while others require more detail about route-finding. In all cases, studying photos of the peaks will familiarize you with the chosen objective. Some of the photos in this book indicate route lines, and a few of the climbs are accompanied by topos.

Descent. Most often, the way up is also the way down. We describe any significant rappels if the descent line deviates significantly from your ascent route.

Note that we avoid specifically listing the best seasons or equipment necessary for each climb. The introductions to each mountain range state seasonal conditions and particular climbs list equipment previous climbers found helpful.

It is our goal that the combination of the route descriptions, grades, resources, and perspectives provided within this text will give you the tools necessary to safely enjoy the mountains of Alaska.

DIFFICULTY RATINGS EXPLAINED
Alaska Grade System
In 1966 Boyd N. Everett Jr., a climber with extensive big mountain experience in Alaska, presented *The*

Organization of an Alaskan Expedition at a Harvard Mountaineering Club seminar. The presentation-turned-book was written in a 2-week period. In the beginning of his book Everett wrote, "There are undoubtedly some inaccuracies, particularly in the final section on routes and the grading of climbs. Corrections and suggestions will be gratefully accepted." In his wisdom Everett recognized the need to create a separate grading system for Alaska, but found it a challenging topic. Everett loosely defined Alaska Grade 1 through 6 and relied heavily on comparison to support his definition. Jonathan Waterman continued to apply the Alaska Grade System in his book *High Alaska*, however the three similar peaks described in his book did not challenge Everett's definition of the Alaska Grade System.

Climbing in Alaska has seen a major increase in popularity in the last 35 years since Everett's original report. As a result, Everett's original system began to show limitations when used to describe the wide variety of climbs and routes being done. Recognizing this limitation, we took it upon ourselves to interpret the original text to more accurately define Alaska Grades 1 through 6, in order to make the definitions better able to communicate a climb's difficulty. Our solution is to present a combination of the updated Alaska Grade System, which reflects the seriousness of the climb with the technical rating given by the first ascentionists.

An Alaska Grade implies that there are unique qualities inherent in the arctic environment and the abundant Alaska wilderness. As described earlier in this introduction, the arctic environment has climbing conditions, such as temperature, snowpack, daylight, and remoteness, which are unlike those on any other mountains in the world. The Alaska Grade emphasizes the overall seriousness involved on the majority of Alaska climbs. Factors that combine to reflect this seriousness are: length of time on route, camping options, length of route, technical difficulty, the sustained nature of the route, difficulty of descent, and difficulty of retreat. The seriousness of a climb is a combination of all the factors listed. Commitment is recognition of this seriousness on the part of the climber and reflects a willingness to undertake the task. All these components manifest to create the unique qualities of the Alaska Grade.

The style in which a climb is undertaken can radically affect the commitment level necessary from the climber, and thus the grade. However, reflected in the grade is the "average time for recent ascents by climbers with experience and physical level compatible to the chosen route." One drawback to the Alaska Grade System is the difficulty in accommodating the effort and means of approach in the grade; therefore you should pay attention to the approach descriptions given for each route.

Alaska Grade 1   Can be climbed in 1 day from base camp and requires third- and fourth-class travel. Remoteness can contribute to seriousness.

Alaska Grade 2   Moderate fifth-class climb that can be accomplished in a day, or a multiday climb involving third- and fourth-class travel. One or more of the following will contribute to the seriousness: altitude, remoteness.

Alaska Grade 3   Difficult fifth-class climb that can be accomplished in a day, or a multiday climb involving fourth- and easy fifth-class travel. One or more of the following will contribute to the seriousness: altitude, remoteness, cornicing, knife-edge ridges.

Alaska Grade 4   Moderate fourth- and fifth-class climb that requires multiple days on route. One or more of the following will contribute to the seriousness: altitude, remoteness, cornicing, knife-edge ridges.

Alaska Grade 5   A climb requiring a high level of commitment with sustained fifth-class climbing; multiple days on route. One or more of the following will contribute to the seriousness: altitude, remoteness, cornicing, knife-edge ridges, limited options for retreat, scarce bivi sites.

Alaska Grade 6   A climb requiring an extreme level of commitment with difficult and sustained fifth-class climbing for more than 4,000 feet requiring multiple days on route. One or more of the following will contribute to the seriousness: altitude, remoteness, cornicing, knife-edge ridges, poor retreat options, scarce and/or hanging bivis.

A plus symbol (+) is added to denote a slightly higher level of difficulty.

Standard Ratings

In addition to the Alaska Grade Syetem, some climbs in this book use standard rating conventions. These include grade (I–VII), which indicates the overall commitment and nature of a climb and specifically how much time it will take; the Yosemite Decimal System (5.0–5.14) for rock climbs; aid climbing ratings (A1–A5), where the higher the number the less secure the protection placements are and the greater the risk of a dangerous fall; and finally ice ratings, which indicate water ice with a "WI," and alpine ice or névé with "AI." A number follows the ice rating; the higher the number, the more difficult the ice climbing.

We have gone to great efforts to be accurate with the route descriptions and grades in this book. However, due to the ever-changing nature of conditions and the sparseness of information expect some inaccuracies. We have tried in earnest to give an idea of what to expect on each route, though it was not possible to verify every piece of information. We urge each climber to proceed with caution, especially in wild, untamed Alaska.

Famed alpinist Doug Scott summed it up well, after he climbed a new route on the south face of Denali with Dougal Haston. He wrote, "All over Alaska much steeper climbs than ours are being made up the granite buttresses and steep ice couloirs which abound in such places as the Ruth Gorge. They are being climbed in the most adventurous styles without fixed ropes and without radios. Every climber has the right to climb this way providing he has accumulated sufficient experience on other mountains over years of climbing. There is no shortcut to safe climbing at high altitude, particularly up here in the Arctic: it is a long and painful apprenticeship." (*Mountain*, no. 52, Nov/Dec 1976).

MINIMUM IMPACT BACKCOUNTRY TECHNIQUES

It goes without saying that guidebooks attract more people, which results in increased impacts. The visual effects of a careless team, or even a single climber, can last for generations. There are still signs of the early expeditions to the Arrigetch Peaks. It is absolutely imperative that climbers in Alaska respect and preserve the pristine quality of their surroundings.

Climbers must be well aware of the current, most effective camping and travelling techniques used to protect the environment. Teams must plan to pack out all trash, avoiding the temptation to just toss it all down a handy crevasse. Consult park rangers at Denali, Wrangell–Saint Elias, Gates of the Arctic, Glacier Bay, Lake Clark, and other national parks to acquaint yourself with environmental concerns of park managers. A good supplemental resource is the Leave No Trace website *www.LNT.org*.

Field Notes from Alaska

Daryl Miller, Denali National Park mountaineering ranger

Alaska has long been regarded as the last frontier having some of the most remote and rugged mountains in the world. The quest for solitude and adventure lures thousands of climbers from around the world into the backcountry each year to test their skills and wilderness experience. Unfortunately, every year there are numerous accidents and some fatalities resulting from poor judgment. A hundred years ago, wilderness survival skills were a way of life in Alaska. The rules were simple and harsh: Survival was your responsibility, no one else's. Since then, we have grown socially and culturally unwilling to accept that primitive education, which dictated that people simply learned or died.

Today, because most people, including most Alaskans, live in urban environments and grow up with an urban culture, wilderness skills are rarely learned. The result is that the wilderness-bound end up depending more and more on equipment and less and less on their own competence when dealing with dangerous situations in wilderness settings. Each year in this state, the National Park Service and other agencies conduct backcountry rescues that never should have been needed. Many of these incidents are a result of people forgetting that the most important trip objective and priority is a safe journey out and back.

Some incidents stem from a lack of judgment and some from a lack of training. Outdoor proficiency should come from a long, mentored apprenticeship that presents the opportunities to deal safely with increasingly precarious situations. But there are few opportunities for such wilderness exposure today. Many factors have conspired to change that. Technology has made it possible to call for rescue from almost anywhere at the same time that it has made backcountry travel easier and faster. This same technology has served to blunt respect for the tests that Mother Nature can still throw at humans. Taking communication on a trip is a part of being responsible, but basing how much risk you take on the existence that communication is negligent at best.

Many times I have tried to warn climbers and backpackers of nature's cold and harsh realities. The Alaska environment can be extremely unfriendly to humans. It is indifferent and unforgiving. On top of that, the scale of Alaska is easily underestimated. Most people set unrealistic expectations. Ten miles cross-country in Alaska is not like 10 miles on trail systems in the lower 48, but more like 30 or 40 trail miles.

Arrogance about the outdoors blinds people to these realities. Unfamiliarity with Alaska's arctic and subarctic conditions and a sometimes total disregard for elementary principles of safety simply compound the problems.

I have seen the results firsthand too many times. It is a sad and painful task to tell family and friends that their loved one is lost or dead in the mountains. It is true that accidents do happen. There are medical emergencies and acts of nature for which no one can plan. But these situations are rare. An examination of climbing accidents in Alaska shows that a great number of rescues involve people who have misjudged the consequences of their decisions and were underprepared for Alaska weather. Furthermore, the remoteness of the Alaskan backcountry makes everyone susceptible to a catastrophic accident or medical emergency. Most accidents result from people making bad decisions because they lack knowledge or are complacent; severe weather and remoteness then compound this bad judgment.

The ability to evaluate hazards in the backcountry is in part linked to the time spent there, but there appears to be a refusal on the part of some to let experience teach them. Some consider their success in the backcountry a reflection of superior outdoor skills, although most wilderness travellers have never been tested in crisis. They forget that experience with crisis is necessary to hone skill. "Near misses," those brief encounters with mortality, are valuable learning tools if properly approached.

Errors in judgment are educational if they send the right message—that turning around at the right time or opting not to go on are decisions that will save your life time and time again. Unfortunately, our virtual-reality society has some problems defining risk. To some degree, we have come to see risk as a quest instead of a warning. The "no fear" philosophy pushes people to navigate in the backcountry regardless of the elements, but it operates on the faulty premise that liabilities and possible injuries are a low priority and that rescue is just a call away. People fail to make the right choices based on their capabilities and they forget that prevention is the rule because treatment is often impractical or impossible. This is dangerous for the people seeking recreation and for the people called upon to rescue them.

My first climb on Denali in 1981 was one of the most traumatic and best learning experiences in my life because of the severe storms we encountered. During the next 19 years I climbed Denali numerous times by various routes and completed a 45-day winter circumnavigation in 1995. As a mountaineering ranger for the past 11 years I have witnessed many worst-case scenarios regarding accidents, along with some of the most determined wills to survive. After many years of leading varied and difficult backcountry patrols in Denali National Park, I offer these thoughts on venturing into the great wilderness of Alaska.

Be Prepared

▲ Everyone has a personal responsibility to maintain self-sufficiency in the wilderness and should always base decisions on getting back on their own.

▲ Failure to recognize your own limitations in the Alaska wilderness can put you immediately in harm's way.

▲ Educate yourself on logistics and current conditions before attempting trips into the Alaska bush.

▲ Prevention, not treatment, is what will ultimately save your life in the wilderness.

▲ A well thought-out and responsible contingency plan for self-evacuation should be established before your trip.

▲ Remember that wilderness rescues in Alaska are often dangerous to the rescuers and are always weather contingent.

▲ Leave important information regarding trip plans with the right people. Failure to do so has cost numerous lives and has resulted in unneeded searches.

Objective and Subjective Hazards

▲ The Alaska scale is easily underestimated in regard to terrain, leaving people unrealistic about trip expectations.

▲ Glaciers and glaciated rivers are significant barriers that should always mandate respect and planning.

▲ Remoteness compounds problems that otherwise might be manageable.

▲ Avalanches are regularly underestimated, especially their speed and power.

▲ Mechanized transportation commonly gives people a false sense of security. During an emergency, people often discover that they are farther into the wilderness than they had realized.

▲ The prerequisite to misadventure is the belief that you are invincible or that the wilderness cares about you.

▲ As a rule, if you die in the wilderness you made a mistake. Careless judgment has a sharp learning curve.

Calculating Risk

▲ There is a notable difference between a calculated risk and a gamble. A calculated risk considers all the odds, justifies the risk, and then arrives at an intelligent decision based on conservative judgment. A gamble is something over which you have no control, and the outcome is just a roll of the dice.

▲ You cannot make intelligent decisions in the wilderness if you do not understand the risks.

▲ Firsthand knowledge of mistakes made on previous trips into the wilderness is often an invaluable tool when making significant decisions regarding your life.

▲ When making decisions, keep in mind the devastating impact that accidents have on friends and loved ones.

▲ Accidents in the wilderness are like bad relationships: They are typically easier to get into than to get out of.

Surviving a Crisis

▲ Your best resource is the ability to think in a controlled manner when a life-threatening crisis is happening.

▲ Panic and confusion have long been inseparable partners and are your constant adversary during an emergency.

▲ The ability to improvise and use available resources is often the key to survival in emergency situations in the wilderness.

▲ Sometimes people perish simply because they fall short on perseverance. Never give up, because the will to live is a valuable asset.

A NOTE ABOUT SAFETY

Safety is an important concern in all outdoor activities. No guidebook can alert you to every hazard or anticipate the limitations of every reader. Therefore, the descriptions of roads, trails, routes, and natural features in this book are not representations that a particular place or excursion will be safe for your party. When you follow any of the routes described in this book, you assume responsibility for your own safety. Under normal conditions, such excursions require the usual attention to traffic, road and trail conditions, weather, terrain, the capabilities of your party, and other factors. Keeping informed on current conditions and exercising common sense are the keys to a safe, enjoyable outing.

The Mountaineers Books

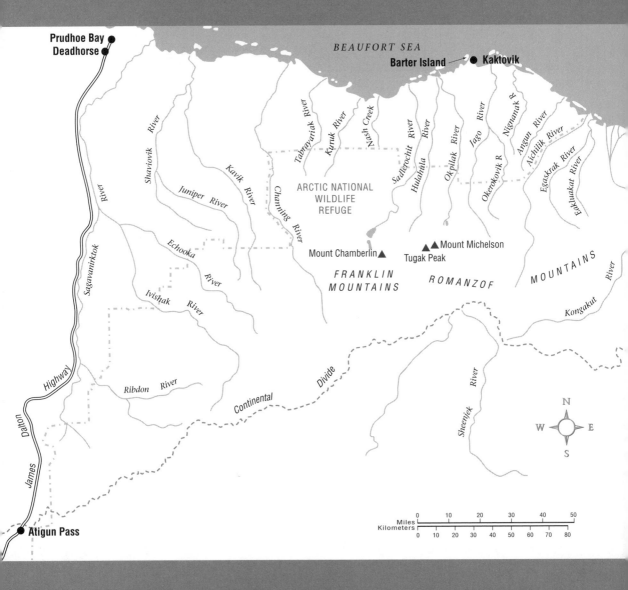

BROOKS RANGE

THE BROOKS RANGE extends across the entire northern third of Alaska, from the Chukchi Sea in the west to the Yukon Territory's British Mountains in the east. Because of the high latitude (the entire range is north of the Arctic Circle), precipitation is low, glaciers are few, and rivers are moderate in size and relatively clear. During the summer, the sun never sets. Ten separate mountain groups combine to make up this low, but wide mountain range—the tallest peaks are just slightly higher than 9,000 feet. The three most popular areas: the eastern Franklin and Romanzof Mountains, the central Endicott Mountains, and the spectacular Arrigetch Peaks in the west were chosen for this book.

With its fragile alpine environment, the Brooks Range is by far the most environmentally sensitive region in this book, and its protection is of the utmost concern for the National Park Service. Strict attention to Leave No Trace camping and travelling are required to protect the area into the future.

FRANKLIN AND ROMANZOF MOUNTAINS

Located in the far northeast corner of Alaska, south of Barter Island and the Innupiat community of Kaktovik, the Romanzofs include many peaks similar to Mounts Chamberlin (9,020 ft) and Michelson (8,855 ft) included in this book. These mountains define "wild and remote" and are home to Dall sheep, wolves, grizzlies, and hundreds of thousands of caribou. The best times to avoid snow and clouds of mosquitoes are late June, August, and early September.

Fairbanks-based air services fly to Kaktovik via Barrow or Deadhorse. From Kaktovik, Alaska Flyers (owned and operated by Walt Audi) flies climbers into the Arctic National Wildlife Refuge, landing on gravel riverbars. There is no public camping, so you may want to ask Alaska Flyers about staying near the hanger until you can fly in. Groceries are available in Fairbanks. From there on out plan on being self-sufficient. It is possible to get a meal and some groceries in Kaktovik, but prices are high and choices limited. Combining climbs with river trips down the Hulahula or Okpilak Rivers can save money and provide a summit to sea experience.

 MOUNT CHAMBERLIN

(9,020 ft; 2749 m)

Route ▲ West Ridge
Difficulty ▲ Alaska Grade 1
Elevation gain ▲ 3,200 ft from the toe of Peters Glacier
Average time ▲ 7–10 Days, 1 day on route
Map ▲ Mount Michelson (B-2)
Resources ▲ *AAJ* 1964, p. 168; *AAJ* 1970; *AAJ* 1971 p. 338; *AAJ* 1991

History: Graham Stephenson, Dennis Burge, and George G. Barnes climbed the north spur to the west ridge, July 24, 1963.

Approach: Fly from Fairbanks to the northern town of Kaktovik with Frontier Air or Wright Air Service.

Mount Chamberlin from the northwest. The West Ridge route is the right skyline. (Photo: Brian Okonek)

From Kaktovik, Alaska Flyers will land a Super Cub on a gravel strip on the south end of Lake Peters. From this strip you can access the mouth of Chamberlin Creek.

Route description: From the south end of Peters Lake, travel east up Chamberlin Creek. The 1991 route travelled to the base of Peters Glacier on the west side of Mount Chamberlin. Climb the east rim of the glacier and join the 1964 route on the North Spur of the West Ridge. From here it is basically ridge walking. Rocky slopes and snow cornices may be encountered on the ridge. Note that, while there is a private research camp at Peters Lake, there is no hut available to climbers.

Descent: Retrace the ascent.

 ## 2 MOUNT MICHELSON

(8,855 ft; 2699 m)

Route ▲ South Face to East Ridge
Difficulty ▲ Alaska Grade 1
Elevation gain ▲ 1,500 ft
Average time ▲ 7–10 days, 1 day on route
Maps ▲ Mount Michelson (B-1, B-2)
Resources ▲ *AAJ* 1958; *AAJ* 1976, pp. 93–95, 436–437; *AAJ* 1981, p. 166; *AAJ* 1992, pp. 125–126; *Descent* 3, no. 4, Jul/Aug 1971

History: John P. Thompson and R. E. "Pete" Isto climbed the mountain on April 23, 1957. There have been a number groups passing through here, and many have mentioned the ease of climbing Mount Michelson and the beauty of its neighbor, Tugak Peak.

Approach: Fly from Fairbanks to Kaktovik with Frontier Air or Wright Air Service. Most parties fly to a gravel strip in the Okpilak River valley just south of the Okpilak Lakes. Walter Audi of Alaska Flyers lands a Cessna 206 there. This approach requires crossing the Okpilak River for routes on Mount Michelson. Another option, good for the Esetuk Glacier route, is to land at 1,500–1,800 feet in the Hulahula River drainage.

Jan Lokken approaching Esetuk Glacier and Mount Michelson from the northwest (Photo: Philip Marshall)

Tugak Peak from 7,500 feet on the Esetuk Glacier (Photo: Philip Marshall)

Parties wanting to climb the north ridge should swing wide around the north side of Mount Chamberlin and cross Karen Creek. A wide plateau soon descends into Katak Creek. Follow Katak Creek down the south side of the river to the Hulahula River. From the Hulahula River, hiking up to the upper East Fork of Esetuk Creek allows for an easy climb of Mount Michelson's North Ridge. From here, it is possible to walk out to Kaktovik.

Route description: Once on the Esetuk Glacier of Mount Michelson, the climbing is moderate to the summit. Expect 45-degree snow slopes lower down on the South Face and just below the summit on the East Ridge. While not at the same scale as most Alaskan glaciers, the glaciers are crevassed.

Descent: Descend the route of ascent unless you want to traverse. Some parties exit with a 5-day raft trip down the Hulahula River, reaching the coast at Barter Island and Kaktovik. Parties have also walked to Kaktovik along the Okpilak River. Other options include walking to the Neruokpuk Lakes landing strip at the south end of Lake Peters.

 3 TUGAK PEAK

(8,500 ft; 2590 m)

Route ▲ North Ridge
Difficulty ▲ Alaska Grade 1
Elevation gain ▲ 1,000 ft
Average time ▲ 7–10 days, half day on route
Map ▲ Mount Michelson (B-1)
Resources ▲ *AAJ* 1976, p. 436; *AAJ* 1981, p. 166; *AAJ* 1982, pp. 141–142

History: Bill Lentsch and George Barnes climbed this peak on August 2, 1963. Another party incorrectly claims the first ascent in the 1981 *American Alpine Journal*. Tugak means "walrus tusk" in the native language.

Approach: Follow the same approach as for Mount Michelson (Route 2).

Route description: This is 1,000 feet of moderate snow climbing along the aesthetic North Ridge with no hidden surprises. The view of Tugak Peak from the base camp for Mount Michelson begs one to climb it.

Descent: Retrace the ascent route.

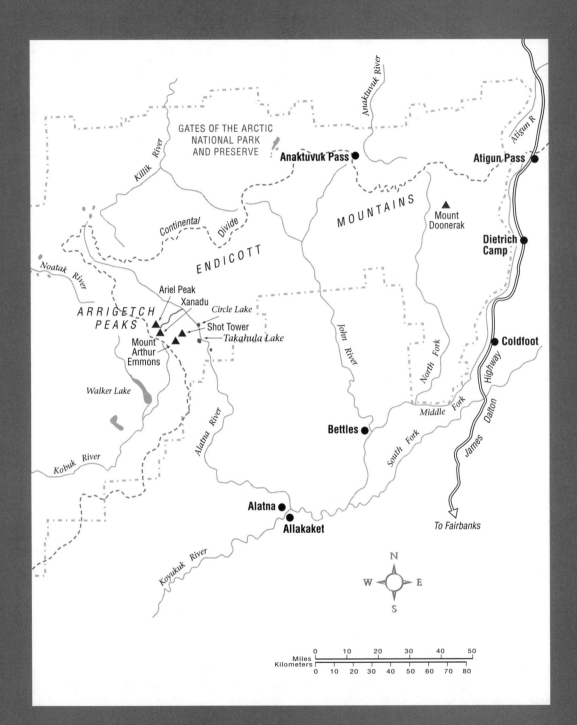

ARRIGETCH PEAKS

Named by the Innupiat, Arrigetch means "fingers of the hand outstretched." Remote, rugged, and beautiful, the Arrigetch has established routes of moderate difficulty as well as many more unclimbed walls, arêtes, and summits.

The earliest recorded visit was by geologist Philip Smith, who travelled through the Arrigetch in 1911 and then again until 1922. Adolph and Olaus Murie saw the peaks on their dogsled trip through the Brooks Range in 1931. Robert Marshall described the Arrigetch in his classic *Arctic Wilderness*. In 1962 Tom Hamilton documented the Arrigetch from a geological perspective, naming the Wichmann Glacier after his wife's family.

The first climbers arrived in 1963. After air-dropping a load of supplies in an apparent talus field, the party of five landed on Takahula Lake, considered at that time the nearest landing spot. Three days of struggling with overloaded packs through thick alders; sharp, loose talus; hordes of mosquitoes; and across glacial meltwater streams, they finally reached the point where they expected to find their re-supply. They quickly realized that the "talus field" seen from the airplane was a boulderfield that had swallowed their airdrop. Unable to recover the vital supplies necessary to continue the expedition, the team left, defeated. The following year, the same members returned to the Arrigetch with a better airdrop plan and hardier climbers to make several first ascents and name the bigger peaks (*AAJ* 1965).

In 1971, David Roberts completed a series of expeditions into the Arrigetch and claimed numerous first ascents, including Shot Tower, possibly the most impressive spire in the range. Roberts wrote several articles for the *American Alpine Journal*. A professor at Hampshire College, he inspired a host of his students to climb there, including the "Arrigetch Kids" Tom Kizzia, Chip Brown, and Jon Krakauer. Their magazine articles about these largely unexplored monoliths have lured climbers ever since.

The Arrigetch's fragile alpine environment makes it the most vulnerable to impact of any place in Alaska addressed in this book. Stringent adherence to Leave No Trace camping and travelling techniques is the only way to protect the lichens, mosses, and other sensitive tundra vegetation from trampling.

The most convenient—although expensive—approach is to fly from Fairbanks to Bettles on a scheduled flight with Wright Air or Frontier Air, then charter a floatplane (Cessna 185 or De Havilland Beaver) to one of three lakes: Kutuk Lake (a Beaver can land, but approach requires river crossing), Circle Lake (closest, but too small for a Beaver to take off loaded), or Takahula Lake (large enough for a Beaver, but farthest away). Several parties have walked into the Arrigetch from the highway, a 3- to 4-week walk and a wilderness adventure all its own.

The Gates of the Arctic National Park and Preserve appreciates if visitors would stop by the Park Service office in Bettles.

 ## SHOT TOWER

(6,069 ft; 1849 m)

Route ▲ West Ridge
Difficulty ▲ IV, 5.8, A2
Elevation gain ▲ 1,500 ft
Average time ▲ 2 weeks, 1 day on route
Maps ▲ Survey Pass (B-2, B-3)
Resources ▲ *AAJ* 1972, pp. 46–50; *AAJ* 1981, pp. 166–167

History: Shot Tower was first climbed by David Roberts and Edward Ward on June 21, 1971.

Approach: The base of Shot Tower can be reached with a long hike up Creek 4662 (Aiyagomahala Creek) after flying in by floatplane to Takahula Lake. Follow the left, or north side of the creek along intermittent game trails. Resist the urge to go high or along the creek bottom. There is a hot spring indicated on the

South Face of Shot Tower. The West Ridge route is in the left skyline. (Photo: Roman Dial)

map, but don't get your hopes up too high. Alternately, fly in to Circle Lake. From there, travel up Arrigetch Creek 3 miles and hike south over a pass, descending to Creek 4662.

Route description: The West Ridge of Shot Tower is an undisputed Arrigetch classic. The narrow arête involves sixteen pitches up protectable cracks and fractured granite. The first three pitches ascend a sharp spine with fat, nut-sucking cracks. The gray-and-orange granite is considered among the best rock in the Arrigetch. The fourth, fifth, and sixth pitches increase in difficulty, but can be protected. Pitches 7 and 8 ease off as they approach the ridge's distinctive mushroom cap. The ninth pitch, the crux-free pitch, follows a left leaning crack beneath the "mushroom." Pitch 10 requires a traverse left. On the first ascent, Ward and Roberts left a piece of fixed line here to protect the traverse. With some finesse, the "mushroom" is passed to a wide ledge. At the top of pitch 13, a stone moat cuts the ridge. This relaxing spot, with ice deep in the cracks, is a great place to absorb the views and prepare for the 60-foot crux aid pitch. Pitch 14 begins as an overhanging wall split by a shallow crack system. This bottoming crack has yet to be free-climbed and will require tenacity to ensure solid protection. It is bolt-free and hopefully will stay that way. From the top of this pitch, two more pitches of moderate climbing along the ridge carry the now-euphoric climber to the summit. Ed Ward and David Roberts both commented, "It was the best rock climb of our lives."

Descent: Rappel the ascent route. Be extra aware of the plated granite, which does a fine job of catching ropes.

5 XANADU

(7,100 ft; 2164 m)

Route ▲ West Face to South Arête
Difficulty ▲ III, 5.7
Elevation gain ▲ 1,500 ft
Average time ▲ 2 weeks, 1 day on route
Maps ▲ Survey Pass (B-2, B-3)
Resources ▲ *AAJ* 1975, pp. 37–42; *AAJ* 1990, p. 163

History: Inspired by David Roberts's photos, Jon Krakauer and Bill Bullard made the first ascent in August 1974. After a failed attempt, they returned the next day and completed the route up the west face and south ridge. Members of their party climbed to the horizontal section of the northwest ridge and came within 200 feet of the summit.

Approach: From Takahula Lake travel up Aiyagomahala Creek (Creek 4662) and over Independence Pass to the south of Wichmann Tower. From Circle Lake, travel 3 miles up Arrigetch Creek and hike south over a pass, descending to Creek 4662.

Route description: Ascend the scree slope to the base of the West Face at 5,000 feet. The route accesses the ridge via a long, right-slanting ledge with a short, vertical 5.7 dihedral to gain the ridge. Once on the ridge, the route continues for two pitches to the base of the arête. Five 50-meter pitches follow the crest of the arête leading to the prominent and intimidating roof. The 5.7 roof is climbed directly on excellent "Gunks"-like granite with buckets and good protection to a great ledge. From the ledge, ascend a short 5.7 section, then a pitch and a half to the summit.

Descent: Rappel the ascent. Be extra aware of the plated granite, which does a fine job of catching ropes.

The West Face and South Arête (right skyline) of Xanadu (Photo: Jon Krakauer)

Bill Bullard on the first ascent of the South Arête of Xanadu (Photo: Jon Krakauer)

6 ARIEL PEAK

(6,685 ft; 2011 m)

Route ▲ South Ridge

Difficulty ▲ Alaska Grade 1

Elevation gain ▲ 2,000 ft from the Arrigetch Basin; 1,100 ft from Escape Pass

Average time ▲ 2 weeks, half day on route

Maps ▲ Survey Pass (B-2, B-3)

Resources ▲ *AAJ* 1970, pp. 68–74

History: Arthur Bacon and George Ripley climbed Ariel on August 17, 1969. David Roberts and Robert Waldrop made the second ascent the following day.

Approach: Ariel sits at the head of Arrigetch Creek, north of Escape Pass. Xanadu is to the south. The approach depends on which creek you take. From Aiyagomahala Creek (Creek 4662) travel over Independence Pass, which is south of Wichmann Tower (6,916 ft) and Peak 6,391. Travel over a pass south of Peak 7,068 (Melting Tower) and north of Peak 6,179. Continue west down the East Fork of Awlinyak Creek to the Northeast Fork. Travel northeast to the pass between the North Ridge of Xanadu and the South Ridge of Ariel. From Arrigetch Creek, hike up to Escape Pass, where the climb starts. This is the eastern approach to the peak. The ascent from the moraine to the pass requires exposed third-class scrambling; the pass is much easier from the west. It is also possible to gain the South Ridge from the pass

Xanadu, Escape Pass, and Ariel (on right) from upper Arrigetch Creek (Photo: Brian Okonek)

north of Ariel, between Peak 6,022 and Ariel.

Route description: This peak is a magnificent climb and one of the least technical in the Arrigetch. The climbing along the ridge is exposed third-class scrambling. The views from the summit are amazing. This is the route Roman Dial wants to climb with his teenage kids. Another nontechnical route to the summit, and an alternative to the South Ridge, is the North Ridge, which can be accessed by travelling up into the cirque below Peak 7,181 (Caliban) and hiking to the pass north of Ariel and south of Peak 6,022.

Descent: Retrace the ascent.

 7 MOUNT ARTHUR EMMONS

(6,556 ft; 1998 m)

Route ▲ West Ridge
Difficulty ▲ Alaska Grade 2, 5.5, AI 3
Elevation gain ▲ 1,500 ft
Average time ▲ 2 weeks, 1 day on route
Maps ▲ Survey Pass (B-2, B-3)
Resources ▲ *AAJ* 1975, p. 37

History: Jon Krakauer and Bill Bullard climbed the West Ridge to the summit for the first ascent on July 4, 1974.

Approach: The base is reached by travelling south (uphill) through another of the numerous boulder and scree slopes from Aiyagomahala Creek (Creek 4662) to the glacier flowing from the north flank of Mount Arthur Emmons. Travel the northwest glacier to the large notch on the west (right-hand) skyline to the start.

Route description: This beautiful route lies hidden at the very head of Creek 4662 and is separated from Independence Pass by Pyramid Peak to the west. The route is one of the few in the range to date that offers ice climbing.

Begin by ascending moderate, 45-degree ice to gain the West Ridge. Once the ridge is gained, the climbing is moderate on good rock to the summit. The entire ridge is fourth class with a few class 5 sections. Beware

of afternoon thunderstorms, which occur frequently in the area.

Descent: Reverse the route of ascent.

ENDICOTT MOUNTAINS

Made famous in the book *Arctic Wilderness* by the early explorer Robert Marshall, the Endicott Mountains form a labyrinth of mountains, rivers, forests, and canyons (see map on page 34). Less remote than most of the Brooks Range, the Endicotts are accessible from the James Dalton Highway, which links Alaska's Interior with Prudhoe Bay. Drive 6 hours on gravel roads north of Fairbanks to Coldfoot, a gas and service station at the foot of the Brooks Range. Rising to the east are the mysterious Philip Smith Mountains and to the west, the Endicotts.

 8 MOUNT DOONERAK

(7,457 ft; 2272 m)

Route ▲ Southeast Ridge
Difficulty ▲ Alaska Grade 1+
Elevation gain ▲ 4,200 ft from Saint Patricks Creek; 1,400 ft on Southeast Ridge
Average time ▲ 7–10 days, 1 day on route
Maps ▲ Wiseman (D-1, D-2)
Resources ▲ *AAJ* 1959, p. 218; *AAJ* 1981, p. 166; *AAJ*, 1974, pp. 140–141; *AAJ* 1976, pp. 435–436; Marshall, *Arctic Wilderness*; Sherwonit, *Alaska Ascents*

History: George W. Beadle, Gunnar Bergman, and Alfred Tissières climbed Mount Doonerak by the Southeast Ridge on June 30, 1952. The first recorded

Mount Arthur Emmons. The West Ridge is the right skyline. (Photo: Jon Krakauer)

visits to this area were in 1929 and 1932, when famous traveller and explorer Robert Marshall travelled extensively around the mountain and made many valiant attempts to climb what he thought to be the highest peak in the Brooks Range. He documented his journeys in his book *Arctic Wilderness*. Marshall's efforts to find a feasible route up the mountain failed, but he contributed greatly to the rich history of the area. Doonerak is a Kobuk Eskimo word meaning "devil" or "spirit." These spirits can foretell good luck or bad, but mainly delight in being mischievous. Bill Sherwonit's *Alaska Ascents* recounts the history of Robert Marshall's expedition around Mount Doonerak. Consider bringing copies of both books to fully enjoy the history of this spectacular area.

Approach: Base camp for the Southeast Ridge is a 20-mile, 2–4 day walk from the James Dalton Highway, following a series of passes from Trembley Creek to Kinnorutin Pass. Park about 50 miles north of Coldfoot and Wiseman at a small pullout opposite the mouth of Koyuktuvuk Creek. Cross the Dietrich River, hike up Trembley Creek and over Falsoola Pass, past Blarney Creek, and finally up Kinnorutin Creek to beautiful Kinnorutin Pass. From the pass hike southwest over a low divide to Saint Patricks Creek. Follow the west fork of Saint Patricks Creek to Midnight Mountain (first climbed by Robert Marshall and Kenneth Harvey in June 1939). The mountain is typically climbed from a base camp at the confluence of Saint Patrick's creek and its west fork, which flows from the east of Midnight Mountain.

Route description: The elevation gain on your summit day will be 4,000-plus feet. The flanks of Midnight Mountain must be scaled to reach the 2 miles of ridge between Midnight Mountain and Mount

Southeast Ridge of Mount Doonerak (Photo: Roman Dial)

Doonerak. This initial 2,800 feet is a spectacular skywalk and scramble. The final 1,400 feet of elevation gain from the 6,150-foot pass is third- and fourth-class scrambling on surprisingly stable shale and schist. A rope is advised for those less comfortable on this type of terrain, or if the weather deteriorates.

Descent: Most parties retrace their ascent route, making the round trip in a long summer day.

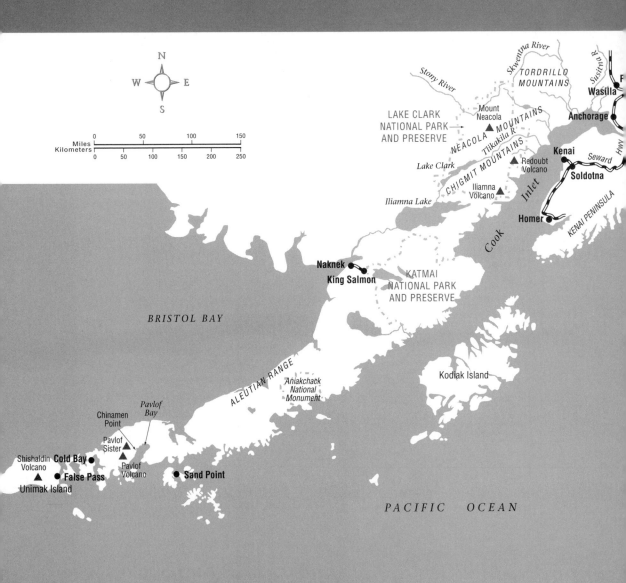

ALEUTIAN RANGE

S tretching 1,500 miles into the Pacific Ocean, the Aleutian Range is Alaska's longest continuous mountain range. The Aleutian Range is divided into four distinct mountain groups: the Alaska Peninsula, the Chigmit Mountains, the Neacola Mountains, and the Tordrillo Mountains.

The weather on the exposed Alaska Peninsula is considered some of the worst in the world. October and May are the wettest months. At least the temperatures do not plummet like they do in the Interior, due to the warming effects of the ocean.

Abundant wildlife, particularly bird life, flourishes in the Aleutians. Grizzly bears inhabit the peninsula and can be found all the way to Unimak Island, the easternmost island of the chain.

ALASKA PENINSULA

The 500-mile Alaska Peninsula starts at Naknek Lake and extends to Unimak Island, the first of the Aleutian Islands. Shishaldin and Pavlof Volcanoes are members of what is popularly known as the Ring of Fire. Steam rising from Pavlof hints at its potential activity. If continuous vertical gain was measured from the ocean bottom, Shishaldin Volcano would be the highest mountain in Alaska at 32,472 feet!

Anchorage-based air services can provide the most convenient access to the peninsula.

 9 SHISHALDIN VOLCANO

(9,372 ft; 2856 m)

Route ▲ East Face
Difficulty ▲ Alaska Grade 1
Elevation gain ▲ 6,000 ft
Average time ▲ 10–14 days, 1 day on route
Maps ▲ Unimak (C-1, D-1), False Pass (C-6, D-6)
Resources ▲ Hubbard, *Cradle of the Storms*, pp. 17–40; Hubbard, *Alaskan Odyssey*, pp. 130–153

History: G. Peterson and two partners made the first recorded ascent on May 16, 1932. The second ascent was not until 1965. The locals claim Shishaldin as the "tallest on the Aleutian Islands," though not to be confused with tallest on the peninsula. Father Hubbard claimed to have climbed this peak.

Approach: Fly with Penn Air from Anchorage to False Pass on Unimak. Hike west up the drainage to False Pass and traverse the north side of Mount Isanotski. The pass between Isanotski and Shishaldin Volcano offers a great camp, but the notorious big winds and "venturi effect" require snow caves.

Route description: The route to the summit is straightforward up 40-degree snow slopes. A rope and running pro may be necessary in icy conditions, but not for crevasses. Under the right conditions, the skiing and the views are excellent. The summit releases the most acrid steam of all the volcanoes, according to the local volcano skiers. "Yet, there is nothing more aesthetic than carving turns down a hard-earned Aleutian peak with nothing but blue sky and ocean

Shishaldin Volcano (Photo: Chris Flowers)

on either side and snowy white symmetry under your skis," says climber and skier Chris Flowers.

Descent: Retrace the route of ascent.

 10 ## PAVLOF VOLCANO

(8,905 ft; 2714 m)

Route ▲ Northwest Face
Difficulty ▲ Alaska Grade 1
Elevation gain ▲ 4,000 ft
Average time ▲ 10–14 days, 1 day on route
Map ▲ Port Moller (B-6)
Resources ▲ *National Geographic*, 1955, pp. 109–134

History: Pavlof was first climbed on June 27, 1928, by T. A. Jagger, J. Gardiner, O. P. McKinley, P. A. Yatch-menoff, and R. H. Stewart. Speculation surrounds this ascent, which was recounted in *National Geographic*. The second recorded ascent was made in June 1950 by T. P. Bank.

Approach: Fly to Cold Bay or Sand Point from Anchorage with either Reeve or Penn Air, then fly to Volcano Bay or Cathedral River with a local pilot. Alternatively, one can get a boat ride across the bay to the north shore of Cold Bay, but no commercial charter is available at the time of writing. From the north side of the bay, start bushwhacking and aim for the foothills of Mount Dutton. On the 30-mile trek in from Cold Bay, there are two hot springs en route: one at 5 miles, and the second about 20 miles into the trek near Emmons Lake. The skiing from nearby Mount Emmons right down to the hot spring is not to be missed. These world class wilderness hot springs have good flow rates and temperatures and can be found in "Geothermal Re-

Pavlof Volcano with Pavlof's Sister in the background (Photo: Chris Flowers)

sources of Alaska," by T. P. Miller (see bibliography). Parties have also flown from Sand Point to Pavlof Bay and landed in an area called Chinaman Lagoon. From here travel west, navigating around Pavlof's sister.

Route description: From the base of the Northwest Face climb upward to the summit on characteristically wind-scoured hard pack or ice. The climbing is straight-forward and the ski descent even better. An awesome feature in this area is the Aghileen Pinnacles, which create a magnificent skyline to the west. March is a favorite time for this area because plenty of snow allows for skis and a sled and the weather is generally more stable.

Descent: Ski to your heart's content!

Nancy Pfeiffer skiing under the magnificent Aghileen Pinnacles (Photo: Chris Flowers)

CHIGMIT MOUNTAINS

The Chigmits are bordered on the west by Iliamna Lake, to the north by Tlikakila River, to the south by Cook Inlet and Redoubt Bay, and to the east by the North Fork River, which separates the Double and Black Glaciers (see map on page 44). Iliamna and Redoubt, are also part of the Pacific Ocean's Ring of Fire.

Alpine Air and Alaska West Air are the most current sources of air access to this area.

 ## ILIAMNA VOLCANO

(10,016 ft; 3052 m)

Route ▲ Northwest Ridge
Difficulty ▲ Alaska Grade 1
Elevation gain ▲ 6,500 ft
Average time ▲ 10–14 days, 1 day on route
Maps ▲ Lake Clark (A-1), Kenai (A-8), Iliamna (D-1)
Resources ▲ *AAJ* 1960, p. 106; *AAJ* 1986, pp. 147–148 (winter ascent); *Scree,* June 1959

History: Ivan Petrof describes a first ascent supposed to have taken place in 1871. R. H. Sargent passed close

enough in 1924 to name the Umbrella Glacier. Not until 1958 did T. H. Davis, K. E. Hart, T. Rejita, and M. Nitsch make an attempt on the southeast face, only to be turned back at 7,500 feet. The first ascent came on June 1–7, 1959, by Helga Balding, Erik Barnes, Gregg Erickson, and Paul Crews. The first winter ascent took place on February 21, 1985, by George Rooney, Rudi Bertschi, Ken Zafren, and Willy Hersman.

Approach: The best access is to fly in to the Tongue Glacier and follow the Upper Tongue Glacier to the base of the Northwest Ridge. The approach to this side of the mountain was first attempted in 1959 when Lowell Thomas Jr. flew the winter ascent team into the Tuxedni Glacier. Upon landing he declared that he would take no more climbers to the mountain due to the poor landing sites and harsh weather. However the landing potential on the Tuxedni Glacier and the Tongue Glacier is good, but up to the pilot's discretion.

It is also possible to approach this mountain by flying in to Chinitna Bay to the south and then hiking or skiing up the West Glacier Creek. The first

The Northwest Ridge of Iliamna Volcano (Photo: Paul Roderick)

ascent party travelled up Umbrella Creek and onto the Umbrella Glacier to reach the Southwest Ridge. The left fork of West Glacier Creek could also provide access.

Route description: Iliamna is an active volcano and had a minor eruption in 1978, venting steam to 10,000 feet above the summit. It is known as a stratovolcano, composed of multiple layers of lava flows and pyroclastic rocks. The climbing on the Northwest Ridge is a mixture of steep and moderate snow slopes. In a couple of places the steeper terrain might be wind-scoured down to blue ice and require belays to negotiate. Overall, the route is a straightforward snow climb.

Descent: Reverse the route of ascent.

 12 REDOUBT VOLCANO

(10,197 ft; 3108 m)

Route ▲ North Face
Difficulty ▲ Alaska Grade 1
Elevation gain ▲ 5,500 ft
Average time ▲ 10–14 days, 1 day on route
Maps ▲ Kenai (B-8, C-8)
Resources ▲ *AAJ* 1960, pp. 106–107; *AAJ* 1979, p. 174 (winter ascent); *AAJ* 1981, p. 164 (Northwest Ridge and glacier system); *AAJ* 1986, p. 147; *Scree*, Aug 1959

History: Redoubt Volcano is the highest of seventy-six major volcanoes on the Aleutian Peninsula and

Islands. This strato-volcano has erupted numerous times since the 1700s, most recently in 1989, when it spewed ash as high as 35,000 feet. Jon Gardey, Gene Wescott, Finley Kennel, and Charles Deehr climbed the East Face to the Northeast Face in 1959. The first winter ascent was from the south on December 26, 1977, by Gary Bocarde and Kevin Duffy.

Approach: There are many approach options for climbing this peak. Your preferred route will depend upon the time of year you want to climb. On the north side the climbing involves landing on the Drift River gravel bars, which are typically clear of ice by May, and then travelling up the toe of the glaciers toward the desired route. Landing on skis in this area will work well, too.

For the southern routes you would either have to fly in during the frozen months so you can land on Crescent Lake and travel up the rivers, or you will have to bushwhack a great deal just to get to the base of the mountain. In the summer it may be possible to land on Crescent Lake, but the bushwhack approach will be painful. Adding to the dilemma, crossing the North Fork of Crescent River can be very dangerous.

Route description: From the north there are two recorded routes. The first-ascent route travelled the eastern glaciers up to the Northeast Ridge (see the left route line on the overlay). This side of the mountain requires more routefinding through crevasses all the way to the summit. The second route travels up the Northwest Ridge to Peak 9,300. Steve Hackett, Toby Wheeler, Daniel Jones, Daniel Hurd, John Samuelson, and Helmut Tschaffert were the first to climb this route in 1973. They landed at the large pass northwest of the route at 3,500 feet. Gary Bocarde and Kevin Duffy approached from Crescent Lake to make the first winter ascent up a new route on the south side. They encountered a straightforward and aesthetic

The East and Northeast Faces of Redoubt Volcano with Drift River in the foreground. The right line ascends from the Drift River landing strip and the left line is the route of the first-ascent party. (Photo: Paul Roderick)

snow ridge to a significant false summit. A snow ridge connects to the true summit.

Descent: Retrace your ascent route, preferably on skis.

NEACOLA MOUNTAINS

The Neacola Mountains represent the northern boundary of the Chigmits. Their southern boundary is Tlikakila River and the North Fork River. The Neacola and Stony Rivers border the north, and the Chakachatna River is to the east (see map on page 44). These mountains hold many unexplored peaks, and we chose the brightest one of them for this book: Mount Neacola.

13 MOUNT NEACOLA

(9,426 ft; 2873 m)

Route ▲ West Face Couloir
Difficulty ▲ Alaska Grade 2, AI 4
Elevation gain ▲ 4,600 ft
Average time ▲ 3 weeks, 1–2 days on the route
Map ▲ Lake Clark (D-9)
Resources ▲ *AAJ* 1980, pp. 529–530; *AAJ* 1992, pp. 71–73, 125; *AAJ* 1996, p. 179

History: James Garrett, Loren Glick, and Kennan Harvey climbed this mountain on May 20, 1991.

Approach: Fly from Kenai to an unnamed glacier on the east side of Mount Neacola.

Route description: Once you are on the glacier at the base of the West Face, the gully of ascent is very obvious. The party that was in the Neacolas for the first time explored this area and discovered this feature (*AAJ* 1979, p. 529). The large gully ascends at an angle to the right (south) and was climbed on the right side by the first-ascent party. They found the rock to not be of the same quality as the rock found elsewhere

Mount Neacola (Photo: James Garret)

in the range. The rock was much more crumbly; however the ice is protectable. At its steepest point near the top the gully reaches 65 degrees. Once on the ridge the climbing is wonderful; kick back for an enjoyable climb to a summit that is a sharp protrusion with an amazing view of the nearby peaks and more distant mountains.

Descent: Descend via the route of ascent.

Pyramid Peak

Four Horsemen

ALASKA RANGE

The Alaska Range is divided into five distinct mountain groups with Denali (20,320 ft) towering at its helm. From its western boundary it begins where the Aleutian Range ends and makes a massive sweep north into Alaska's Interior. The Alaska Range includes: the Revelation Mountains, Kichatna Mountains, Central Alaska Range, Eastern Alaska Range, and the Delta Mountains at its far-eastern end.

REVELATION MOUNTAINS

Seldom noticed or written about, the Revelation Mountains have remained relatively unexplored. To date, fewer than a dozen expeditions have travelled to their core, weather being the greatest detractor. Located 100 miles northwest of Anchorage, this heavily glaciated group lies north of the Neacola Mountains and Neacola and Stony River drainages, east of Big River, and west of the Kuskokwim River (see map on page 56).

With hardly a dozen climbing expeditions recorded, the Revelations remain dormant and pristine. A glance at the first-ascent teams reveal low-profile pioneering spirits like Tom Walter and Fred Beckey. The granite is no different than in most areas, ranging from solid to so horribly fractured and decomposed you could frontpoint.

Fly from Anchorage, Nikiski, Girdwood, or Talkeetna. Because this area lies close to the coast, prepare yourself for bad weather and a solitary experience.

The Four Horsemen (Photo: Greg Collins)

14 FOUR HORSEMEN

(8,600 ft; 2621 m)

Route ▲ West Couloir to South Ridge
Difficulty ▲ Alaska Grade 2, 5.6, AI 4
Elevation gain ▲ 3,100 ft
Average time ▲ 2–3 weeks, 1 day on route
Maps ▲ Lime Hills (C-3, D-3, C-4, D-4)
Resources ▲ *AAJ* 1968, pp. 27–35; *AAJ* 1988, p. 119

History: David Roberts explored this area in 1967. The next party to focus in this area was a team of National Outdoor Leadership School instructors who repeated quite a few of Roberts's routes and added a few more difficult lines to their achievements. These guys climbed many new routes in the Revelations, mostly up snow-and-ice gullies to rock ridges. Tom Walter and Greg Collins climbed a route on the Angel's Southeast Buttress, which consisted of mixed terrain to 80 degrees and had some unprotected climbing on a crumbly rock band that was climbed free at 5.10.

Approach: It is possible to fly from Girdwood or Nikiski, south of Anchorage. It is also possible to fly to the Revelations from Talkeetna; however this is a long trip and will undoubtedly be more expensive.

Route description: The West Face couloir begins as a wide couloir to the col and leads to the South Ridge for 3,100 feet of AI 4. Once on the ridge there is moderate fifth-class climbing to the summit. The routes on the Four Horsemen are examples of the classic gully climbing and mixed potential that abound on the exquisite granite in the range. The Revelations are a virtually unexplored mountain range, and the climbing around the Revelation Glacier is still

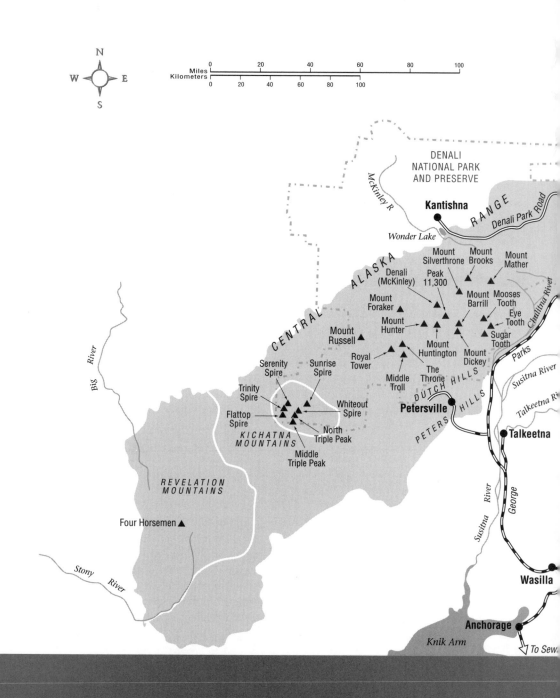

untapped. The weather in this mountain group will dictate the climbs you undertake, but the earlier in the season you arrive, the more likely that the weather will be consistent.

Descent: Retrace your route of ascent.

KICHATNA MOUNTAINS

Boasting the most rugged terrain in the smallest area of any place in Alaska, the Kichatna Mountains are the crown jewels of the Alaska Range and offer an end-less amount of climbing (see map on page 56). Steep granite rock faces, snow- and ice-filled gullies, and nothing over 9,000 feet characterize the group. June, July, and August offer the best conditions, but prepare for only three pleasant days in thirty of horizontal rain, snow, or sleet. The Kichatnas are an ornery bunch.

The Kichatnas were first sighted in 1899 by explorer Joseph Heron, who named the three distant peaks to the north of his position near Rainy Pass Mounts Augustin, Gurney, and Lewis. Seven years later, in 1906, infamous fibber Dr. Fredrick Cook made it to the headwaters of the West Fork of the Yentna River for a better view, but still the Kichatnas remained virgin.

A view of the Kichatna Mountains from the south. Left to right: Flattop Spire; Mount Nevermore; South, Middle, and North Triple Peaks; and Kichatna Spire. (Photo: Paul Roderick)

It was not until the 1960s that attention again turned to this region. Ed LaChapelle, Harvey Manning, and Austin Post circulated a dramatic, but unnamed photo Post had taken on a scenic flight showing the Kichatnas popping up through the clouds. Remembered as the "Riesenstein Hoax," this cryptic Garden of Eden was searched for in vain by many alpinists. Even Fred Beckey gave up on the quest.

New York climbers Al DeMaria and Brownell Bergen finally cracked the nut after tenaciously searching the American Alpine Club library. They rallied for a trip to the "unexplored mountains west of Denali" and catalyzed the Golden Age of the Kichatnas. Word spread through climbing circles of an immense vertical wilderness buried deep in the Alaska Range, and Royal Robbins, David Roberts, Charlie Porter, and Michael Graber took up the call, armed with Yosemite-style tactics.

Their skills, open minds, and hardness were rewarded with outstanding first ascents, but not without enduring the area's legendary foul weather. Forming a low point, weather systems from the north and south sides of the Alaska Range collide over the Kichatnas, creating a "venturi effect." Hundred-mile-an-hour winds and plummeting temperatures more characteristic of Denali can whip up and make one think hard about the consequences of being stuck high on a wall.

Getting there requires plopping down a sack of money for the flight from Talkeetna, which deters most visitors. Given good visibility, landings are not a problem on east and north glaciers; good snow conditions prevail late into the season. You can also land on gravel strips outside the mountains, but you face a longer approach on foot. The surrounding tundra, with its scattered limestone and granite boulders, offers excellent bouldering and views of Dall sheep. It is straightforward to walk up any of the compact glacier toes. If you get stranded by poor weather and have to get to a telephone, bushwhack south to a lodge at Rainy Pass, which has the closest amenities of civilization, but be prepared for river crossings and bears.

15 FLATTOP SPIRE

(8,400 ft; 2560 m)

Route ▲ Southeast Pillar
Difficulty ▲ VI, 5.10, A3
Elevation gain ▲ 2,300 ft
Average time ▲ 3–4 weeks, 2–3 days on route
Map ▲ Talkeetna (B-6)
Resources ▲ *AAJ* 1995, p. 31

History: The first ascent of Flattop Spire was on June 19, 1977, by Michael Graber, Alan Long, and George Schunk via the Northeast Face and North Ridge. Mike Pennings and Doug Byerly climbed the magnificent line on the Southeast Pillar on July 8, 1994. This is a wild-looking peak that looks completely different from all aspects.

Approach: Fly in from Talkeetna to the Tatina Glacier. From the pass at the head of the glacier there are two approach routes. The first is to travel down the Monolith Glacier under the West Face of Middle Triple Peak, but the west fork of the Monolith Glacier is very broken, and it could be difficult to get into the upper basin. The other choice is to travel from the pass. Go to the west between Mount Nevermore and Never-again Peak, then rappel into the upper west fork of the Monolith Glacier basin.

Route description: The Southeast Pillar is a demanding route filled with high-end free climbing and some aid, but "this route would make a mega free climb; I bet it'd go free," proclaims Pennings. The beginning pitches are unprotected climbing that may rattle your cage if not solid on the rock, but this soon gives way to amazing free climbing in a sweet crack that sails upward for several pitches at 5.10. In the spots where the crack gets shallow or the flares are too thin, solid aid moves can break up the free climbing. Once at the top of this initial crack system (top of pitch 8), a traverse on flakes out to the left and then right brings you to the last crack, which carries you to the top of the buttress. A short ridge-walk on easy snow brings you to the summit. (See accompanying topo based on an original drawing by Doug Byerly.)

Southeast Pillar of Flattop Spire (Photo: Michael Pennings)

FLATTOP SPIRE
Southeast Pillar

12 10 m
5.9, A1 (5.10*)
11 45 m
5.9
10 50 m
5.9, A1 (5.11*)
Upside-Down Staircase
40 m 9
5.9, A1 (5.10*)
The Navel
8
60 m
5.9, A1 (5.10*)
60 m 7
5.9, A1 (5.10*)
* denotes probable free rating
6 60 m
A1 (5.10*)
A3
Missing Link Traverse 5 5.10
5.9
4
A2
Salathe Simulator
3
5.10, A1
A3
2
5.9, A1
A2+ hooks
1
5.9

Pennings and Byerly recommend two sets of Friends and nuggets, two cliffhangers, and a few knifeblades.

Descent: Rappel the route to the base.

16 NORTH TRIPLE PEAK

(8,400 ft; 2560 m)

Route ▲ Northwest Couloir to West Ridge
Difficulty ▲ Alaska Grade 2, 5.6, AI 4
Elevation gain ▲ 1,900 ft
Average time ▲ 3–4 weeks, 1 day on route
Map ▲ Talkeetna (B-6)
Resources ▲ *AAJ* 1979, p. 167; *AAJ* 1981, p. 161; *AAJ* 1994, p. 122

History: Peter Sennauser and Richard Ellsworth climbed this couloir to the ridge and summit during a 25-hour push on May 2, 1978. More than a decade later, in June 1993, Doug Byerly and Calvin Hebert climbed this couloir. Mike Pennings soloed the route soon after on July 12, 1993.

Approach: Hire an air service and fly from Talkeetna to the Tatina Glacier.

Route description: From the top of the pass that overlooks the Monolith Glacier at the head of the Tatina Glacier, find your way over the bergschrund and begin climbing up the gully. It can be snowy, but there is blue ice in there somewhere. The couloir can be protected with ice screws and with rock protection, utilizing the rock on the side of the couloir. The climbing in the couloir lasts for twelve 50-meter pitches. Once on the col on the ridge, climb the remaining ridge for three pitches up mixed ground to the summit.

Descent: Retrace the route of ascent.

From the Tatina Glacier, North Triple Peak (left) with the Northwest Couloir ascending to the West Ridge. The West Face of Middle Triple Peak is on the right. (Photo: Mike Wood)

17 SERENITY SPIRE

(7,500 ft; 2286 m)

Route ▲ Southeast Face
Difficulty ▲ IV, 5.10
Elevation gain ▲ 1,200 ft
Average time ▲ 3–4 weeks, 1 day on route
Map ▲ Talkeetna (B-6)
Resources ▲ *AAJ* 1981, pp. 160–164; *AAJ* 1994, p. 122; *Climbing*, no. 64, 1987

History: Andy Embick and Alan Long made the first ascent in June 1980.

Approach: Fly to the Tatina Glacier from Talkeetna. From the Tatina Glacier walk up into the west fork of the Upper Tatina Glacier under the awesome looking East Face of Flattop Spire. Serenity Spire is between Tatina Spire and Trinity Spire. The magnificent Flattop Spire is at the head of the cirque.

Route description: There may be two to three routes on this face. The original was climbed on the East Face for ten pitches up a prominent right-facing dihedral. The rock quality was reported to be excellent, and the climb went mostly free at 5.9 with a little A2. Another route reported on this face in 1993 by Mike Pennings and Jeff Hollenbaugh may be the same line

Trinity Spire (left) and Serenity Spire (right) from the Tatina Glacier (Photo: Mike Wood)

as the Embick/Long route; they suspect this due to their discovery of some old gear on the route. They reported climbing the southeast-facing side, following the left-most (southernmost) right-facing dihedrals up the face. The climbing was mostly 5.9 to 5.10 on excellent rock. Also in 1993, Doug Byerly and Calvin Hebert climbed the right-most of the three obvious lines on the face. Their route was mostly free at 5.10.

Descent: Rappel the route.

 ## 18 TRINITY SPIRE

(7,500 ft; 2286 m)

Route ▲ Southeast Face
Difficulty ▲ IV, 5.10, A0
Elevation gain ▲ 1,500 ft
Average time ▲ 3–4 weeks, 1 day on route
Map ▲ Talkeetna (B-6)
Resources ▲ AAJ 1981, pp. 160–164; Climbing, no. 64, 1987

History: Andy Embick and George Schunk did the first ascent of this route on June 21, 1980. The climb was notable to Schunk: he actually exclaimed that the route "is among those few climbs in the Kichatnas that would be pleasant to repeat."

Approach: Fly to the Tatina Glacier from Talkeetna. From the Tatina Glacier walk up into the west fork of the Upper Tatina Glacier. Trinity Spire is the large spire in the middle of the three prominent spires in the Flattop cirque and is located just south of Serenity Spire.

Route description: The accompanying route overlay shows the start of the route. This climb was completed with eleven 50-meter pitches, on good rock, following crack systems that were free-climbed at 5.10. A short point of aid (A0) was used to get through a section, but for the most part this climb goes free.

Descent: Rappel the route.

 ## 19 WHITEOUT SPIRE

(7,600 ft; 2316 m)

Route ▲ West Face to North Ridge
Difficulty ▲ Alaska Grade 1
Elevation gain ▲ 1,500 ft
Average time ▲ 3–4 weeks, half day on route
Map ▲ Talkeetna (B-6)
Resources ▲ AAJ 1966, pp. 27–29; AAJ 1976, p. 435; AAJ 1981, pp. 160–164

History: This peak was most likely climbed on July 15, 1965, by John Hudson and Peter Geiser when they tried to climb Vulgarian Peak. It was pretty stormy, so it is hard to say for sure. Their route description most closely describes Whiteout Spire (7,600 ft) as it is noted in the 1981 American Alpine Journal (p. 162). In 1975, Paul Denkelwalter and Gary Bocarde climbed the spire, encountering exciting glacier travel leading to the climb. Once on the climb there was snow and a little ice climbing, which brought them to this very cool summit. On July 10, 1993, Mike Pennings and Jeff Hollenbaugh skied to within a few hundred yards of the summit and had great views and great skiing.

Approach: Hire an air service and fly from Talkeetna to the Tatina Glacier.

Route description: From the Tatina Glacier it is a short hike or ski up the northern, or left-hand, of the two icefalls. Start climbing on the west face, 40–45 degrees, to gain the north ridge. Once on the ridge, it is fourth-class travel to the summit. This is one of the easiest peaks in the range, and the views and the skiing are worth it, plus you need to climb to the top of something once in a while.

Descent: If snow conditions are right, you can ski off the ridge; the slopes on both sides of the ridge are 40–45 degrees. Alternately, hike back to your camp on the glacier.

20 SUNRISE SPIRE

(7,900 ft; 2407 m)

Route ▲ Northwest Couloir (Going to the Sun Couloir)
Difficulty ▲ Alaska Grade 2, 5.6, A1, AI 4
Elevation gain ▲ 2,000 ft
Average time ▲ 3–4 weeks, 1 day on route
Map ▲ Talkeetna (B-6)
Resources ▲ *AAJ* 1979, pp. 168–171; *AAJ* 1981, p. 168

History: Andy Embick and Andy Tuthill first climbed this route to the summit in July 1978. The west face has remained relatively untouched, except by Robert McDougall and his partner Kjell Sweden, who attempted a route that ascended nine pitches up awesome rock. Lower down on the route they found good cracks at 5.10, and higher they found thin flakes and thinner cracks at A2. They were forced to descend due to poor weather. Jeff Hollenbaugh and Mike Pennings also attempted this face in a single push, but were thwarted a dozen pitches up by bad weather. Pennings exclaims "I think the west face would make an out of this world, high-standard free climb!"

    Approach: Fly in to the Cul-de-sac Glacier from Talkeetna. The base of the route is at the head of glacier.

    Route description: This route is straightforward. Once over the bergschrund the slope sweeps upward at about 55 to 60 degrees. The couloir requires a total of nineteen 50-meter pitches that can be protected with rock protection and ice screws. The top of the gully averages about 80 degrees, and the terrain becomes a bit more mixed. There is snow and thin ice over the exit rocks to gain the col at the ridge. The two remaining rock pitches are moderate and bring you to the summit.

    Descent: Rappel the route, or descend the back side to the Shelf Glacier, which would be a long walk back around to camp.

Whiteout Spire (left) and Vulgarian Spire (right) from the Tatina Glacier (Photo: Mike Wood)

Sunrise Spire from Tatina Glacier, with Going to the Sun Couloir on the left. Kichatna Spire is hidden by clouds in the background. (Photo: Mike Wood)

21 MIDDLE TRIPLE PEAK

(8,835 ft; 2692 m)

Route ▲ East Buttress
Difficulty ▲ V, 5.10, A2
Elevation gain ▲ 3,600 ft
Average time ▲ 3–4 weeks, 3–4 days on route
Map ▲ Talkeetna (B-6)
Resources ▲ *AAJ* 1973, p. 409; *AAJ* 1977, pp. 103–105; *AAJ* 1986, pp. 145–147; *AAJ* 1995, pp. 140–142; *Climbing*, Oct/Nov 1991

History: To date this climb has seen fewer than a half-dozen ascents. The first team of Andrew Embick,

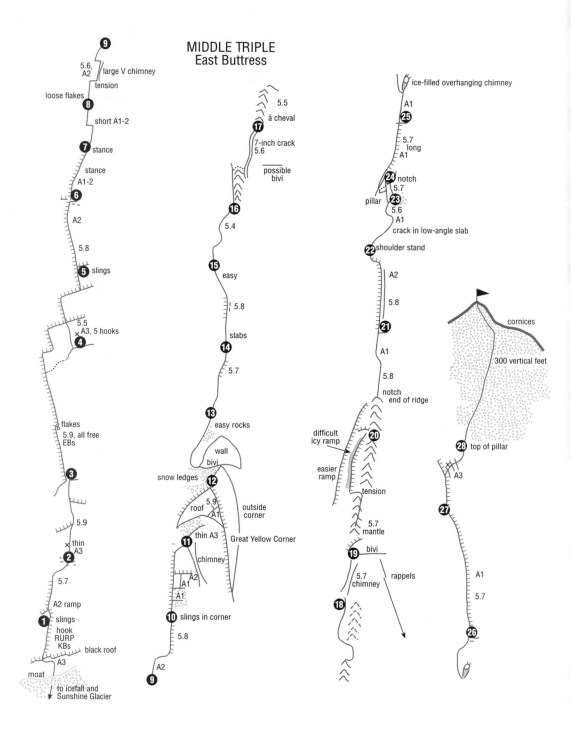

MIDDLE TRIPLE
East Buttress

9

5.6, A2 — large V chimney

tension

loose flakes

8

short A1-2

7 stance

stance
A1-2

6

A2

5.8

5 slings

5.5
4 — A3, 5 hooks

flakes
5.9, all free
EBs

3

5.9

2 — thin A3

5.7

A2 ramp
1 — slings
hook
RURP
KBs — black roof
A3
moat
to icefall and
Sunshine Glacier

5.5
17 — à cheval

7-inch crack
5.6
possible bivi

16

5.4

15

easy

5.8

slabs

14

5.7

13 — easy rocks

wall
bivi

snow ledges — 12

roof — 5.9
A1

thin A3 — 11

chimney

A2
A1
A1

10 — slings in corner

5.8

9

A2

outside corner

Great Yellow Corner

ice-filled overhanging chimney

A1

25

5.7
long
A1

24 — notch
5.7
23

pillar — 5.6
A1

crack in low-angle slab

22 — shoulder stand

A2

5.8

21

A1

5.8

notch
end of ridge

difficult
icy ramp

20

easier
ramp — tension

5.7
mantle

19 — bivi

18 — 5.7
chimney — rappels

cornices

300 vertical feet

28 — top of pillar

A3

27

A1

5.7

26

The East Buttress of Middle Triple Peak (Photo: Paul Roderick)

Michael Graber, Alan Long, and George Schunk climbed this awesome and notorious route on the East Buttress of Middle Triple Peak on June 2–9, 1977. Conrad Anker and Seth Shaw climbed the buttress on May 10, 1991. They finished via an ice gully to the left of the final headwall. Mike Pennings and Jon Allen made the third ascent of this route in a 36-hour push. They climbed the majority of the route free, with Pennings taking a 40-foot fall while making some difficult aid moves after a section of run-out free climbing, then jumping right back on it to the top. On July 29, 1994, Joe Reichert and Michelle Morseth climbed the East Buttress for the fourth ascent, and on July 3,

1997, Matt Culberson and his partner made the fifth ascent of this route.

Approach: The majority of the people who travel to the Kichatnas for the East Buttress typically land on the Shadows Glacier and travel over the pass at the head of the Shadows Glacier to the top of the Sunshine Glacier. Descend about 2 miles and head up the west fork of the Sunshine Glacier to the base of the route. Pennings and Allen approached from the Tatina Glacier, using a pass just east of North Triple and found that a good way to go as well.

Route description: The route begins at the base of the buttress a bit right of center and follows an obvious dihedral system. In the first pitch there is a large roof, and on pitches 3–5 there are large roofs, which are skirted to the right. The route entails many dihedrals, flakes, and protectable crack systems. It is quite common to climb and fix the first three or four pitches. Once at the top of the initial 1,200-foot rock buttress, there is a nice bivi ledge at the base of the ridge. The ridge climbing is a mixture of fourth-class routefinding and easy fifth-class pitches. The final bivi site lies at the top of the seven- to eight-pitch ridge, just above a final 5.7 chimney. This is typically two pitches or so below the start of the upper pillar. The climbing on this upper rock section is fantastic and can go all-free in good weather at 5.10+ This upper section can be anywhere from ten to fourteen pitches until it tops out at the base of the final 300-foot snow slope.

Descent: Travel back down the snowfield, then rappel the upper pillar back to the bivi site. From here most parties have rappelled down the north side of the ridge for eight to ten rappels to the glacier below. Short rappels may keep the rope from getting caught so frequently in this section. Once on the glacier below, make your way through the crevasses back to camp.

CENTRAL ALASKA RANGE

Most of the Central Alaska Range lies within Denali National Park and Preserve, where, as the name implies, Denali (Mount McKinley) resides. Historically the most sought after mountains in Alaska, the Central Alaska Range has been the number-one climbing destination in the state (see map on page 56). The western boundary of the Central Alaska Range is the west fork of the Yentna River. Flatlands mark the range's southern and northern borders, and Broad Pass marks the eastern boundary, where the headwaters of the Nenana and Chulitna Rivers flow north and south respectively.

The park was established in 1917 to protect all the wildlife from ravenous market hunters wanting to sell to buyers in Fairbanks, but as the popularity of climbing increased, the National Park Service (NPS) adopted regulations to manage climbers as well. In a continued effort by those who care (particularly President Jimmy Carter) to protect wildlife by protecting the greater ecosystem, the original park has been expanded several times to its present 6 million acres. Congress later designated the land within the original park boundary as a wilderness area, protecting it from motorized vehicles and plane landings.

Climbers heading to the Central Alaska Range must familiarize themselves with the park boundaries and current regulations governing climbing and camping. Currently, all climbs on Mount Foraker and Denali require preregistration with the NPS office in Talkeetna 60 days in advance, with a non-refundable $25-per-person deposit. This application fee is then credited toward a $150-per-person special-use fee. Only one additional member may join the climb after the 60-day deadline and not at all during the last 30 days of this period. While not mandatory, climbers should register with the NPS for other climbs in the Central Alaska Range and leave an itinerary in the event of an accident. Backcountry permits for the park's north side are issued on a first come, first served basis.

The entrance to Denali National Park and Preserve is located at mile 230 on the George Parks Highway at McKinley Village. The Denali Park Road travels 91 miles west into the historic mining town of Kantishna and scenic Wonder Lake and provides overland access for Mounts Silverthrone, Brooks, and Mather (Routes 39, 40, and 41) on the north side of the Central Alaska Range. The park road is open from June to mid-September and closed the rest of the year. Private cars can travel as far as Savage River, 14 miles from the park entrance. Summer travel beyond this point must be on one of the commercially licensed buses that operate on the park road. The visitor center at the park entrance can make reservations for the bus.

A remote area on the south side of the Central

Alaska Range has earned the name Little Switzerland. This beautiful and aptly named area encompasses the entire inner bend of the Kahiltna Glacier, just 20 miles from the glacier's snout. The unofficially named, but widely recognized Pika Glacier flows past the most popular and centralized grouping of towering granite spires, including Royal Tower, The Throne, and Middle Troll.

Brian Okonek and Roger Robinson were the first to travel into this remote area and snagged a few first ascents including The Throne via the Northwest Ridge in 1976. In 1977, Brian Okonek, Roger Robinson, and Ken Cook returned to the Pika Glacier to make first ascents of Royal Tower, South Troll, Your Highness, Dragons Spine, Italy's Boot, and the group made a second ascent of The Throne.

The area is easily accessed via airplane, or—with more difficulty—by walking in from the end of Petersville Road, located at mile 114.5 on the George Parks Highway. In general, climbers heading to these and other climbs on the south side of the Central Alaska Range fly from Talkeetna.

22 MOUNT RUSSELL

(11,670 ft; 3557 m)

Route ▲ North Ridge
Difficulty ▲ Alaska Grade 2+
Elevation gain ▲ 3,500 ft
Average time ▲ 7–10 days, 1 day on route
Map ▲ Talkeetna (D-4)
Resources ▲ *AAJ* 1959, p. 228; *AAJ* 1963, pp. 390–395; *AAJ* 1967, pp. 344–345; *AAJ* 1973, pp. 407–408; *AAJ* 1982, p. 135; *AAJ* 1990, pp. 21–27; *AAJ* 1994, pp. 120–121 (winter ascent); *AAJ* 1999 p. 256; *Scree* 24, no. 6, 1981

History: This is one of the most amazing peaks in Alaska simply for its beauty, and it is completely overlooked by so many who visit the Alaska Range. Mount Russell lies to the west of its giant siblings, on the cusp of the Central Alaska Range, and it has had only six recorded ascents to date. The first ascent by Hellmut Raithel and party from the Chedotlothna Glacier up the West Face on May 28, 1962, is a fascinating account that appeared in the 1963 *American Alpine Journal*. The second ascent began from the upper Yentna Glacier basin, which is now the standard departure site for attempts on the North Ridge. Thomas Kensler, Peter Brown, John Hauck, Dick Jablonowski, and Dan Osborne climbed the North Ridge between July 4 and 13, 1972.

Approach: Fly from Talkeetna to the 8,000-foot plateau of the Yentna Glacier on the northeast side of Mount Russell. It is illegal to land inside the Denali Wilderness Area boundary that crosses this basin.

Route description: The landing strip up here is right on the border of the old park, with the old park boundary running off the summit of Mount Russell. From the landing site, the route follows mellow-angled slopes that can be skied for the most part up to 8,700 feet. At this point your skis may need to be replaced by crampons to reach the high camp, which is located near the knob (10,000 ft) just north of the pass and "Knob 10,005." It is easy to gain a ton of elevation quickly. Remember this when coming from 340 feet in Talkeetna to the 8,000-foot basin then to high camp; it is really easy to get a headache. From the high camp it is feasible to summit in a day.

The ridge that connects "Knob 10,005" to the main rock ridge on the map at 9,700 feet is quite negotiable on the ridge proper. It is common to get lured down off the ridge. Near the end of the ridge traverse, it may be necessary to drop right off the crest and cross the top of steep slopes that average 60–65 degrees. It will then become obvious that you can get off the ridge and travel west under the bergschrund until it looks the mellowest. It may be attractive to go directly up the ridge and not traverse the bergschrund to the easier spot, but it isn't all that easy. Climbing the bergschrund requires some snow

The North Ridge of Mount Russell, marked by the sun/shade line (Photo: Mike Wood)

aid moves to get onto the 45- to 50-degree ice face. From here you can traverse up and left to the east to gain the ridge. Once on the ridge the travel is really enjoyable and appears to have changed quite a bit since the first ascent of the ridge in 1972 and other more recent accounts. It actually seems to be getting easier, but it is hard to say for sure. The routefinding is quite interesting on the ridge itself, with some bouldering ice moves, but then the slope eases back and is a 45-degree walk to the summit on super-cool wind sculptures. The summit is very small and has a "killer" view of the Kichatnas and Mount Foraker.

Descent: To get back down, retrace your ascent route; however, instead of traversing back across the ice slope to gain the part of the bergschrund you came up, it may be easier to follow the ridge straight down. Expect to do a wild rappel over the bergschrund. This must be well calculated because there is quite a drop, and it is hard to figure the best place to do this when looking down from the top.

23 ROYAL TOWER

(8,130 ft; 2478 m)

Route ▲ East Buttress (Gargoyle Buttress)
Difficulty ▲ IV, 5.10
Elevation gain ▲ 2,300 ft
Average time ▲ 2 weeks, 1 day on route
Map ▲ Talkeetna (C-3)
Resources ▲ *AAJ* 1987 p. 179; *AAJ* 1994, p. 120; *AAJ* 1999, pp. 193–194; *AAJ* 2000, pp. 214–215; *Climbing*, no. 196, Aug 2000

History: On June 19 and 20, 1977, Brian Okonek, Ken Cook, and Roger Robinson made the first ascent of Royal Tower. It is hard to say who made the actual first ascent of the Gargoyle Buttress. Many people may have climbed at least up to the sixth pitch. However, Dave Anderson and his partner Rob Feeney reached the top on June 6, 1999, and were able to supply some great information.

Fly-in approach: Fly from Talkeetna to the Pika Glacier in the Little Switzerland area. From the airstrip on the glacier, travel west 0.25 mile downglacier to the base of the route.

Walk-in approach: Travel north past the Talkeetna spur road at mile 99 on the George Parks Highway to Trapper Creek at mile 114.5, the intersection of the highway and Petersville Road. The Petersville Road runs 33 miles to the parking area just north of Peters Gap. This is a very unimproved road at present. In the winter and spring months the road is plowed for only 14 miles to Kroto Creek. From the parking area hike on tractor trail along Peters Creek, and continue past Bird Creek, which flows into Peters Creek from the west. Once over a shallow pass, drop down into the drainage of Bear Creek and head north to the confluence of Bear Creek and Wildhorse Creek. Follow Wildhorse Creek to its headwaters and on to the pass known as "Rivendell," 13 miles from the parking area.

From the pass descend northwest to Granite River and onto the Granite Glacier. Follow the glacier 9 miles to Exit Pass (5,850 ft), the saddle at the head of Granite Glacier's west fork, also known as the Exit Fork. From the top of Exit Pass, which can be quite rocky and scree-covered in summer months, drop down and cross a bergschrund that can be difficult to negotiate in August and September due to a lack of snow bridges. Once over the bergschrund, travel down the glacier and onto the main Pika Glacier at 5,000 feet, just north of The Throne, one of many impressive granite towers in the area.

Route description: This route is a completely stunning buttress that is the most obvious feature on the Royal Tower. The other routes on this peak are a bit difficult to find due to the available route descriptions, but they are all there and hopefully we will be able to sort this out in the future. You won't have a problem finding this aesthetic route.

The climbing begins at the base of the ridge, about halfway up the slope leading toward the entrance to the large gully separating the north and south peaks. Dave Anderson calls the climbing "enjoyable" and on good granite. It is fractured, as is most mountain granite, but the protection is all there and the rappel routes are as well. The upper snowfield at the top of the route to the south summit doesn't get climbed often. The

Royal Tower from the Pika Glacier (Photo: Mike Wood)

climbing is in the 5.10 range with many more moderate pitches. In places the rock can be a little crispy or flaky. (See accompanying topo based on an original drawing by Dave Anderson.)

Descent: Rappel the route, or descend along the South Ridge, making occasional rappels to the col near a rock pinnacle known as The Munchkin, then walk back down Pika Glacier to camp.

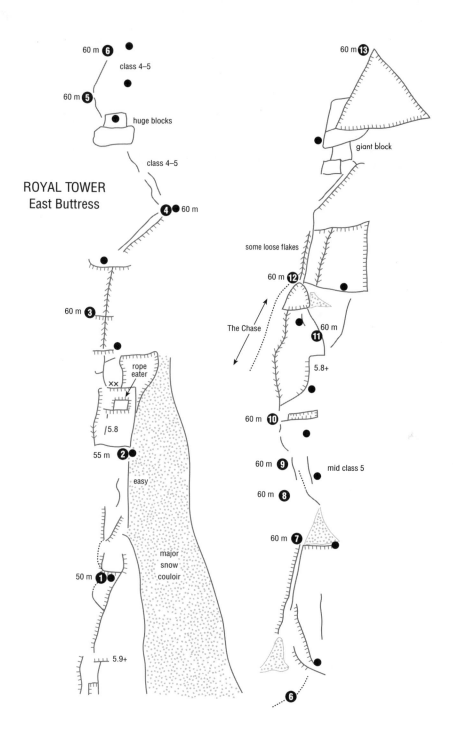

60 m **6**

class 4–5

60 m **5**

huge blocks

ROYAL TOWER
East Buttress

class 4–5

4 60 m

60 m **3**

rope
eater

××

/ 5.8

55 m **2**

easy

major
snow
couloir

50 m **1**

5.9+

60 m **13**

giant block

some loose flakes

60 m **12**

The Chase

11 60 m

5.8+

60 m **10**

60 m **9**   mid class 5

60 m **8**

60 m **7**

6

The Throne with the West Face shaded and the South Face sunlit. The line indicates the Alkaitis/Byer/Mayo route. (Photo: Mike Wood)

24 THE THRONE

(7,390 ft; 2252 m)

Route ▲ South Face
Difficulty ▲ III, 5.9+
Elevation gain ▲ 1,500 ft
Average time ▲ 2 weeks, 1 day on route
Map ▲ Talkeetna (C-3)
Resources ▲ *AAJ* 1978, pp. 511–512; *AAJ* 1985, p. 179; *AAJ* 1989, p. 137; *AAJ* 1991

History: There are a huge number of routes on this most impressive peak. Many of the routes have only been climbed for the first few pitches, while others go all the way to the summit. First ascents of identical routes on this face have been reported. This peak needs a Yosemite-style topo map to keep track of all the ascents since 1976.

The South Face is less steep than the West Face, but it offers some excellent climbing on fine granite. Beginning just past the corner separating the South and West Faces, documented routes on the South Face (from west to east) are as follows. In 1981 Nick Parker climbed a route to the west of *Lost Marsupials* on the prominent, rounded ridge to the west of the South Face gully. *Lost Marsupials* itself is the rock rib to the west of the obvious snow gully on the face. It had a recorded ascent in 1996. The South Face gully received two "first ascents": one in 1980 and the second in 1990.

East of the gully lie the two routes presented in the route description. The first obvious dihedral leading to lower-angled rock and on to the summit was climbed on July 31, 1976, by Okonek and Robinson. The next route to the east is a dihedral just west of the beautiful white dihedrals on the far-east side of the south face. Mike Alkaitis, Henry Byer, and Molly Mayo climbed this route in 1998.

Approach: Fly to the Pika Glacier in the Little Switzerland area, or walk in via the approach for Royal Tower (Route 23).

Route description: Travel up to the pass between

The Throne and the North Troll about 200 meters from the small spire known as The Plunger to the north of the pass. The Okonek/Robinson route begins by climbing the low-angle rock up to the corner system on the lighter-colored rock. This stunning dihedral leads to the low-angle slope above, and third- and fourth-class travel weaves to the summit in twelve pitches.

The Alkaitis/Byer/Mayo route is just to the east and begins on low-angle rock to another left-facing dihedral in the dark rock corners. The dihedral exits onto lower-angle terrain but then continues to climb directly to the ridge for some final steep pitches. This route was named *Lord Knows* and is rated 5.9+.

Descent: Rappel the route or *Lost Marsupials* farther to the west on the South Face.

25 MIDDLE TROLL

(6,900 ft; 2103 m)

Route ▲ South Face
Difficulty ▲ III, 5.9
Elevation gain ▲ 1,500 ft
Average time ▲ 2 weeks, 1 day on route
Map ▲ Talkeetna (C-3)
Resources ▲ *AAJ* 1985, p. 179; *AAJ* 2000, pp. 214–215; *Climbing,* no. 196, Aug 2000, pp. 90–96

History: The first party to climb Middle Troll included Pete Pollard and John Rich in June 1984. They recorded climbing the South Face on "nice rock."

Approach: Fly from Talkeetna to the Pika Glacier

North Troll, Middle Troll, and South Troll from Pika Glacier (Photo: Matt Smith)

On-route up Middle Troll (Photo: Dave Anderson)

in the Little Switzerland area, or walk in via the approach for Royal Tower (Route 23).

Route description: The route up Middle Troll is one of the most fun and provides some of the most spectacular views in the Alaska Range. The route starts in the snow gully between Middle and South Troll. As with most climbs in this area, the bergschrund and/or moat can be the most difficult obstacle to overcome, but once on the route the climbing unfolds before your eyes. The climbing is up to 5.9, but the majority of the route is lower fifth class with some fourth-class climbing interspersed. There is loose rock in the typically fractured granite of the range, but the protection is good and plentiful. Once at the top of the face there is a great ridge that you must straddle to get to the very top, and a diving board–like perch exists below the summit for you to shimmy out onto.

Descent: Rappel the route or descend one of the snow gullies to the north or south.

26 MOUNT FORAKER: SULTANA RIDGE

(17,400 ft; 5303 m)

Route ▲ Northeast Ridge (Sultana Ridge)
Difficulty ▲ Alaska Grade 3
Elevation gain ▲ 10,500 ft along 9 miles of ridge
Average time ▲ 3 weeks, 10–18 days on route
Maps ▲ Talkeetna (D-3), Mount McKinley (A-3)
Resources ▲ *AAJ* 1980, pp. 521–522; *AAJ* 1982,
    p. 133 (ski descent); *AAJ* 1984, p. 153 (winter
    ascent)

History: Charles Houston and his team first climbed Mount Foraker in 1934 via the Northwest Ridge. The Upper Northeast Ridge was climbed in 1966 by a Japanese team, but this route is heinously scary due to the "death hangers" (i.e., unstable hanging glaciers) along the whole route. (The avalanche in the photo on page

Sultana Ridge on Mount Foraker. The horizontal route line ascends Mount Crosson's described Southeast Ridge. From the far right, the route doubles back to reach the vertical route line ascending Sultana Ridge. (Photo: Brian McCullough)

19 runs across this route.) Finally, Brian Okonek, Roger Cowles, and Dave Johnston climbed the ridge in March 1979. This was the second winter ascent of the peak and the first time the ridge had been climbed in its entirety. This experienced and strong team of climbers was on their third attempt of the ridge when they finally succeeded.

Approach: Fly to the 7,200-foot base camp on the southeast fork of the Kahiltna Glacier. To reach the base of Mount Crosson, travel west down the southeast fork and across the Kahiltna Glacier to the base of Crossen's Southeast Ridge on the other side of the glacier. There are a few crevasses, but you can clear these quite easily for a total distance of 3 miles.

Route description: This wonderful route is the safest and most accessible route up Mount Foraker, involving 9 miles of ridge climbing from the base of Mount Crosson. The route begins at the base of Mount Crosson at 6,900 feet, and the choices for getting onto the Southeast Ridge of Mount Crosson are many. Much depends upon the snow conditions and the wind direction that has deposited the snow. The south side of the ridge does offer some short gullies that greatly reduce your exposure time to avalanches. Once on the ridge, however, the snow conditions are typically pretty wind-scoured and offer great cramponing.

At 8,200 feet and again at 9,500 feet, there are great camping spots on the Southeast Ridge. These spots offer low-angle camping sites, and if you poke around, decent snow to make walls can be found. The routefinding on Mount Crosson gets a little trickier toward the top, but once over the 12,800-foot summit the descent to the col requires only a bit more routefinding, as the broad ridge narrows in places. Going directly over Peak 12,472 may be necessary to avoid avalanche hazards, but it is possible to traverse below the summit if conditions allow to avoid gaining extra and unnecessary elevation.

The next portion of the climb heads almost due south along an undulating ridge where well-hidden crevasses often run parallel to the rope, due to the glacier tension pulling them down the slopes on either side. It may go without saying, but it is worth wanding the whole ridge route almost from the time you ascend above the last rocks on the Southeast Ridge of Mount Crosson.

The majority of the route is on the divide of the Alaska Range and is ravaged by every weather system that blows through. In all, you lose 3,670 feet of elevation from the top of Mount Crosson just to get to the base of Mount Foraker's summit ridge. It is here at 12,200 feet that the last camp is typically put in before the summit push. This is a great campsite, as the slopes above get steeper and do not lend themselves to camping easily.

The day ahead is a doozy with some big elevation gain to reach the summit and descend back to camp. The route to the summit is straightforward, but this massive, broad ridge, which is somewhat nondescript and monotonous, could become exceedingly difficult to negotiate in poor weather. It is prudent to place plenty of wands during your summit bid.

Descent: Retrace your line of wands to reach Kahiltna base camp. It must be noted that it is definitely not worth trying to take shortcuts and descend any of the "death variations" such as the 1966 Japanese route.

27 MOUNT FORAKER: INFINITE SPUR

(17,400 ft; 5303 m)

Route ▲ Infinite Spur
Difficulty ▲ Alaska Grade 6, 5.9, AI 4
Elevation gain ▲ 9,000 ft to south summit
Average time ▲ 4 weeks, 7–14 days on route
Maps ▲ Talkeetna (D-3), Mount McKinley (A-3)
Resources ▲ *AAJ* 1978, p. 359; *AAJ* 1990, pp. 28–35; *Climbing*, no. 44, 1977; *Coast Magazine*, Aug 2000

History: Alex Bertulis and a partner made the first attempt on this face in 1968. It was 3 o'clock in the morning on June 27,1977, when Michael Kennedy

Mount Foraker's Infinite Spur. Near the top, the original Kennedy/Lowe route is on the right and the left line is a variation. (Photo: Carl Tobin)

and George Lowe left their base camp on the Lacuna Glacier to begin climbing the Central Spur of the South Face of Mount Foraker. It took them a total of 7 days to climb this route, having been pinned down for a day at their high camp. They descended via the Southeast Ridge to a cache they had left on the approach. They named this route the "Infinite Spur" after the endless nature of the route. On June 14, 1989, Jim Nelson and Mark Bebie made a 10-day ascent of the Infinite Spur. They were stuck high on the route for 4 days before they could climb to the top and descend via the Southeast Ridge. In June 2000 two parties climbed the Infinite Spur simultaneously. They both descended via the Sultana Ridge over Mount Crosson to reach the Kahiltna Glacier.

Approach: Fly to the 7,200-foot base camp on the southeast fork of the Kahiltna Glacier. From there, travel south down the southeast fork, aiming for the small glacier to the north of Peak 8,460 and the base of the southeast ridge of Mount Foraker. At the head of this glacier is a pass that is easily ascended and drops down onto the Lacuna Glacier. From the base of this pass on the Lacuna Glacier, travel up the glacier a short distance to circumvent some crevasses and head for a low spot in the ridge to the west. There may be some awkward climbing to get over this pass, and it has the potential to avalanche as well. Once on the other side, drop down again to the Lacuna Glacier and travel to a safe camp below the Central Spur of the South Face. This cirque has very active icefall, and care must be taken to ensure a safe route to the base of the climb.

Route description: This 9,000-foot route with some sixty to eighty-odd pitches requires the highest in alpine climbing standards. It says quite a bit about the route that it received its second ascent 9 years after the first, and didn't see another ascent for 11 years. Many ambitious but ultimately unsuccessful parties have found the route to be intimidating, the climbing challenging, and the descent long. The final approach to the base of the spur is subject to considerable icefall hazard. There are two obvious icefall runouts on both sides of the main spur. These should be avoided

as quickly as possible as you head for a 1,500-foot snow and ice slope that arcs to intersect the spur.

From the top of this initial slope the route weaves through mixed ground and 5.8–5.9 rock for full 60-meter rope-lengths until you are on the ridge at about 9,400–9,500 feet. The granite is wonderful on the lower part of the route, and it is interspersed with snow and ice. The middle sections of the climb, between 9,500 and 11,000 feet, become more mixed and the rock quality becomes less solid in the sections of black rock. The climbing here generally follows the spur over mixed ground that can frequently be ascended via simul-climbing, although there are also sections of fifth class that require belays. A large rock buttress is passed to your left 600 feet beyond a large rock wall that intersects the ridge at 11,000 feet. This offers a safe bivouac site.

From 11,000 feet, climb around the rock buttress to a snow ridge and the snow slopes above, heading for a very distinct black rock band. From this point there are many different route options. Originally, Lowe and Kennedy passed the band to the right. The left-hand option was taken by Barry Blanchard and Carl Tobin. The center line, which heads directly up a narrow gully into some mixed terrain, leads to some steep pitches of waterfall ice. Above the rock band, where the route once again intersects the ridge, the exposure to the west increases, and a traverse farther west under a steep rock buttress on 55-degree snow and ice ends in a very sharp snow arête. Above here, the terrain eases, allowing for more simul-climbing until you reach a hanging ice cliff at 14,000 feet. This spot can be a very good bivi site. The remaining climbing takes you up 55-degree slopes in the final couloir until about 15,200 feet, from which point you can walk to the 16,800-foot south summit.

Descent: Half the parties that have climbed this route have come down the Southeast Ridge. Each party felt that this was a very difficult and dangerous descent. The two parties in 2000 came down on the Sultana Ridge over Mount Crosson to reach the Kahiltna Glacier. This long descent may not be attrac-

Mount Hunter with the Kahiltna Glacier in the foreground, as seen from Mount Foraker's Sultana Ridge. The right line follows Beckey's West Ridge route and the left line is the Bocarde variation. (Photo: Brian Okonek)

tive for most people due to its length, but we believe you will soon find it is the best option.

28 MOUNT HUNTER: WEST RIDGE

(14,573 ft; 4441 m)

Route ▲ West Ridge
Difficulty ▲ Alaska Grade 4+, 5.8, AI 3
Elevation gain ▲ 7,600 ft; 4.5 mile-long ridge climbing
Average time ▲ 2 weeks, 7–10 days on route
Map ▲ Talkeetna (D-3)
Resources ▲ *AAJ* 1955, pp. 44–45; *AAJ* 1959, pp. 222–224; *AAJ* 1964; *AAJ* 1967, p. 343; *AAJ* 1984 p. 153; Roper and Steck, *Fifty Classic Climbs*, p. 14–18; Waterman, *High Alaska*

History: Fred Beckey, Heinrich Harrer, and Henry Meybohm climbed this peak on July 5, 1954—the same year that they completed a first ascent of Mount Deborah and the first ascent of Denali's Northwest Ridge. When they finished the climb, the glacier was too melted out for Don Sheldon to pick them up with a ski plane, so they walked out via the Kahiltna Glacier to reach the Petersville Road to return to Talkeetna.

Approach: Fly in to the landing strip on the southeast fork of the Kahiltna Glacier. From there, travel west down "Heartbreak Hill" and turn left at the main branch of the Kahiltna Glacier. Travel the remaining 1.5 miles down the Kahiltna Glacier to the first rock ridge coming off Mount Hunter's West Ridge. Ascend the tiny tributary glacier south of the ridge.

Route description: The route climbed by the first-ascent party is the most commonly ascended route on Mount Hunter. It is not, however, a "beginner's route" by any means. This route is fraught with many miles of corniced ridge, avalanche-prone slopes, and crevasses. Over the years there have been some variations made to the beginning of the original route. These have their advantages and disadvantages, but we describe the first-ascent route and leave the variations up to you.

The West Ridge route begins by ascending the most northern of the small glaciers that pour off the end of the West Ridge. The climbing is straightforward, but beware that there is an icefall that can deposit avalanche debris onto the line of ascent. This glacier is followed to a saddle at 8,950 feet that provides a really nice camp (Camp 1). From here it is a short climb to a rock spire from which steep downclimbing and rappelling are necessary to gain the col to the east. Once on this col it is necessary to traverse the slopes and follow the ridge (while avoiding the cornices) to the top of the next high point (9,500 feet). This is an excellent vantage point to study the route ahead. Downclimb to the next saddle, repeating a theme that will become very common on this route. Traverse along the ridge, climbing a thin line between being above a cornice fracture or below an avalanche crown. This saddle is a great place for a camp before the next section is explored.

The granite rock step rising 500 feet in front of you requires about three rope-lengths of roped climbing. Traverse about 100 feet below the rock ridge crest. In the middle section of the rock band, crack-climbing on excellent granite brings you back to the ridge crest at the base of the crucial, 50-foot Beckey Chimney. Beyond the chimney are several pitches of mixed climbing before more corniced ridge and snow slopes demand your attention.

The Bocarde variation is intersected on the ridge at 10,200 feet, where there is a large, flat place to camp. From here the ridge continues to rise and fall to the base of a slope at 10,700 feet. Just east of Point 10,820 there is an excellent place to dig in that may serve as a high camp. The next slope offers steeper ice climbing followed by wild cornices before the ridge finally broadens. There is one final obstacle ahead before reaching the upper ramparts of Mount Hunter. A huge crevasse defines the edge of the summit plateau, spanning the entire width of the slope. This final section at 13,500 feet is often difficult to nego-

tiate. Cross the summit plateau, where the way is defined by routefinding around crevasses and perhaps wanding it well in the event that poor weather moves in. This 0.5 mile can be arduous due to deep snow conditions. It is up to you to find the easiest way up the final snow slope to reach the 14,573-foot summit.

Descent: Retrace your steps down the West Ridge to the Kahiltna Glacier.

29 MOUNT HUNTER: MOONFLOWER

(14,573 ft; 4441 m)

Route ▲ Moonflower
Difficulty ▲ Alaska Grade 6, 5.8, A3, AI 6
Elevation gain ▲ 6,100 ft
Average time ▲ 3 weeks, 7–10 days on route
Map ▲ Talkeetna (D-3)
Resources ▲ AAJ 1980, pp. 523–524; AAJ 1981, p. 155; AAJ 1982, pp. 118–123 (Stump); AAJ 1984 (Bibler/Klewin); AAJ 1985 (McNerthney/ Newsome); AAJ 1993, p. 138 (DeKlerk/ Brugger); AAJ 1995, pp. 134–135 (Rackliff/ Belcourt); AAJ 1996, pp. 175–178 (North Face); AAJ 1997, p. 174 (Lowe/Anker); Climbing, no. 64, 1981; Climbing, no. 67, 1981 (Stump/ Aubrey); Climbing, Jun 1986 (Newsome); Climbing, no. 105, 1987; Climbing, no. 146, 1994; Climbing, no. 150, 1994; Waterman, High Alaska

History: The history of attempts on the Moonflower route on the North Buttress of Mount Hunter is fascinating and a veritable Who's Who of Alaska mountaineering. A valiant attempt by Pat and Doug Klewin with Todd Bibler was made in 1979. In 1980 Pat and Dan McNerthney, Rob Newsome, and Doug Klewin returned as "White Punks on Dope." The following year the same team of the McNerthney brothers, Doug Klewin, and Newsome returned as "Back in Black."

The first 4,000 feet of the Moonflower *route on the North Buttress of Mount Hunter (Photo: Brian Okonek)*

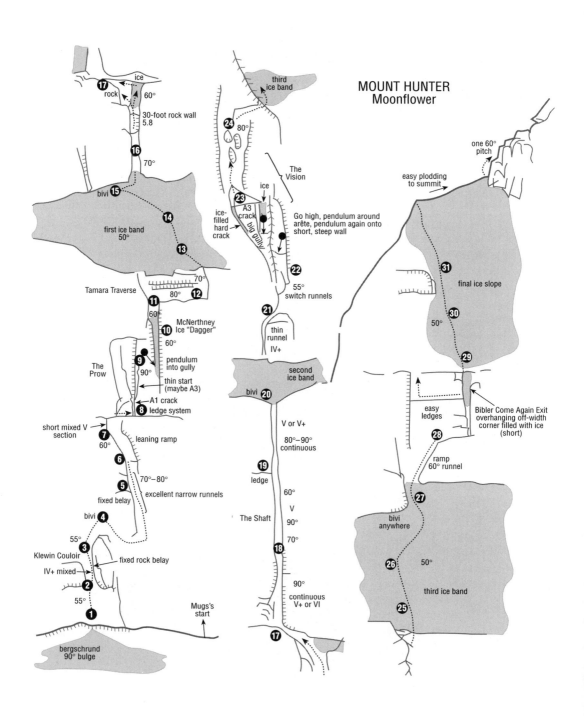

MOUNT HUNTER
Moonflower

ice
17
rock
60°

30-foot rock wall
5.8

16
70°

bivi 15

first ice band
50°

14

13

Tamara Traverse

70°
80°
12
11
60°

McNerthney
Ice "Dagger"

10
60°

9
pendulum
into gully

The
Prow
90°

thin start
(maybe A3)

A1 crack

8
ledge system

short mixed V
section
7
60°

leaning ramp

6

5
70°–80°

excellent narrow runnels

fixed belay

bivi 4

55°
3

Klewin Couloir

IV+ mixed
2

fixed rock belay

55°

1

Mugs's
start

bergschrund
90° bulge

third
ice band

24
80°

The
Vision

ice

23
A3
crack

Go high, pendulum around
arête, pendulum again onto
short, steep wall

ice-
filled
hard
crack

big gully

22
55°
switch runnels

21

thin
runnel

IV+

second
ice band

bivi 20

V or V+

80°–90°
continuous

19
ledge
60°

V
90°

The Shaft

18
70°

90°
continuous
V+ or VI

17

one 60°
pitch

easy plodding
to summit

31

final ice slope

30
50°

29

Bibler Come Again Exit
overhanging off-width
corner filled with ice
(short)

easy
ledges

28

ramp
60° runnel

27

bivi
anywhere

26

50°

third ice band

25

Onto the stage entered Mugs Stump, who intended to give it a solo attempt, but reconsidered and hooked up with Paul Aubrey. The Back in Black team reached a high point from which they retreated momentarily. Meanwhile Stump began climbing a line to the right of theirs that soon traversed to the left and directly into the "prow" or "keel" and the Back in Black team's intended ascent line. Mugs Stump and Paul Aubrey solved the puzzle of the *Moonflower* route and climbed to their high point on the last snowfield, deciding to forgo the summit.

In 1983 Todd Bibler returned with Doug Klewin to complete the route, ascending the left side of the face at the beginning of the route and continuing to the summit of Mount Hunter. Finally in 1984 Pat McNerthney and Rob Newsome climbed *Moonflower* to the summit as well. The tenacity of the core group of Doug Klewin, Todd Bibler, Rob Newsome, and Pat and Dan McNerthney is remarkable. So too, the number of attempts made by such noted climbers as Charlie Porter, Gary Bocarde, Dale Bard, and Jim Bridwell during this exciting period of time for the route. The weather, the route conditions, the technology in alpine climbing, and the knowledge gained by each party finally came together for a celebrated ascent of a magnificent testpiece. The route description can best be understood using the topographic map and the photo provided.

Approach: Fly in to the landing strip on the southeast fork of the Kahiltna Glacier. The North Buttress is a difficult feature to overlook due to its extremely accessible proximity to the landing strip. The approach to the base of the North Buttress is not difficult, but there is a fair bit of crevasse hazard and a huge amount of serious serac-fall danger if you get too close to the east side of the glacier. Powder blasts are commonly witnessed running across the southeast fork of the Kahiltna Glacier.

Route description: The buttress itself rises steeply from the glacier for 4,000 feet to the ridge at the top of the buttress and continues for another 2,000 feet to the summit of the west peak of Mount Hunter.

This is an extremely technical route, and the condition that the route is in very much dictates its safety and the likely success of the party. The route's proximity to the airstrip may prompt more people to try this route and lends to it a false sense of safety. Every year there is a line of very experienced climbers and alpinists attempting *Moonflower*; only the most technically proficient make it. In technical difficulty, it is a grade harder than the Cassin Ridge of Denali. This route is the culmination of many different types of climbing that have taken years to hone and apply to the Alaskan environment. Although most people may want to know the difficulty of each pitch, it is impossible to reassure our readers with the grade of each individual pitch because of the route's ever-changing conditions.

The spindrift formed on the upper slopes of the mountain is nearly constant, and it is possible to have small pockets of slab, especially at the base of the route below the bergschrund. Unique features that form on the North Buttress are "snow pods," incredible snow mushrooms that lurk under overhangs and may be formed by the combination of updrafts and downdrafts. If you are unlucky enough to be under one when it falls, it will surely ruin your day—and they will fall at some point. Unfortunately the most notorious pod grows just at the top of the gully used to access The Shaft, and exposure to the monster is inevitable. Once past this snow mushroom and above The Shaft, the objective hazards that remain are the avalanche potential on the upper slopes and a storm while on the route.

Descent: The descent of this route is a matter of personal preference. Rappel the whole route (quickest), or travel to the summit and down the West Ridge (see Route 28). The first option takes much less time, but is fraught with its own special set of problems involved in rappelling a 4,000-foot face.

The West Ridge consists largely of horizontal downclimbing with only a few rappels. However, cornices, avalanche slopes, and complicated routefinding on this long ridge make it a very involved climb unto itself. Though this option does take longer, parties that have been up the West Ridge may be able to find the easiest route down more quickly.

30 DENALI: WEST RIB

(20,320 ft; 6193 m)

Route ▲ West Rib
Difficulty ▲ Alaska Grade 4, AI 3
Elevation gain ▲ 9,000 ft
Average time ▲ 3–4 weeks, 4–7 days on route
Map ▲ Mount McKinley (A-3)
Resources ▲ *AAJ* 1960, pp. 1, 113; *AAJ* 1973 (alpine style); *AAJ* 1978 (solo); *AAJ* 1984 (winter ascent); *AAJ* 1990, p. 50; Waterman, *High Alaska*

History: On June 19, 1959, Peter Sinclair, Jake Breitenbach, Barry Corbet, and Bill Buckingham climbed the West Rib. The climbers' average age was 23 years old, and Breitenbach was the only one who had any big mountain experience—from Denali's West Buttress the previous year. Their ascent is written up in the 1960 *American Alpine Journal* and they even made the cover! In 1977 Ruprecht Kammerlander completed the first solo ascent of the route. Then on February 28, 1983, Charlie Sassara, Robert Frank, Steve Teller, and Chris Hraback flew in to attempt Denali's West Rib. On March 11, Sassara and Frank left from high camp at 18,000 feet. They reached the summit, then, while descending from 19,600 feet, Sassara heard Frank yell. Suddenly, he slid into Sassara, tumbling him about 100 feet before he self-arrested. Frank continued to tumble for 7,000 feet to his death. Unfortunately, this is the way many climbers have come to their deaths on the West Rib: descending the upper slopes after a summit push.

Approach: Fly in to the Kahiltna Glacier. To reach the base of the Chicken Couloir where the route begins, travel up the northeast fork of the Kahiltna Glacier. Ice avalanches have been witnessed travelling across the entire glacier, so move quickly. Only one group has been killed in this fork in all these years, but there is no rhyme or reason to serac-fall. The routefinding has a tendency to push you to the right, under some of the worst "hangers" (i.e., cornices or hanging seracs) in the valley. There is a reasonably safe camp halfway up the northeast fork. At about 10,500 feet, navigate through an icefall just before you reach a camp. The camp is to the west of the couloir at the base of the incredibly beautiful golden granite.

Route description: Perhaps due to its close proximity to the Cassin Ridge, this beautiful route has unfortunately been overlooked by the majority of climbers coming to Denali. It has inspired climbers who desired a taste of a more technical route on the mountain and who wanted at the same time to avoid the more heavily travelled West Buttress route.

There are many different schools of thought on how best to climb the West Rib, ranging from the traditional expedition-style ascent, acclimatizing on the route, to going up the West Buttress route and acclimatizing at the 14,200-foot base camp. From the 14,200-foot basin, make forays up the mountain to acclimatize and get stronger. When weather and group dynamics all come together, descend to 7,900 feet on the Kahiltna Glacier, grab supplies, and travel up the northeast fork to the base of the Chicken Couloir at 11,200 feet. This allows you to climb the whole route from the northeast fork to the summit and down during a 2- or 3-day high-pressure system.

The other alternative is to forgo the lower Rib Chicken Couloir start and climb the upper West Rib or "Riblet" from the 14,200-foot basin intersecting the upper West Rib at 16,200 feet. Unfortunately this means missing 5,000 feet of really great climbing. In either case, one of the safest features of the West Rib route is the option to leave the route and retreat to the relative safety of the 14,200-foot base camp and a cache that had been placed (by your party) prior to the ascent.

The route begins at the head of the Kahiltna Glacier's northeast fork, at 11,200 feet in the Chicken

Denali's West Rib route (left) and Cassin Ridge route (right) (Photo: Bradford Washburn, neg. no. 4847)

Couloir. Climb upward for 1,500 feet on slopes ranging from 30 to 50 degrees. Rock protection can be used on the left side of the couloir, supplemented with ice screws or snow pickets where necessary. There is a tendency to want to travel to the right too soon; it is advisable to travel straight up and hit the ridge proper.

Once on the ridge there are two snow domes or bulges to negotiate. These are quite often icy and require belayed climbing or simul-climbing protected by ice screws. Once at the top of the last snow dome the route flattens out at 13,300 feet. This is a great place to camp, and safe walls can be put in to avoid the storms that can rage in this exposed area. The views of the Cassin Ridge from this camp are awesome as well. It is also possible to camp higher up, at around 14,000 feet in a nice bergschrund that has sheltered many climbers through some terrible storms.

The climbing above travels to the east (climber's right) and over snow slopes. The climbing weaves through the rocks that eventually link up to the ridge. This climbing is fun and requires routefinding with a real mixed-climbing feel. The ridge turns to snow by 16,000 feet. At this point start looking for a place to settle into a good camp. There are some small but very protected spots in the rocks up high at 16,200 feet, near the base of the couloir that leads through the diamond-shaped rock band. It is also possible to camp tucked against the rocks just below this couloir to the east of the ridge. These camps look right down onto the base camp at 14,200 feet; this is a great place to bail from if you have had enough.

Above this camp the couloir into the rock band is very straightforward with some old fixed line in it. The rocks above provide good running protection and some fun climbing. Once you reach the upper Balcony Camp, it is good to continue. This is a super-exposed campsite and the remains of old tents tattered by the wind prove this point. Climbing higher will soon bring you to the end of the rocks at 17,800 feet. The original West Rib route travelled to the left of the rock band above. Two little gullies exist to the west of the largest rock outcrop, topping out a bit lower than the larger gully to the east of the rock band. This is a good and safe way to go because you can protect with rock anchors and reach flat ground sooner. The other choice is to cruise straight up to the right of the rocks in the very large gully that has a cornice on the upper right-hand side. This is also protectable on the left with rock pro and pickets in the snow. Topping out here can be steep for about 30 meters, which means you may need to belay the top section and place a few more pickets.

Once over the top you are now on the Football Field at 19,200 feet and can travel a short distance to the north to meet the West Buttress "trail." Be pre-

pared for severe wind that can cause whiteout conditions. Travelling to the west is the descent for the West Buttress back to Denali Pass. Travelling to the east is the ascent to Kahiltna Horn (20,000 ft) and from there the last 300 vertical feet to the summit.

Descent: Descend the West Buttress route. We assume that climbers attempting the West Rib route have acclimatized on or have already climbed the popular West Buttress route. It is a complex route in its own right, with book-length descriptions. Refer to Colby Coomb's *Denali's West Buttress*. Knowledge of the West Buttress route is critical because of the whiteout conditions often encountered on the Football Field; you must be already familiar with the descent route in order to find it.

The greatest number of deaths on Denali have occurred when exhausted climbers attempt to descend the West Rib route. Travelling roped with no running protection allows for a total group catastrophe. The snow is super hard, making it impossible to arrest a fall with just an ice ax. Descent down the West Rib is not recommended!

 ## 31 DENALI: CASSIN RIDGE

(20,320 ft; 6193 m)

Route ▲ Cassin Ridge
Difficulty ▲ Alaska Grade 5, 5.8, AI 4
Elevation gain ▲ 9,000 ft
Average time ▲ 3–4 weeks, 3–5 days on route
Map ▲ Mount McKinley (A-3)
Resources ▲ *AAJ* 1962, p. 27; *AAJ* 1968 (Japanese variation); *AAJ* 1972; *AAJ* 1977 (solo); *AAJ* 1983, p. 93 (winter ascent); *AAJ* 1979, p. 164; *Climbing*, no. 67, 1981; *Climbing*, no. 72, 1986; *Climbing*, no. 73, 1987; Roper and Steck, *Fifty Classic Climbs*; Cassin, *Fifty Years of Alpinism*, p. 158; Waterman, *High Alaska*

History: Denali's Cassin Ridge is surely important. It may even be the most important route in North

Colby Coombs climbing at 13,200 feet on the Cassin Ridge (Photo: Mike Wood)

America, based on appearance and location alone. The historical bit is interesting as well, from Cassin himself to Mugs Stump. The ascent of the South Ridge is a testimony to the marvelous skill Riccardo Cassin and his team had developed in order to ensure a safe and successful revolutionary ascent on July 19, 1961. Bradford Washburn introduced the South Ridge route to Cassin, who was interested in climbing a major new route in Alaska. The initial couloir that is now the standard beginning of the Cassin route was climbed as a variation in 1967 by the Japanese. It was, however, climbed from the upper half to the ridge by Cassin's party on their original ascent. So the Japanese couloir is only half-new.

Since that time the route has been a major testpiece for climbers from around the world. In the summer of 1976 the soloist Charlie Porter climbed the Cassin route in a 36-hour push to the summit. In March 1982 the route received a winter ascent by Mike Young, Roger Mear, and Jonathan Waterman. In 1991 the incredible Mugs Stump soloed the Cassin in a remarkable 15-hour push, a total of 27.5 hours round trip, from 14,200 feet on the West Buttress. In 2000, even with the advances in alpine equipment technology and the breaking of mental barriers, this route still sees fewer than four ascents a year. Each spring there is a line of talented alpinists that are "gonna climb the Cassin," but they are denied due to the combination of the mountain's great scale, the route, cold, altitude, weather, or coming to their senses and realizing that climbing Denali is by no means casual.

Approach: Fly in to the Kahiltna Glacier. To reach the base of the Cassin Ridge it is necessary to travel up the glacier from the southeast fork to the northeast fork. Once at the northeast fork there is a dilemma: Do you take snowshoes or skis to the base of the route, or do you walk in? You will have to retrieve your skis or snowshoes if you take them up the fork. Typically there is so much icefall off the hanging glacier between the West Rib and the Cassin Ridge that it is easy to travel with only crampons to the base of the Japanese Couloir. The reputation of the northeast

fork of the Kahiltna Glacier as a shooting gallery is well deserved; quick travel and proper routefinding are critical.

Route description: Beginning at the bergschrund at 12,200 feet, climb 55-degree snow slopes to the Japanese Couloir. Halfway up, the couloir becomes constricted. At this point it is possible to climb the ice to the right, which is about 75 degrees, or go around on the rock. Fixed pins and old fixed lines will help identify this spot. This is a good route around, but it is deceivingly more difficult than it looks.

Once around this obstacle follow the couloir to the ridge, using ice screws and rock protection. Top out in the Japanese Couloir and head to the left, belaying among the rocks. From this belay, climb up to the base of the cliff that lies ahead and traverse under the rocks to the right. (If you go left you will find the Cassin Ledges.) Continue around to the east until it looks like you will go out of sight. Around the corner is a moderate-angled gully that turns into a bit of a squeeze near the top with a scrap of old fixed line (see photo on page 89). Once over this short crux there is a good belay. From this belay, climb up a steep snow-and-ice face to gain the ridge that begins the 1,000-foot, knife-edge ice traverse. This is well protected with pickets and ice screws. At the top of this section the ground mellows out considerably, and good camping can be found.

In past years it was possible to walk straight up to the bergschrund at the base of the first rock band. However, due to active glacial movement, it is now necessary to rappel from the far-left side. At the bottom of the 80-foot rappel the slope is 70 degrees and must be traversed around the corner to a not-so-secure belay. As of May 2000 a slot on the right-hand side of the bergschrund has developed, allowing one to walk right through to negotiate this obstacle. The slope above this ice cliff is about 45 degrees, and if there is avalanche danger, it could lurk on this slope. Once in the bergschrund at 15,200 feet you are totally installed in a very safe and cozy camp.

Leaving from this camp only requires moving out

to the right and heading up toward the weakness in the rocks. An identifying characteristic is an M-shaped rock formation. As of 1998 there was a weathered wooden shaft from an old ice ax still buried in the snow as a stake. This is a great landmark if it is still there. Once among the rocks it is a matter of weaving around and up to find the easiest route, which requires no rock climbing. Narrow gullies open into a broader slope with an intimidating rock band that has tons of dihedrals. These dihedrals, though daunting, do not need to be climbed. In the slope there is a triangular rock with and old pin in it (as of 1998). From here travel to your left (west) about 60 meters and up a very small gully. When the gully dead-ends, climbing over the left edge will get you around and onto much quicker mixed ground. Weave up and through the rocks, keeping to the right as you ascend small gullies and around rocks, eventually ending up on the ridge above the first rock band. The snowy ridge will easily bring you to the base of the second rock band. This too looks intimidating, but climb straight out to the west and you will see the major weakness that travels through the second rock band. This climbing is great fun with moderately steep terrain and protection in the rocks.

The angle soon eases off a bit before the last little crux of the route: the rock band that stretches across the slope pinches down to a 20-foot section of rock that must be climbed. There is an old no. 2 Friend stuck in the crack that will be useful. The crack itself wouldn't feel so difficult if it were 10,000 feet lower and could be climbed without a pack. At the top of this short rock section, head out to the left, then back around to the right where only another 90 meters brings you to the top of the second rock band.

Between 15,200 feet and the top of the second rock band at 17,800 feet there really isn't any ideal camping. Once the snow slope above the second rock band has been traversed to the point where rocks intersect the slope, a relatively sheltered camp can be made on a rib in the rocks. The snow slope that travels up to the summit cornice is subject to wind loading and is

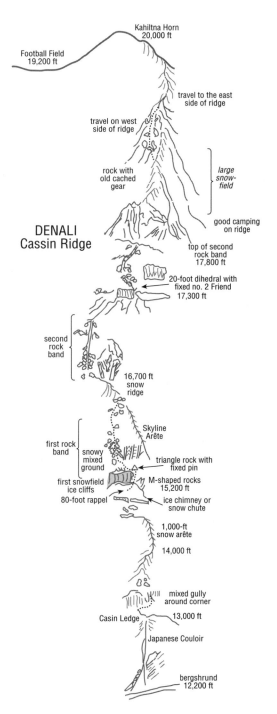

DENALI
Cassin Ridge

Kahiltna Horn
20,000 ft

Football Field
19,200 ft

travel to the east
side of ridge

travel on west
side of ridge

large
snow-
field

rock with
old cached
gear

good camping
on ridge

top of second
rock band
17,800 ft

20-foot dihedral with
fixed no. 2 Friend
17,300 ft

second
rock
band

16,700 ft
snow
ridge

Skyline
Arête

first rock
band

snowy
mixed
ground

triangle rock with
fixed pin

first snowfield
ice cliffs

M-shaped rocks
15,200 ft

80-foot rappel

ice chimney or
snow chute

1,000-ft
snow arête

14,000 ft

mixed gully
around corner

Casin Ledge

13,000 ft

Japanese Couloir

bergshrund
12,200 ft

the perfect angle to create an avalanche. The rocks above the camp can be protected for running belays if the slope is questionable.

The last 2,000 feet is a mixture of traversing along the ridge and travelling to the left just off the ridge. This is mostly steep walking where you wouldn't want to stumble. Travel very high on the snow slope to the left of the ridge until there is a weakness that allows a return to the ridge proper. From here travelling through steep rock boulders on ice will bring you to the final snow crest that leads to the top of the route on Kahiltna Horn (20,000 ft).

Descent: The most straightforward way down is to descend the route to Denali Pass and then walk down the West Buttress route. We assume that climbers attempting the Cassin Ridge route have acclimatized on or have already climbed the popular West Buttress route. It is a complex route in its own right, with book-length descriptions. Refer to Colby Coomb's *Denali's West Buttress*.

 32 MOUNT HUNTINGTON

(12,240 ft; 3730 m)

Route ▲ West Face Couloir
Difficulty ▲ Alaska Grade 3+, AI 4
Elevation gain ▲ 3,000 ft
Average time ▲ 2 weeks, 2–4 days on route
Map ▲ Talkeetna (D-2)
Resources ▲ *AAJ* 1979, p. 165; *AAJ* 1990, pp. 43–49; *AAJ* 1991, pp. 157–158; *AAJ* 1992, p. 122 (winter ascent); *AAJ* 1994, p. 116; *Climbing*, no. 68, Sept/Oct 1978

History: The history surrounding Mount Huntington is a fascinating trip into Alaska's mountaineering past. This "little" mountain was first the desire of French alpinist Lionel Terray, who from season to season waited to hear if anyone had scooped this prized virgin Alaska summit. He was finally able to arrive in Alaska and climb the aesthetic Northwest Ridge

(French Ridge). Lionel Terray reached the summit of Mount Huntington in 1964.

In 1965 David Roberts, the Harvard mountaineer who had been focusing on Alaskan first ascents, set his sights on the rib that splits the West Face and arrives at the upper snowfields. This first ascent had its epic moments, and one member of the party, Ed Bernd, was killed during the descent. Nevertheless, the route soon became a prize for the Alaska hard men. The development of the two routes now climbed on Mount Huntington signified a switch in interest from the larger giants to smaller, more technical climbs. For years, people have completed ascents around the entire mountain, but it wasn't until 1978 that attention was focused on the line between the French Ridge and the Harvard Route.

The couloir on the West Face is perhaps the most controversial in terms of first ascents in Alaska. It is most likely the easiest line of ascent on the mountain, but for years it thwarted the first three ascent parties, beginning with John Evans, Denny Hogan, and Vic Walsh who first climbed the West Face Couloir to the intersection of the Harvard Route in April 1978. In June 1978, Steve and Ron Matous with Bruce Adams climbed to the summit slopes and onto the summit ridge. In 1979 Denny Hogan, Peter "Cado" Avenali, and Peter Lev climbed to the Harvard confluence. All were able to climb the 1,500-foot couloir, only to get turned back on the upper snowfields. In 1987 Dave Nettle and James Quirk climbed the route a good 10 years after the first ascent. In the 1990 *American Alpine Journal* they stated that they had accomplished a first ascent on Mount Huntington. The controversy surrounding this ascent has ironically labeled the couloir the Nettle–Quirk route. It is this example of claiming first ascents that has cemented the idea that in Alaska, people do climbs and don't document them. This is true of one local climber, Christopher Mannix, who made an ascent of this route to the summit ridge in 1979 with Stacy Allison (the first American woman to summit Everest) and Bobby Knight to gain the fifth ascent of the face "with the 'old gear' by the way!" as

Mount Huntington. The corniced French Ridge descends into the foreground; the West Face is bathed in sunlight.
(Photo: Paul Roderick)

Mannix enjoys pointing out. In 1991 a four-person team of John Bauman, Leo Americus, Dave McGivern, and Charlie Sassara climbed the couloir and bivied just 700 feet from the summit for 4 days in a storm. They made one final push, climbing 300 feet above their camp before the winds forced them to retreat.

Bring plenty of food because the Tokositna Basin has been the scene of many long storm days and stranded climbers. The best story to date is the time when a grizzly miraculously showed up at the 8,300-foot base camp and raided the camp of Steve Mascioli and Mike Dimitris, keeping them at bay for a night, and forcing them to abandon their climb.

Approach: The west fork of the Tokositna Glacier at 8,300–8,400 feet is the most commonly used landing site to access the West Face. People have made it into the west fork of the Tokositna Glacier from the west fork of the Ruth Glacier, but this approach does not sound or look that easy. The icefall draining the west fork of the Tokositna Glacier is quite broken—to the point that nobody has been able to walk down through, but it has once been avoided by a pretty treacherous skirting along the east side.

Route description: The route up the West Face Couloir begins in the upper Tokositna Basin and travels up snow slopes for 800 feet. When you reach the rocks, traverse left to the base of the couloir. The belay for the first pitch of ice is in the rocks to the left of the couloir. Climb the first ramp of 60-degree ice, finishing the pitch with a short, but steep step. Belay at the top of this step. It is not advisable to stay in the left-hand (and narrowing) fork of the couloir, which appears to connect to the main couloir up higher. Difficult pro and loose rock make this option a bit dangerous.

For the next pitch lead up and right, getting around the rock blocks and out into the wide, main couloir: Easy Street. The overall angle of the couloir is 55 to 60 degrees with a few short steps of 80 degrees. The couloir is 1,200 feet in length. At the top of the couloir there can be some snow fluting that will need be climbed to get out of the upper section. Start traversing over to the broken rock that lies to the south as you exit the top of the couloir. This is the intersection with the Harvard Route.

At the intersection of these routes, it may be possible to find a bivi among the rocks, or to rappel less than one rope-length (about 80–100 feet) and get to the Roof Pitch on the Harvard Route. This is a relatively safe place to bivi in bad weather, however it is difficult to find good places to camp on this route.

The upper snow- or ice field is the most common reason for being thwarted on this beautiful peak. The upper slopes are on average 50 degrees, but the avalanche hazard has deterred many climbers from travelling to the summit. Once this snow-and-ice face has been climbed to the ridge, the remaining ridge climbing has cornices that must be avoided by traversing below the ridge to the summit.

Descent: Return via the ascent route.

 33 PEAK 11,300

(11,300 ft; 3444 m)

Route ▲ Southwest Ridge
Difficulty ▲ Alaska Grade 4, 5.9, AI 3
Elevation gain ▲ 4,100 ft
Average time ▲ 2 weeks, 3–4 days on the route
Maps ▲ Mount McKinley (A-2), Talkeetna (D-2)
Resources ▲ *AAJ* 1968, pp. 372–373; *AAJ* 1969, pp. 372–373; *AAJ* 1977, pp. 155–156; *AAJ* 1981, p. 157; *AAJ* 1985, pp. 174–177; *Climbing*, no. 84, 1981; *Climbing*, no. 105, 1987

History: Swiss climbers Niklaus Lötscher and Heinz Allemann completed the first ascent of the Southwest Ridge on July 21, 1968.

Approach: Fly in from Talkeetna to the Don Sheldon Mountain House on the Ruth Glacier. Travel (ski) 7 miles up the west fork of the Ruth Glacier to the base of the Southwest Ridge. If conditions are favorable you may be able to land on the west fork at the base of the route.

Route description: The route starts on a broad snow slope on the northwest side of the ridge and joins the crest of the ridge after several hundred feet of 40-degree snow climbing. The gully on the southeast side of the ridge is more accessible and convenient for recovering your skis on the descent, but a cornice

Peak 11,300 from Mount Huntington's French Ridge. The Southwest Ridge is the sun/shade line; the Southeast Ridge forms the right skyline. (Photo: Brian McCullough)

with obvious wind loading in the gully can make this option more dangerous. This gully can also have awkward rock climbing at the top.

From the ridge crest, the route moves horizontally onto the Northwest Face and then up a thin couloir to regain the crest of the ridge, where the route continues over some rotten rock that can be slabby and snowy at times. Some rock steps can be encountered on this section, with short mixed climbing and easier snow sections. Sticking to the right of the ridge crest eventually leads to a rock pitch that ends at a large col that provides spacious camping on the ridge at 8,000 feet.

Continue up the ridge on steepening snow, then traverse left to reach a broad, 65-degree ice-and-snow couloir. From a belay in the snow scoop next to the south side of the huge block that is on the ridge crest proper, climb up the block's right side to the crest. Climb northeast through a little snow arête that comes up from the right (south) side of the ridge. Climb down the other side of this arête, then head up to the true ridge crest.

Once at the crest of the ridge you will find a horn with a ton of slings that are used to rappel into the col. A bivi in the notch at 9,800 feet is possible, but beware of the cornice that can form in this area. From the notch, belay from the other side and exit to the left, rock-climbing on some awkward terrain. This soon eases a bit to a steep snow rib that will bring you to the ridge again. Beyond here obstacles can once again be passed on the right side of the ridge. From this point there are several pitches of mixed climbing and rock steps along the ridge to an 80-foot rappel or downclimb into a gully to the right. Regain the ridge crest, then climb along some easier, snowy, mixed terrain. This leads to the final 750-foot ice face, which decreases in steepness as you get closer to the summit. The summit is very flat, and offers great (if not exposed) camping. Often times along the route you may find yourself descending below the ridge to dodge ob-

stacles, but don't get lured too far off the ridge.

Descent: From the summit of Peak 11,300, descend the Southeast Ridge to 9,000 feet, staying to the right (south) side of the ridge. The ridge gets steeper and more defined as it narrows upon approaching the rocks. When you are finally forced to rappel, use bollards or ice-hourglasses. Rappel, angling toward the ridge as much as possible. On the ridge or just below is a bench that can be a possible bivi at 9,400 feet. The ridge begins to widen and gets less steep, so stay along this as much as possible until forced to rappel one more rope-length down steep ice. Continue climbing along the rock band until you are again forced to rappel another eight to ten times. Stay along the ridge crest as much as possible until you reach the glacier below that leads down between the Southwest and Southeast Ridges over some crevassed terrain to your skis. The rappels are down loose rock that is very catchy on the ropes. There have been many rappels through this rock as well and you may find slings, but be prepared to leave slings and possibly some gear.

34 MOUNT BARRILL

(7,650 ft; 2331 m)

Route ▲ East Face (Cobra Pillar)
Difficulty ▲ VI, 5.10+, A3
Elevation gain ▲ 2,650 ft
Average time ▲ 2–3 weeks, 5–7 days on route
Map ▲ Talkeetna (D-2)
Resources ▲ *AAJ* 1989, pp. 74–83; *AAJ* 1992, pp. 59–64; *AAJ* 1993, p. 138; *Climbing*, Oct/Nov 1991

History: According to Bradford Washburn, the first ascent of Mount Barrill may have been completed by a

East Face of Mount Barrill (Photo: Colby Coombs)

group of The Mazamas from Portland, Oregon, in 1910. The second ascent of Mount Barrill was in 1953 by Fred Beckey, John Rupley, and Herb Staley. The first winter ascent of Mount Barrill was in February 1976 by Paul Denkelwalter, Dr. Jim Olsen, Dr. William Brant, and Ed Olmstead. Jack Tackle and Jim Donini climbed the Cobra Pillar June 5–10, 1991. This was the second time they went to the Ruth Gorge with the intention of climbing the East Face before they finally succeeded.

An interesting fact is that the ice under Mounts Barrill and Dickey is 3,800 feet thick and moves 3 feet a day. If the ice were to melt out of the gorge, the depth from the tops of the peaks to the valley floor would be twice that of the Grand Canyon.

Approach: You can easily fly in and land at this route's base or just a touch farther down the gorge. The other option is to get dropped off at the Don Sheldon Mountain House landing strip on the Ruth Glacier and hike down to the base.

Route description: The majority of the climbing on this route is entirely free at 5.10+ on some of the finest rock in the Ruth Gorge. However, there are still plenty of friable rock sections, which are quite common on the lower-angle sections of the rock faces flanking the Ruth Gorge. The crack climbing in the center of the pillar itself and the dihedral at the top of the pillar, above the large bivi ledge, is beautiful. Originally, the large, left-facing dihedral drew Donini and Tackle in, leading to a face that required too much aid. So the team headed down and found a great weakness that traversed to the crack in the center of the pillar. This is protected with natural gear and one bolt, which was placed by Donini and Tackle.

From here the climbing is spectacular to a great bivi ledge seventeen pitches off the ground. Above the bivi site lies some more sustained climbing, including some 100 feet of aid supplemented with three bolts for protection. From here seven pitches

of mixed climbing bring you to a snowfield that can be travelled quickly. The only remaining obstacle is the cornice at the top; this may vary in size and difficulty depending on the condition of the face.

Descent: The descent off the peak is down the back side on the north-facing slopes that lead to the Mountain House landing strip. This can go very quickly, but watch for avalanche danger.

35 MOUNT DICKEY

(9,545 ft; 2909 m)

Route ▲ West Face
Difficulty ▲ Alaska Grade 1
Elevation gain ▲ 2,500 ft
Average time ▲ 2 weeks, 1 day on route
Map ▲ Talkeetna (D-2)
Resources ▲ *AAJ* 1956, pp. 47–50; *AAJ* 1977, p. 156; *AAJ* 1980 (winter ascent); *AAJ* 1981, p. 157 (ski descent)

History: Bradford Washburn and David Fischer climbed the West Face on April 19, 1955. This first-ascent route has become the most popular route up and down this massive peak. In February 1979 Brian Okonek and Roger Kowels climbed the West Face route.

The East Face of Mount Dickey is more than 1 mile high of vertical granite! This impressive face has seen equally impressive ascents, reserved for only the most experienced technical climbers. A little trivia: the ice under Mount Dickey's 5,000-foot East Face is 3,800 feet thick. Glacial melt caused by global warming would leave future generations with a face in the Ruth Gorge of 8,800 feet of amazing granite.

Approach: It is most common for parties to fly into the strip at the Don Sheldon Mountain House on Ruth Glacier and descend the glacier into the Ruth Gorge. It is possible during the early spring and summer months to land right in the gorge below Mount Dickey and set up a base camp.

It is not recommended to approach this route via Pittock Pass due to the huge potential for icefall. People have endured the mental strain or walked through, oblivious, but if you find it necessary to travel under

Route up Mount Dickey's west slopes (Photo: Paul Roderick)

the seracs, do it on descent when you are travelling faster and thus minimizing exposure to icefall.

Another option is to travel in or out via the Backside Glacier on the west side of the Ruth Gorge. The glacier flows behind Mounts Bradley, Johnson, Wake, and Church, and Dickey is at its head. From your landing spot, descend the Ruth Glacier into Ruth Gorge to the toe of the Backside Glacier. Then follow the glacier to its head. This would definitely provide some great Alaskan travel opportunities.

Route description: This route is in the book because it seemed that the multitude of folks who go up the East Face needed a little help after their taxing ascent. The West Face route is one of the very best ascents in the Ruth Gorge and allows for beginners to ascend a peak in this area. For all its fantastic beauty, the Ruth Gorge does not generally lend itself to beginner climbing.

From 4,500 feet on the Ruth Glacier at the base of Mount Dickey, the route travels west into the cirque between Mount Dickey and Mount Bradley (9,100 ft). The pass that lies in front of you is known as "747 Pass." Pilots commonly excite tourists in their planes by flying through the pass, giving the illusion that they are going to smack right into the rock walls. This pass does have potential avalanche hazard. Once over the pass, however, you are now on the Backside Glacier and the routefinding begins.

Leaving 6,400 feet the route stays pretty close to the South Ridge and doesn't wander too far out onto the face. The beginning of the routefinding requires some challenging searching around crevasses and onto the more wide-open plain of Mount Dickey. Around 7,500 feet there is one little step that is actually steep enough to have to negotiate with front points and *piolet* traction, but once beyond this section the rest of the route unfolds in front of you to the summit. Camps can be easily dug in up here on this open plateau with spectacular views.

Descent: Retrace your route back down the slopes of Mount Dickey. It may be helpful to follow your wands back down, especially around the tricky spots.

36 SUGAR TOOTH

(8,000 ft; 2438 m)

Route ▲ West Face
Difficulty ▲ V, 5.10+, A2
Elevation gain ▲ 2,000 ft
Average time ▲ 2 weeks, 2–3 days on route
Map ▲ Talkeetna (D-2)
Resources ▲ *AAJ* 1995, pp. 137–138

History: Andi Orgler, Tommi Bonapace, and Raimund Haas climbed this route in late June and early July 1994. When reading the accounts of the climb one cannot help but be impressed by the conditions encountered while climbing the route. Quite often it was snowing or raining, but they managed to continue climbing at a high technical standard.

Approach: Planes can land in the Ruth Gorge below Mount Dickey, except during July and August, when snow is scarce on the glacier.

Route description: This route has sixteen pitches. See the topo (based on a topo drawn by Andi Orgler) for details. Orgler, Bonapace, and Haas started the route in the rain, and after two pitches decided to retreat and try it the next day. The next morning it snowed, and there was verglas on the rocks, but they continued, undaunted. "Although the face was not perpendicular (UIAA VI, A2), the climbing was demanding, since water flowed over the edges of the roofs and soaked us," they reported.

From the bivi they proceeded up three more beautiful pitches to reach the South Ridge. The weather was looking better, so they travelled to the summit and spent another evening. This route was 5.10b/c with only short sections of A2 when these climbers did the route.

Descent: Rappel the line of the route.

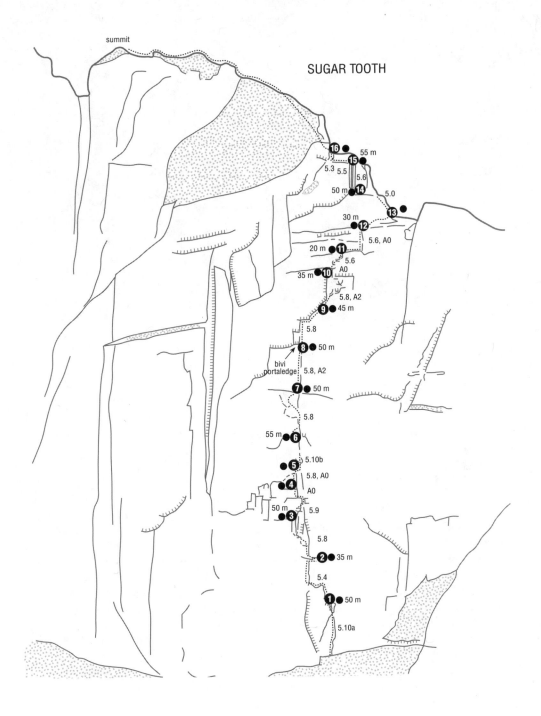

summit

SUGAR TOOTH

16 ●
● 15   55 m
5.3 5.5
     5.6
50 m ● 14   5.0
              ● 13
      30 m ● 12
              5.6, A0
20 m ● 11
        5.6
35 m ● 10   A0

        5.8, A2
● 9   45 m

        5.8
● 8   50 m

bivi   5.8, A2
portaledge
● 7   50 m

        5.8
55 m ● 6

● 5   5.10b
        5.8, A0
● 4
        A0
50 m ● 3   5.9

        5.8
● 2   35 m

        5.4
● 1   50 m

        5.10a

Eye Tooth (left) and Sugar Tooth (right), as seen from the great gorge of the Ruth Glacier (Photo: Joe Reichert)

37 EYE TOOTH

(9,000 ft; 2743 m)

Route ▲ West Face (Dream in the Spirit of Mugs)
Difficulty ▲ V, 5.10
Elevation gain ▲ 2,800 ft
Average time ▲ 2 weeks, 2–3 days on route
Map ▲ Talkeetna (D-2)
Resources ▲ *AAJ* 1989, pp. 90–93; *AAJ* 1995, pp. 137–141

History: This is a beautiful piece of granite at the head of the cirque directly across from Mount Dickey. In the 1995 *American Alpine Journal*, Andi Orgler wrote, "Mugs Stump and I had in 1987 made an agreement not to interfere in the projects of the other. The peaks around the gap were to be left for him, but tragically Mugs was lost two years ago, and so the peaks were 'free.'" On July 30, 1994, Andi Orgler, Tommi Bonapace, and Raimund Haas climbed the West Face of the Eye Tooth. Orgler writes that, "Mugs would have been enchanted with the route, and we have named it 'The Dream in the Spirit of Mugs.'"

Approach: Planes can land in the Ruth Gorge below Mount Dickey, except during July and August, when snow is scarce on the glacier. Eye Tooth and Sugar Tooth are located in the same cirque, directly across the Ruth Gorge from Mount Dickey. There is a bit of routefinding necessary to avoid crevasses in order to access this cirque.

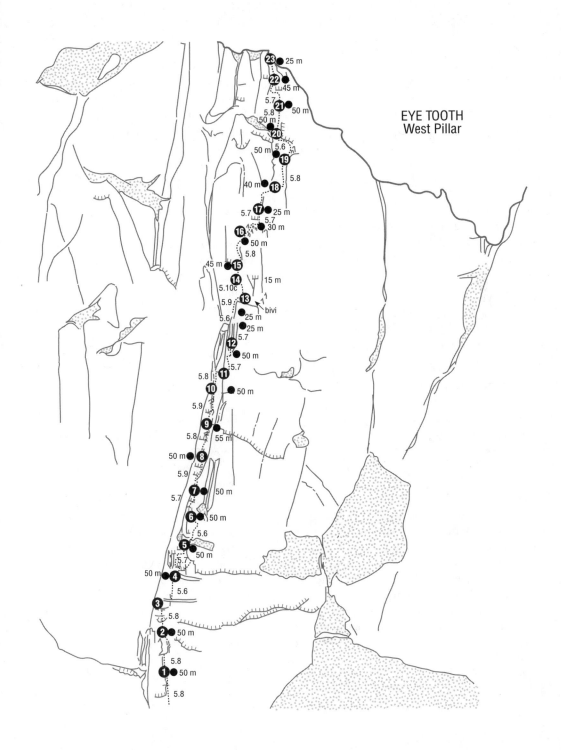

EYE TOOTH
West Pillar

Route description: This route has twenty-three pitches. Orgler and partners climbed in July and experienced some inclement weather. It was during some marginal breaks in the weather that the three were able to climb the route. They climbed fourteen pitches and ended up at a ledge that would have been a good bivi, but the weather continued to change for the worse, so they quickly climbed the remaining nine pitches to the top of the route. The granite is beautiful, and the climbing is spectacular, with the whole route completely free-climbed. At its hardest it is 5.10c, but the majority of the route is in the 5.8 range. See the topo for details.

Descent: With a few deviations, rappel the line of the route.

38 MOOSES TOOTH
(10,300 ft; 3139 m)

Route ▲ Ham and Eggs Couloir
Difficulty ▲ Alaska Grade 3+, 5.9, AI 4
Elevation gain ▲ 2,800 ft
Average time ▲ 2 weeks, 2–3 days on route
Map ▲ Talkeetna (D-2)
Resources ▲ AAJ 1976, pp. 285–293; AAJ 2000, pp. 212–213

History: Jon Krakauer, Thomas Davies, and Nate Zinsser climbed this peak July 16–18, 1975. They do not brag about being the most experienced at the time of ascent and Krakauer will laugh when recalling the foibles encountered while climbing this couloir. Their story is briefly described in the route description, mixed with more current information.

Approach: Fly in to the landing strip in the small basin. The landing strip was pioneered by Paul Roderick, the owner and operator of Talkeetna Air Taxi, and accounts for this route's increased popularity. Flying in has reduced the hazardous and arduous approach from the Ruth Gorge to a 10-minute walk to the base of the route. If conditions don't allow for air transport and you end up stuck, you may have to walk out of the basin to the Ruth Gorge. To get down or up into the basin, the most common route is to hug the wall to the north and travel the icefall that drops 2,500 feet in 2 miles, making the routefinding pretty tricky.

Route description: Since its first ascent in July 1975, this route did not see much traffic until the late 1990s. By today's standards the route is technically within many budding alpinists' abilities, mainly due to the shortened approach, once again proving that approach and relative ease of access are half the battle in Alaska. The Ham and Eggs Couloir is also the most direct line to the true (east) summit of the Mooses Tooth.

Start this route at the far-left side of the couloir, a spot that the inexperienced may not readily recognize. During the first ascent in mid-July, Krakauer and partners found the first three or four pitches to be mainly rock with thin cracks to protect and short aid moves, which led to "mashed potato" snow and thin, hollow ice runnels. In recent years climbers have found that conditions on the route are better early in the season; however, if you attempt it too early, you will find the couloir full of snow.

Farther up, where the couloir splits, take the right-hand gully up 45-degree ice. The ice gets steeper, then turns to snow. At this point look for the right-facing corner on the right side of the gully. The first few moves are the hardest, then you will find a hand-sized crack. Steve House advised that, as of May 2000, this is "normally" an ice pitch, and that you can climb ice in either the right- or left-hand fork. "This season the left fork was all ice, but very 'punky' ice. I elected to climb the harder, but protectable rock in the right fork. There is also ice here sometimes. I saw [the first-ascent party's] old bolt, out left near the top of the right-hand fork, but it doesn't make sense to go that way. There is a good fixed anchor in the rock, followed by 40-degree snow climbing above the rock."

The Southwest Face of Mooses Tooth from the summit of Mount Dickey. The Ham and Eggs Couloir ascends to the left of center. (Photo: Brian Okonek)

Thomas Davies and Nate Zinsser at the top of the Ham and Eggs Couloir on the first ascent (Photo: Jon Krakauer)

the hardest pitches on the route, with consistent 65- to 70-degree ice. The route remained a consistent 55 degrees with short, steep steps all the way to the top of the couloir, for a total of twenty-one pitches.

All the belays are on rock in this couloir. At the very top of the couloir there is a great bivi site to the climber's left upon exiting the top of the gully. The site may not be obvious to the untrained eye. It lies about 300 feet left from the top of the gully, near a big boulder; it does require some digging and chopping, but not too much. From the notch at the top of the couloir, travel along the corniced summit ridge, which can be protected with rock and ice protection.

Descent: Return to the top of Ham and Eggs Couloir, then rappel the route. It is reported that there are great rap anchors every 60 meters down the couloir to the base of the route. Some of these may require ice-hourglasses, but most are fixed pieces.

 39 MOUNT SILVERTHRONE

(13,220 ft; 4029 m)

Route ▲ North Ridge
Difficulty ▲ Alaska Grade 1+
Elevation gain ▲ 4,700 ft
Average time ▲ 2 weeks (Wonder Lake to Silverthrone Col and back), 1 day on route
Maps ▲ Mount McKinley (A-2, B-2)
Resources ▲ *AAJ* 1976, p. 433; *AAJ* 1979, pp. 166–167; *AAJ* 1981, p. 158; *AAJ* 1988, p. 117 (winter ascent)

On pitch 9 during the first ascent, the party placed a bolt to help protect a short aid pitch while trying to pass a roof. On pitch 11 the party found the first 90-degree ice. This only lasted for a short distance. It was pouring rain when they tried to climb this section and it was from this point that they bailed off the route to return a few days later.

On the next try Krakauer and party cruised the first eleven pitches to find the first vertical sections on pitches 11 and 12 rotting away. Pitches 11–15 were

History: In 1944 Bradford Washburn, Major R. Bruce Bass, Captain Robert P. Sharp, and Lieutenant Alvin Ivler spent the days between October 17 and December 9 on and around Mount Silverthrone testing winter survival gear for the United States Air Force. During this time they climbed Mount Silverthrone and explored many of the surrounding peaks. From March 5 to 21, 1987, Brian Okonek, Diane Calamar Okonek, and Rick Ernst climbed Mount Silverthrone

Mount Silverthrone from 9,750 feet on the Brooks Glacier (Photo: Brian Okonek)

for the first "official" winter ascent.

Approach: The North Ridge of Mount Silverthrone is most easily reached by walking in from the road on the north side of Denali National Park and Preserve. The northside entrance to the park is located at mile 230 on the George Parks Highway at McKinley Village. Denali Park Road leaves this highway and travels 91 miles west to the historic mining town of Kantishna and scenic Wonder Lake.

Wonder Lake Campground is the trailhead for the approach to Silverthrone. From the campground travel down the newly improved trail to the McKinley River bar. This is only one of a very few improved trails within the park, due to heavy visitor use—otherwise, Denali is a trailless park. The McKinley River bar is the greatest hazard on this route, as it is more than a mile long, with swift-moving currents that fluctuate diur-

nally. The backcountry ranger's desk at the park's main visitor center will often have current water volume reports, but these can be unreliable, due to the ever-changing nature of the river.

Once across the river, hike due south on the remnants of an historic horse trail to the east side of Turtle Hill. Continue to Clearwater River and on to Cache Creek. The trail wanders through tundra with a few alder-whacking sections, mainly along Cache Creek. After a final crossing of Cache Creek, proceed to a crossing of Oastler Creek where it meets Cache Creek. The trail becomes steeper as it winds up into the hills toward McGonagall Pass. Once at the pass enjoy the breathtaking view of the Muldrow Glacier below.

Negotiate the Muldrow Glacier to the Brooks Glacier, then travel up the Brooks Glacier to 7,500 feet, where another glacier pours into it from Mount

Deception to the east-southeast. From here, many variations have been taken to reach the lower basin below Mount Silverthrone at 8,200 feet. The east side of the glacier has a nice compression to follow, but this course has a tendency to push you under some dangerous icefall, and, beyond the compression, the route requires a great deal of routefinding around large crevasses. We have become convinced that in this area it is worth spreading out on the ropes a great deal due to the size of the bridges spanning the crevasses.

The lower basin offers great camping well out of the avalanche run-out zones—if the campsite is selected with care. Travelling through the Brooks Glacier's firn zone later in the season can be especially challenging, especially around 7,500 feet and higher; the bridges are large and the crevasses are deep. The upper plateaus are safe from avalanche run-out, but care must be taken to ensure safety. Be sure to dig in, because the weather up here can really howl.

On the next leg of the trip, travel almost directly west into a large basin at 9,100–9,300 feet under the South Face of the Central Pyramid. From here, head toward Silverthrone Col to the upper basin at 10,200 feet. The routefinding through the crevasses to arrive here will challenge the most seasoned glacier traveller and greatly excite the aspiring alpinist. The upper basin is the base camp for your summit push and a fantastic site, offering commanding views of Mounts Deception and Mather.

Route description: Once at the 10,200-foot basin there are two ways to get to the upper North Ridge of Mount Silverthrone. The first is to climb up to Silverthrone Col, hang a left (south), and travel along the broad ridge. The other option is to travel up the east side of the North Ridge out of camp to hit the North Ridge proper at 11,200–11,300 feet. The routefinding is straightforward and will keep you to the north of a small knoll and pull you closer to the face leading to the upper North Ridge. A bergschrund at 12,200 feet will have to be negotiated, and the face can be climbed more to the left (north) side. This face can be an avalanche concern, so be cautious.

Once on the ridge the view becomes even more spectacular, and the ridge becomes narrow and corniced, making it exciting for all. The final summit is quite frequently capped by a large cornice, so take caution when evaluating your desire to stand on the tippy-top. The views of Denali and the Ruth Gorge will be ingrained in your memory forever—if the day dawns clear enough to see this spectacular country.

Descent: From the summit perch, reverse the route back down the ridge and face to the base camp in the 10,200-foot basin. Travelling up and down these glaciers through the crevasses is most safely done in weather with good visibility, enabling you to avoid being pushed under seracs and avalanche slopes. Bring enough food so you aren't forced to descend during periods of low-to-no visibility. The extra cooking fuel and food will always pay off.

40 MOUNT BROOKS

(11,940 ft; 3639 m)

Route ▲ North Ridge
Difficulty ▲ Alaska Grade 1+
Elevation gain ▲ 6,500 ft
Average time ▲ 2 weeks, 1–2 days on route
Map ▲ Mount McKinley (A-2)
Resources ▲ *AAJ* 1951–53, pp. 425–433; *AAJ* 1954, pp. 200–203; *AAJ* 1955, pp. 78–83; *AAJ* 1959, p. 215; *AAJ* 1975, p. 116; *AAJ* 1976, p. 433; *AAJ* 1990, p. 158; *AAJ* 1993, p. 140; *AAJ* 1996, p. 178; *Scree,* Dec 1966; *Descent,* May 1994

History: Thayer Scudder, Winslow Briggs, John S. Humphreys, and David Bernays climbed this beautiful ridge on July 5, 1952. They remarked in their write-up that they were surprised that this relatively easy ascent had remained unclimbed until this time. Bradford Washburn made the second ascent of the North Ridge of Mount Brooks on July 19, 1953.

Approach: Follow the walk-in directions for

Mount Brooks from the Muldrow Glacier. The North Ridge ascends the left skyline. In the foreground, note the glacier "canyon" carved by an ice' river. (Photo: Brian Okonek)

Mount Silverthrone (Route 39). From McGonagall Pass, head down the Muldrow Glacier to the moraine at the base of the North Ridge. It is not worth giving a detailed route to the base of the climb due to the ever-changing nature of this terrain. The 20-mile hike up the Cache Creek Trail to McGonagall Pass usually takes about 2 days, with another day to get to the base of the route.

Route description: The route begins at the Northeast Ridge of Mount Brooks, on the moraine at the confluence of the Muldrow Glacier and the Brooks Glacier. The first 1,000 feet are up undefined ridge line and talus slopes. Then pass through some broken rock onto the ridge proper. Some rock fall has been observed at this point, and if there is a large accumulation of snow, be aware of avalanche potential. Once on the

ridge the climbing is wicked enjoyable on a relatively broad ridge with great climbing. At 9,000 feet the Northeast Ridge intersects the North Ridge, where a 65-degree slope is encountered for about 80 feet. From this point, the climbing is mainly on the west side of the ridge. The slope angle increases gently to the point that, if the snow were of unstable nature, it would cause reason for concern. The ridge broadens between 10,500 feet and 11,000 feet, where crevasses intersect the ridge. The final steep pitch delivers climbers onto the summit, where there is a small amount of rock and an awesome view of the range—weather permitting.

The ridge can be climbed from the moraine to the summit in a long day. However, there is a beautiful shoulder to camp on at 7,520 feet, 2,000 feet above the moraine camp.

Mount Mather, with Wedge Peak in the foreground and The Matherhorn in the background (Photo: Paul Roderick)

Descent: The descent is the route in reverse. Follow your wands back down the slope to that sweet little spot on the moraine: your sleeping bag.

 41 MOUNT MATHER

(12,123 ft; 3695 m)

Route ▲ North Ridge
Difficulty ▲ Alaska Grade 3
Elevation gain ▲ 6,500 ft
Average time ▲ 2 weeks, 2–3 days on route
Map ▲ Mount McKinley (A-1)
Resources ▲ *AAJ* 1984, p. 156; *AAJ* 1995, pp. 136–137

History: The first-ascent party was Thayer Scudder, Winslow Briggs, John S. Humphreys, and David Bernays. They climbed the West Ridge from the cirque above the Brooks Glacier on July 21, 1952. In 1979 Jim Bouchard and partner climbed the Northeast Ridge from the Muldrow Glacier to intersect the North Ridge at 10,000 feet. Finally on June 30, 1994, Mike Litzow and Jeff Benowitz completed the most direct ascent of the North Ridge from the small cirque on the south side of the Muldrow Glacier.

Approach: Foot power is the only way at present to reach the base of Mount Mather's North Ridge. It will take 2 or 3 days to reach the base of the climb from Eielson Visitor Center at mile 65 on the Denali Park Road or Wonder Lake Campground. Follow walk-in directions to McGonagall Pass given for Mount Silverthrone (Route 39).

The Muldrow Glacier is burly and unpleasant to walk on due to the huge amount of scree and moraine piles everywhere. There are also huge rivers on the glacier, which roar into the septic system of the glacier as they thunder down a moulin. And for those who think travel would be faster on the lateral moraines, well have fun! The flowers are beautiful over there, and the pools of snowmelt can be a fun dip to numb your aching bones, but don't be in a hurry.

Route description: The fourth cirque to the east from the north ridge of Ragged Peak marks the entrance to the glacier that must be ascended for 0.5 mile to the 5,200-foot level. Stop at the obvious, east-facing couloir. This couloir, which rises to the ridge, is relatively well protected from the rock and ice fall on either side. The bergschrund is small and easy to cross, leading to scree and talus slopes up low-angled ice for 2,000 feet. The ice gives way to lower-angled snow, then, just before the ridge, there is a 50-degree ice and snow slope leading to a bowl on the ridge. From here the views spread out nicely, and the climbing along the ridge is mainly walking, with the occasional ice bulge. A good place to camp can be found on the ridge below Sub-Peak 10,030.

A spur of the Northeast Ridge meets the prominent North Ridge at this point. This is where the 1979 route climbed by Bouchard and partner intersects the ridge. The North Ridge now begins to sharpen as it goes horizontally for quite a way until it meets a nondescript headwall at about 12,000 feet. A series of false summits lines the horizontal, knife-edged ridge. Two larger cornices form on the ridge, punctuating the overall corniced nature of the climbing encountered on the way to the summit. The climbing is absorbing and the views fantastic from the ridge. It is recommended that the final summit be reached on a belay, one climber at a time.

Descent: Return via the ascent route.

EASTERN ALASKA RANGE

Big, remote, difficult to access, and largely unknown, the Eastern Alaska Range is an obsession among Alaskan climbers, but mostly overlooked by the rest of the world. On a clear day, Fairbanks climbers get inspired by views of Mount Hayes (13,832 ft), the highest peak in this mountain group. The range begins east of Broad Pass and ends at the mighty Delta River. The north and south boundaries are the tundra plains of Alaska (see map on page 57).

Lack of easy access is responsible for the comparative lack of activity in the Eastern Alaska Range. Most people enter the area on skis in the spring when the rivers are frozen. By summer, a raft or boat is needed to cross the rivers. In the past one could fly from Delta Junction, but the current absence of local air taxis requires most climbers to take an expensive 1.5 hour flight from Talkeetna. Bring books; bad weather has left some parties stranded for weeks.

 42 MOUNT DEBORAH

(12,339 ft; 3760 m)

Route ▲ Northwest Ridge
Difficulty ▲ Alaska Grade 3+, AI 3
Elevation gain ▲ 5,600 ft
Average time ▲ 3 weeks, 2–3 days on route
Map ▲ Healy (C-1)
Resources ▲ *AAJ*, 1965, p. 404; *AAJ*, 1972, pp. 106–107; *AAJ*, 1975, p. 117; *AAJ* 1977, p. 116; *AAJ* 1978, p. 514; *AAJ* 2000, p. 215; *Climbing*, no. 46, 1978

History: Fred Beckey, Henry Meybohm, and Heinrich Harrer climbed this peak in 1954 via the South Ridge on their whirlwind season in Alaska. They also did the first ascents of the Northwest Ridge on Denali and the West Ridge of Mount Hunter in the same season. The Northwest Ridge of Mount Deborah was first attempted by Richard Nolting, Floyd Frank, and Joe Smyth in 1971 from the Gillam Glacier. In August 1976 Richard Nolting, John Cady, Barry Nash, and Ray Watts returned to successfully complete the North-Northwest Ridge. On April 14, 1977, James Brady, Peter Hollis, Clifton Moore, and Carl Tobin climbed a

The massive massif of Mount Deborah. The Northwest Ridge forms the left skyline of the more distant peak. (Photo: Roman Dial)

variation to the Northwest Ridge, the West-Northwest Ridge from the Yanert Glacier. This is the route described below.

Fly-in approach: The Yanert Glacier is the best access for the Northwest Ridge of Mount Deborah. At the present time it is most common to fly in to the glacier from Talkeetna, as there are no commercial air taxis in the Delta Junction area to access the Eastern Alaska Range. There is a great landing spot at 6,700 feet and a very short ski to the base of The Frozen Hurricane, as Fred Beckey described this icefall on his first ascent of Mount Deborah. Keep in mind that Mount Deborah's distance from Talkeetna makes it difficult to tell what the weather is doing in the Eastern Alaska Range.

Walk-in approach: To walk in or out, the Yanert River is your best choice. From the George Parks Highway near McKinley Village to the base of the route entails about 50 miles of riverbar and glacier travel. In the spring overflow, ice can really help speed travel. Later in the season, however, the river could present a problem due to high water volume. Beware not to bother the locals on your way; it wouldn't be appreciated. They live in this solitary environment for a reason.

Route description: Begin at 6,700 feet at the base of The Frozen Hurricane. At the time of this writing, the easiest way around this 2,300-foot monster ice-

Northwest Ridge of Mount Deborah with Gillam Glacier in the background (Photo: Matt Porter collection)

fall is on the left side. The objective hazard here is high, with icefall and avalanche hazard above you. The travel above the initial chute is quite straightforward, with only a few crevasses to negotiate. Originally, a camp was placed at 7,600 feet, but at 9,000 feet, at the base of the Northwest Ridge, there is a great and safe place to camp. Stay lower down rather than higher up in the valley to avoid avalanche run-outs. From this higher camp you can choose between the original ascent route up the ice gully to a chossy rock rib that leads to the ridge, or follow the 50-degree snow and ice up the face to the ridge at 11,000 feet.

The North Ridge and West Ridge converge at 10,800 feet. At this point or slightly higher, a very exposed camp can be set on the ridge. The remaining 1,500 feet of climbing is along the exposed ridge on snow and rock, traversing on cornices. The April–May 1978 party used 1,500 feet of fixed line, which they removed on the descent. This climbing can be well protected with pickets and ice screws on the ridge. It is very exposed, and the ridge is extremely knife-edged in places. It does back off nicely within 300 feet of the summit. Beware: There is a large cornice that protects the very summit of this peak, so if the summit really is *that* important, be prepared! In 1999 it took local boy Matt Porter and partner 7 hours to climb the route from their tent to the summit via the Northwest Ridge, and 8 hours to descend. This may not be common, but it does illustrate the "going-down factor."

Descent: The easiest and quickest way down is to head directly down the most commonly attempted route: the West Face, which consists of 50-degree ice and snow. Make twenty 150-foot rappels or downclimb. The last rappel over the bergschrund can be quite a doozy. Ice-hourglasses can be used on the upper face, but once the snow gets too deep to dig down to the ice, resort to snow bollards. Downclimbing and rapping off pickets is the most useful way down.

43 MOUNT HAYES

(13,832 ft; 4215 m)

Route ▲ East Ridge
Difficulty ▲ Alaska Grade 2+
Elevation gain ▲ 6,400 ft
Average time ▲ 2–3 weeks, 2–3 days on route
Maps ▲ Mount Hayes (C-6)
Resources ▲ *AAJ* 1942; *AAJ* 1972, pp. 105–106;
   AAJ 1997; *AAJ* 1974, p. 138; *Descent,* Apr/May
   1972; *Descent,* Oct/Nov 1972; *Descent,* Nov/
   Dec 1973; *Descent* 5, no. 3, 1974; *Descent* 9,
   no. 3, 1977; *Descent,* Nov 1987; *Climbing,* no.
   103, Aug 1987

History: Bradford and Barbara Washburn, accompanied by Benjamin Ferris, Sterling Hendricks, Henry Hall, and William Shand made the first ascent of Mount Hayes via its North Ridge in 1941. This was a landmark climb due to the difficulty of the route at the time. The East Ridge was first climbed on May 22, 1972, by Mark Hoffman, Tom Hollis, James Brady, and Dan Osborne.

Fly-in approach: Fly in to the Trident Glacier from Talkeetna. The only available air taxis at this time are located in Talkeetna, which presents a small problem: unlike the Central Alaska Range, it is more difficult to assess the weather and flight conditions in the Eastern Alaska Range due to its distance from Talkeetna. Once again be prepared to spend a bit longer than expected (i.e., take plenty of food and fuel).

Walk-in approach: This may also be the walk out! The approach begins at the Donnelly Campground between miles 237 and 238 on the Richardson Highway. Travel across the Delta River, west and then south to the mouth of McGinnis Creek. Travel up McGinnis Creek on the north side, looking for a well-worn tractor trail about 1 to 1.5 miles up the creek. The trail will suddenly head north

*East Ridge of Mount Hayes, as seen from Levi's Bump
(9,800 ft) (Photo: Georgie Stanley)*

The East Face of Mount Hayes rising from the Trident Glacier (Photo: Bradford Washburn, neg. no. 2936)

and up in elevation from the 2,000-foot and 3,000-foot contour lines. Once topped out on the 3,000-foot contour, travel directly west for 3.5 miles, passing south of Hill 3,935. Another 2.5 miles brings you to the most northwestern fork of an unnamed creek, which leads to a pass at 5,000 feet. At this point there is a bit of up and down in elevation, but travel directly west for 4 miles from the 5,000-foot pass. The Trident Glacier will drop into view almost literally, and from here the routefinding up the glacier is a matter of mountain sense. The Trident Glacier is littered with moraine and many severe icefalls that remain blown clear throughout the winter. The to-

tal distance from the roadhead to 7,000 feet on the Trident Glacier is 30 miles.

Route description: Beginning on the Trident Glacier at 7,000 feet, travel north 3,000 feet up the prominent rib to Levi's Bump (9,800 ft). The ridge ascending to Levi's Bump can be avalanche prone, especially after a north wind. A camp can be placed on the ridge between Levi's Bump and the 4,000 feet to the summit. The ridge leading to the summit consists of 50-degree slopes of snow and ice. Crevasses intersect the ridge at many points along the way.

Descent: From the summit reverse the route down the East Ridge, following your wands to 7,000 feet.

44 MOUNT MOFFIT

(13,020 ft; 3968 m)

Route ▲ Western North Ridge
Difficulty ▲ Alaska Grade 4, AI 3
Elevation gain ▲ 8,000 ft
Average time ▲ 2–3 weeks, 3–5 days on route
Maps ▲ Mount Hayes (C-4, C-5, C-6)
Resources ▲ *AAJ* 1940–42; *AAJ* 1977; *AAJ* 1997, pp. 160, 180–181; *Descent,* Dec/Jan 1972; *Descent* 25, no. 1, 1996

History: Benjamin Greely Ferris Jr., Sterling Hendricks, and Bill Shand made the first ascent of this peak on August 12, 1942. These guys accompanied Bradford and Barbara Washburn, along with Henry Hall, on the North Ridge of Mount Hayes on its first ascent. Bradford, Barbara, and Hall had to leave, so Ferris, Hendricks, and Shand cruised over to attempt the Western North Ridge of Mount Moffit. On the summit day, Washburn flew around the peak, making one of his photographic flights. In the pictures he took, two dots can be seen just below the summit; these dots are the three climbers. It was later suggested that this peak be named Mount Shand in honor of first ascensionist Bill Shand, who was killed shortly thereafter in a car crash while on his way to the Tetons. Unfortunately, the proposed name was mistakenly applied to the 12,660-foot peak to the south.

Randy Waitman and Mike Litzo completed a well-deserved first winter ascent in 1996. This was Waitman's third time to the peak and Litzo's second.

Fly-in approach: Fly from Talkeetna to the Trident

Mike Litzow descending to a snow cave on Mount Moffit's Western North Ridge (Photo: Randy Waitman)

Mount Moffit with Mount Shand to the right and the West Ridge of McGinnis Peak to the left (Photo: Bradford Washburn, neg. no. 2930)

Glacier. From the glacier, walk 8 miles down the glacier to the base of the Western North Ridge. Most people walk in.

Walk-in approach: Follow directions to the Trident Glacier given for Mount Hayes (Route 43).

Route description: The technical climbing begins at 5,000 feet. The route follows the moderate ridge up snow-covered scree slopes to 7,500 feet. From this point the route follows the glaciated ridge line for the rest of the climb. A nice campsite can be found between 9,700 feet and 10,000 feet. Above the campsite

the climb becomes steeper. The crux slope is a 600-foot long, 65-degree snow and ice slope, which is attained after crossing a large bergschrund. At the top, the slope gives way to a 500-foot narrow snow ridge. The ridge displays cornicing and rock gendarmes that are easily surmounted. The rest of the ridge to the summit is impressively corniced. The summit is about 150 feet long and 25 feet wide with a large crevasse running lengthwise.

Descent: Reverse the route from the summit and make sure to follow your wands down.

45 McGinnis Peak

(11,400 ft; 3474 m)

Route ▲ Northeast Ridge
Difficulty ▲ Alaska Grade 3+, AI 3
Elevation gain ▲ 6,000 ft
Average time ▲ 7–10 days, 1–3 days on route
Maps ▲ Mount Hayes (C-5, C-6)
Resources ▲ *AAJ* 1977, pp. 163–165; *AAJ* 1995, p. 144 (winter ascent); *Descent* 3, no. 3, 1971; *Descent* 9, no. 3, 1977; *Descent* 24, no. 1, 1994; *Climbing*, no. 151, 1995

History: Larry Muir and Tom Knott climbed the West Ridge on August 5, 1964. James Brady and John Garson climbed the Northeast Ridge on June 14, 1975. There are quite a few variations to the Northeast Ridge, and these are explained in the route description below.

Approach: This is a peak that has seen quite a number of ascents due to its closeness to the Richardson Highway. It is only 15–20 miles from the road to the base of the mountain. To hike in you must travel across the Delta River, which is not easy in the summer when it is a raging torrent. The crossing can be the crux of the approach. In the winter or early spring the crossing isn't bad at all, either on the ice or in clear shallow water. Late in the summer, when the nights are freezing up higher it can also be easier to cross. Travel up McGinnis Creek onto the McGinnis Glacier and head up the northeast fork. This route brings you to the base of the Northeast Ridge and the Cutthroat Couloir, an obvious couloir first climbed by Roman Dial and Chuck Comstock in March 1975. Travel up the north fork of the glacier if you plan to access the North Ridge.

Route description: The Northeast Ridge has seen the most climbing traffic of any route on the mountain. It is the route of the second ascent of the mountain by James Brady and John Garson in 1976. When

Matt Porter and Kirby Spangler rappelling into the traverse below the crux gendarme on the Northeast Ridge of McGinnis Peak (Photo: Mike Wood)

they climbed the peak, they ascended the Northeast Ridge from the northeast fork of the McGinnis Glacier, heading up the first ice tongue that pours into the main tributary.

In October 1976 Geoff Radford and Jim Jennings made the most complete ascent of the Northeast Ridge, beginning at Peak 7,055 and intersecting the Brady-Garson route at the col between Points 9,010 and 9,280. The next variation was climbed on February 21, 1994, when Jeff Benowitz and Ian McRae did the first winter ascent. They followed the ridge from the northeast fork of the McGinnis Glacier and took

McGinnis Peak's Northeast Ridge route, showing the approach at the bottom. The dotted line indicates the route is hidden from view. (Photo: Jeff Benowitz)

the upper-most glacial tongue in the fork, up the right side of the cirque to gain the ridge at 8,700 feet, bypassing a fair bit of knife-edge ridge. This, too, intersects the Brady-Garson route, which is the remainder of this route description.

From this col a long knife-edge ridge continues upward to a notch at 10,400 feet, where it is possible to put in a snow cave bivi. From here the crux of the climb begins with a two-pitch traverse around a rock gendarme on the ridge. Radford and Jennings bypassed the obstacle on its southeast side, but Brady and Garston went around the northwest side. Only 600 vertical feet of 45-degree snow or ice climbing separates you from the summit.

Descent: The majority of parties who have climbed the mountain in recent years agree that the Northeast Ridge ascent route is the best bet for descent. One rappel is necessary from the top of the gendarme onto the northwest side, intersecting the crux traverse. From here the descent route puts you on your path to exit the mountains via McGinnis Creek and out to burgers and beverage! Radford and Jennings descended the Northwest Ridge, thus completing the first traverse of the mountain.

DELTA MOUNTAINS

The Delta Mountains mark the eastern terminus of the Alaska Range, and Mount Kimball and The Thorn are the farthest-east peaks in the Delta Mountains featured in this book. The Delta River forms the western boundary, tundra plains border the south, and the Tanana and Nebesna Rivers form a northeastern border (see map on page 57).

Less remote than other areas of the Alaska Range, most of the glaciers in the western Deltas stop within a mile of the Richardson Highway. The Deltas are a regular tromping ground of Fairbanks climbers, who built huts in the area. There are a great variety of peaks and routes for all levels of ability, from beginner to expert. Positioned in the rain shadow of the Wrangell Mountains, good weather frequents the Deltas, but beware of lightning storms, which roll in from the plains. For years, the Black Rapids Military Training Camp used the Gulkana Glacier for training missions, so be particularly cautious of the water quality there.

46 WHITE PRINCESS
(9,800 ft; 2987 m)

Route ▲ West Ridge
Difficulty ▲ Alaska Grade 1
Elevation gain ▲ 4,000 ft
Average time ▲ 7–10 days, 1 day on route
Maps ▲ Mount Hayes (B-3, B-4)
Resources ▲ *AAJ* 1961; *Descent 2*, no. 2, 1970; *Descent 9*, no. 3, 1977

History: The photographer Austin Post and his party first climbed this peak via the South Ridge. The second ascent of the mountain was via the North Ridge in April 1960. The ascent party included Les and Teri Viercek, Ron DeWitt, Moonok Sonwod, Pete Dzikiewicz, Lou Schere, Galen McWilliams, and Gene Wescott.

Approach: From the Richardson Highway travel up the Castner Glacier for 6 miles, then take the south fork for about 3 miles to the base of the route. The Thayer Hut, operated by the Alaska Alpine Club in Fairbanks, is located on the point above the confluence of the north and east forks of the Castner Glacier. The slope leading to the hut is steep and potentially avalanche prone during winter months. From the hut, travel up the south fork of the Castner Glacier for 5 miles to reach the base of the West Ridge.

Route description: This route is mellow snow climbing, almost walking. It is the perfect warm-up to

White Princess from the south fork of the Castner Glacier, with Leo Americus preparing a midwinter camp (Photo: John Bauman)

the Deltas and allows you to assess the conditions of the area. This area and this peak have been favorites for Fairbanks climbers for years. Technically this West Ridge of White Princess is not a super-demanding route, but the ridge climbing is fun and the views can be great. This is an especially great route in the winter, when hanging out in the cold to belay is much too uncomfortable.

The bottom of the ridge is scree and talus and may even be blown clear in the winter or melted out in the summer. The steeper slopes in the middle of the ridge can create avalanche hazards and show some cornicing. Once near the top of the climb, there are glaciers that hide deep crevasses under a thin covering of windswept snow. It may be necessary to wand the route to help retrace your steps when the going gets cloudy.

Descent: Retrace your steps back down the route, following your awesome wand placements to that snug camp on the glacier below.

The Thorn's East Face from the north fork of the Robertson Glacier (Photo: Jeff Benowitz)

47 THE THORN

(9,200 ft; 2804 m)

Route ▲ East Face (100 years of Solitude)
Difficulty ▲ Alaska Grade 4, 5.5, WI 5
Elevation gain ▲ 3,000 ft
Average time ▲ 7–10 days, 2–3 days on route
Maps ▲ Mount Hayes (A-3, B-1, B-2, B-3)
Resources ▲ *AAJ* 1999, pp. 248–250; *Coast Magazine,* Oct 2000, p. 19

History: Rick Studley and Jeff Benowitz climbed this remote peak on March 5–6, 1998. This first ascent—in winter—took 8 days round trip from the Alaska Highway.

Approach: Park on the east side of the Robertson River bridge on the Alaska Highway. Ski about 28 miles up the West Fork of the Robertson River. Ski another 12 miles up the north fork of the Robertson Glacier to the base of The Thorn. Expect overflow on the river and deep snow until you get to the Robertson Glacier proper.

Route description: Start up the low-angle snow couloir to the left of the central rock buttress. The couloir steepens and narrows as it rises. Climb two pitches of steep-and-thin mixed ground (5.5, WI 5). We fixed these pitches with one 200-foot rope and a bunch of long slings. A narrow snow-cave bivi can be dug into a snow arête below and north of the main couloir. This is an awesome bivi site with a view of Mount Kimball.

Ascend your fixed line and climb lower-angle,

thicker ice for about 600 feet. Exit the couloir via steep, vertical-to-overhanging ice going up and left. Two pitches of very scary snow-tunneling and cornice-chimneying brought us to a final arête below the East Ridge. Follow this snow-and-rock arête to the junction with the East Ridge. Follow the rime-covered East Ridge for a short distance to the tiny summit. Jeff Benowitz suggests the following gear for this route: 8 ice screws, 2 pickets, 6 cams up to 0.75 size, and 12 assorted pitons.

Descent: From the summit drop down the West Ridge for a pitch or three. Traverse north under the summit cap of The Thorn. Downclimb the North Ridge to reach a large couloir that drops back down to the east. The couloir will take you back to your skis at the start of the climbing. If the couloir is loaded with snow, avoid it because of avalanche hazards. An alternative descent would be to follow the North Ridge all the way down to a pass between the Johnson and Robertson glacial systems. This would be a longer and more difficult proposition. The descent from the top can be completed in about 3–5 hours.

48 MOUNT KIMBALL

(10,300 ft; 3139 m)

Route ▲ Southwest Ridge
Difficulty ▲ Alaska Grade 2+
Elevation gain ▲ 3,300 ft
Average time ▲ 10–14 days, 2–3 days on route
Maps ▲ Mount Hayes (A-2, B-2)
Resources ▲ *AAJ* 1969, pp. 374–375; *AAJ* 1970, pp. 75–78

History: Mount Kimball was finally climbed on the ninth try (!) on June 13, 1969, by Grace Hoeman, Tom

Paul Turecki and Ian McRae prepare for an ascent of Mount Kimball's Southwest Ridge (Photo: Randy Waitman)

Kensher, Dan Osborne, and Mike Sallee after many difficult attempts by them and other experienced Alaskan mountaineers. This is a very remote peak, well protected by the difficult ridges leading to the summit. This is a wilderness journey, and to this day Mount Kimball remains rarely climbed, in part due to the difficulty of the approach. The first route climbed was the West Ridge, and it was not until 4 years later that Doug Buchanan, Jerry Johnson, and Ken Irving succeeded on the North Ridge. We describe the Southwest Ridge here.

Approach: The approach is a burly, 30-mile, overland trip from the Richardson Highway. The roadhead is on Isabel Pass, at the toe of the Gulkana Glacier. From this parking spot travel east across Gunn Creek to the toe of the Gakona Glacier. Continue east to the Chistochina River and head northeast up Slate Creek to the Chistochina Glacier.

Route description: Pilot Harvey Wheeler flew Randy Waitman, Ian McRae, and Paul Turecki onto the north fork of the Chistochina Glacier in February, a cold month. The party's goal was to climb Kimball's Southwest Ridge. The three climbers have decades of experience of climbing in Alaska among them, and for once they were rewarded with unusual and very inviting snow conditions on the ridge. The cramponing was great and quickly brought them to the first obstacle on the ridge: a rock gendarme, which can be negotiated across the snow face on the south side. Once around this, the ridge remains steep and some mixed ground above can hold avalanche potential. Halfway up the ridge 35-degree slopes bring you to a rock step. This is the technical crux of the route and can be overcome with two or three moves.

The next famous feature is the Golf Ball. This historically intimidating and non-negotiable feature was easily avoided by the first-ascent party via an easy snow ramp on the east side. Once around this feature the ridge turns into a large plateau that leads to the summit knob. This can be surmounted with a bit of grunting, front pointing, digging, and swimming. A perfectly classic way to end a true Alaskan peak climb.

Descent: Retrace your route of ascent. The descent may require a rappel to pass the "swim and grovel" slope just below the top. The short rock step may also need to be rappelled.

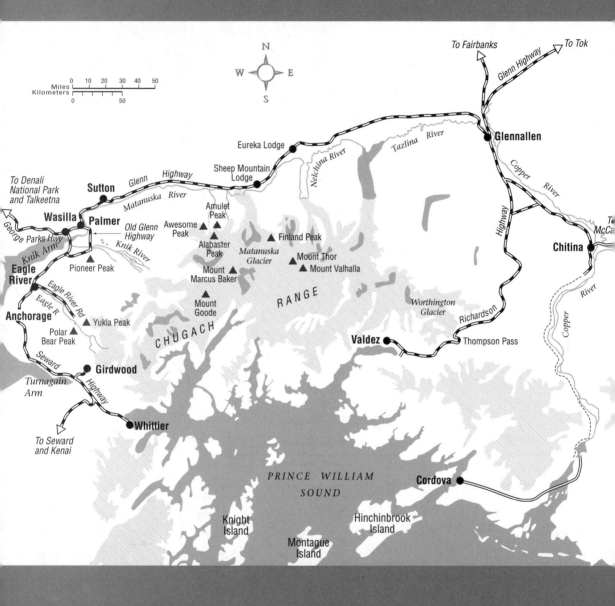

CHUGACH RANGE

The Chugach Range forms a 300-mile-long range in southcentral Alaska. The range is bordered by the Copper River to the east, Prince William Sound to the south, the Nelchina and Tazlina Rivers to the north, and Turnagain Arm and the Portage Valley as far as Whittier to the west.

The western border of the Chugach is the most popular among climbers and other backcountry users. The southern boundary has fascinated marine travellers for years with its major tidewater glaciers calving into Prince William Sound. Dense vegetation and major river crossings heavily defend the northern part of the Chugach, while massive glaciers define the eastern and central portion of the range. Enormous ice fields like the Tazlina and Nelchina Glaciers flow to the north, as others like the University Glacier flow south into Prince William Sound. At 42 miles long, the Columbia Glacier is one of North America's largest tidewater glaciers, but it is retreating quickly. It is the last of fifty-two tidewater glaciers in Alaska that still fills the length of its fiord. The tallest mountain in the Chugach is Mount Marcus Baker (13,176 ft), first climbed by Bradford Washburn (and originally called Mount Saint Agnes). With the range's close proximity to the Pacific Ocean, it is no wonder where such glaciers came from; this also means wet and stormy weather.

The early pioneers of the Chugach Range were dog mushers and gold miners who travelled the Iditarod Trail from the port at Seward, north through the Kenai Mountains to Portage and on to Girdwood. Once in Girdwood, they travelled over Crow Pass Trail into the Eagle River drainage. From here they travelled along the southern edge of the Knik Arm of Cook Inlet and up to the Matanuska or Susitna Valleys.

The early climbers began their trips and rambles in the western mountains. Many of these climbers would train in the Chugach for future climbs on Denali. Two of the most prolific local climbers were Vin Hoeman and his wife Grace. Vin claimed first ascents on many large and remote mountains throughout Alaska, but, sadly, died in an avalanche on Dhaulagiri in 1969 at age 29. He was working on a guidebook to the mountains of Alaska at the time.

The Chugach mountains are comprised of Chugach National Forest and Chugach State Park lands. It is one of the few mountain ranges in Alaska that is not under National Park Service jurisdiction. Access into the Chugach is relatively easy, but native lands border some areas and cannot be trespassed on, particularly on the north side of the range in the Matanuska Valley.

Travel into the mountains can follow a number of different modes of transportation. To walk or ski in is not particularly difficult, especially in the winter when many of the raging rivers are low and frozen. On the south side of the range, it is possible to charter a boat in Prince William Sound to transport you to a destination. Kayaks are also a great means of access for this part of the range. Even snowmobiles can access this country—all to well! There is a well-travelled route from the Nelchina Glacier over the divide at its head and down to the Valdez Glacier. This route, however, proved nearly fatal for at least three snowmobilers when they all plunged into the same crevasse, on top of one another.

The great standby is to fly in to the mountains, but flights are weather-dependant. It is a very good idea to be prepared to hike out if the weather prohibits a pick-up flight. Reading Bradford Washburn's account of his ascent of Mount Marcus Baker is educational on this point.

There are a number of air taxis that can fly you and your gear into the Chugach. Where you want to go generally dictates who takes you and your gear, and from where. The only place you cannot legally land with a plane in the Chugach is in the state park land around the Eklutna, Whiteout, or Eagle Glaciers. The entire Eklutna traverse is on state park land and is off-limits to landings.

From the south it is probably best to fly out of Girdwood with Alpine Air. You may find a pilot in the Anchorage area, but currently Alpine Air is the only service of which we are aware.

For the north side of the Chugach it may be possible to use Alpine Air as well. However, Alpine Air's distance from the Chugach's north side makes it difficult to assess weather conditions prior to take off. In our experience, the very best pilot for accessing the northern Chugach and the central Chugach is Mike Meekin, of Meekin's Air Service. Meekin has three generations worth of knowledge in the

Matanuska Valley, and he can do things with his Super Cub that you cannot imagine.

49 YUKLA PEAK

(7,535 ft; 2296 m)

Route ▲ East Face to Northeast Ridge
Difficulty ▲ Alaska Grade 1
Elevation gain ▲ 2,000 ft
Average time ▲ 1 day on route
Map ▲ Anchorage (A-6)
Resources ▲ *AAJ* 1965, p. 403; *AAJ* 1966, p. 101;
    AAJ 1969, p. 376

History: This is the highest peak in the Eagle River drainage. The word "yukla" means "eagle" in one of the native languages. United States Geological Sur-

Yukla Peak (Photo: Richard Baranow)

Polar Bear Peak (Photo: Richard Baranow)

vey employee Walter C. Mendenhall, during his 1898 trip through the area, noted this peak. Art Davidson and John Bousman climbed it for the first time on July 15, 1964.

Approach: Park at Chugach State Park's Eagle River Nature Center at the end of Eagle River Road. Start hiking east, then south up the North Fork of Eagle River, following that super-sweet trail for about 6 miles. Yukla Creek drains out of the Icicle Glacier just north of the West Ridge of Yukla Peak. This is where you embark on the more authentic Alaskan adventure and begin bushwhacking. Four miles of uphill struggle brings you onto the Icicle Glacier and to the base of the Northeast Ridge.

Route description: The climbing on the route consists mostly of scrambling on scree and talus up to the ridge. Once on the ridge there is more scree, but most likely it is covered with snow. Higher up there are permanent snowfields that are steep enough that you need to remain attentive and composed to avoid a serious fall if you slip.

Descent: Carefully retrace your steps back down the route to your base camp and enjoy the view.

 50 POLAR BEAR PEAK

(6,614 ft; 2015 m)

Route ▲ Northwest Face
Difficulty ▲ Alaska Grade 1+
Elevation gain ▲ 2,600 ft
Average time ▲ 1 day on route
Map ▲ Anchorage (A-6)
Resources ▲ *AAJ* 1967, pp. 345–346; *AAJ* 1987, p. 157

History: Vin Hoeman and C. Serfoss climbed Polar Bear Peak on September 5, 1966, by the Southeast Ridge and descended the Northwest Face. Charlie Sassara and Steve Davis made the first ascent of the Northwest Face route February 15–17, 1986.

Approach: Begin at Chugach State Park's Eagle

River Nature Center at the end of Eagle River Road. Hike the well-marked trail up the North Fork of Eagle River for approximately 6 miles, until it is time to cross the Eagle River at the Icicle Creek confluence, which flows into Eagle River from the north. Beware of the depth of the river; it is definitely an objective hazard of this trip. Once you have crossed the river, bushwhack a short way into the valley that drains Organ Glacier. From here it is about 2.5 miles up to the base of the climb. Ascend the valley, trending left (southeast) to a rounded shoulder at the base of the face.

Route description: Climb third-class mixed terrain of snow, ice, and low-angle rock to the hanging glacier directly below the summit pyramid. Ascend the hanging glacier for 800 feet of 50-degree snow, aiming for a right-trending weakness in the summit block. Rope up at the base of the rock and climb two easy, mixed pitches to the summit. This route offers exposed third-class climbing with great views of the Alaska and Chugach Ranges.

Descent: You can retrace your steps back down the route or descend the original route of ascent down the Southeast Ridge. The latter would put you on the opposite side of the mountain, however, and it would add at least another 3 miles to your walk out. On a more positive note, this route is a total scramble and would be very fast.

 ## 51 PIONEER PEAK

(6,398 ft; 1950 m)

Route ▲ North Face
Difficulty ▲ Alaska Grade 1+, AI 2
Elevation gain ▲ 4,500 ft
Average time ▲ 0.5 to 1 day on route
Map ▲ Anchorage (B-6)
Resources ▲ *AAJ* 1966, pp. 98–104; *Scree* 3, no. 107, 1961

History: Somebody most likely climbed Pioneer Peak from the Matanuska Valley colony in earlier years.

The earliest recorded ascent was by John Billman, Steve Foss, Helga Balding, and Jim Messick on June 18, 1936. The first ascent of the North Face is difficult to discern due to a lack of detailed route description and conflicting accounts of first ascents. The second recorded ascent was by Paul Crews Sr., Warren Crosby, and Harry Pursell via the North Gully on August 16, 1953.

Approach: This is the easiest approach in all of Alaska! Just drive the Old Glenn Highway to the base of the peak, just past the Knik River bridge. Park under the large avalanche slope. Take note of the "No Parking—Avalanche Area" signs!

Route description: Timing on this route is crucial. The best time of year to catch this face in shape is in late April and early May. The snow at this time of year has turned into a nice névé, but there are runnels down the face that carry wet slide avalanches later in the day. These runnels are great to climb in, but needless to say, they are also gun barrels.

Beginning at the base of the route, follow the large gully—usually strewn with avalanche debris—up to the rocks. Earlier in the season, the gully is frozen and there is a sweet route up the left side on low-angle ice, but when melted out the avalanche debris can be cumbersome. You can avoid the debris by climbing the gully's rib, but then you have to pass through very trying devil's club and alder.

The gully leads to a broad snow slope and the snow remains at a moderate angle up the face. About halfway up, the snow face starts to get pinched into a rock band. Follow the snow to the highest point of the face, then if it is early enough in the season and the ice is good, follow a very narrow piece of ice that weaves its way up the cliff for 150 feet. If this is running water when you get there, it can be avoided by climbing the slope directly to the right of the couloir.

Once over this part the slope continues at a moderate 40-degree angle. Then the slope goes to 55–60 degrees and the summit is very much in view. There is a double summit, and it is important to aim for

North Face of Pioneer Peak (Photo: Thomas Bol)

the middle point for a while. As you start getting closer, look for a ramp that angles up and left through a few scattered rocks. This left-slanting ramp moves over some rocks and is probably the steepest part of the whole North Face route. The slope increases in angle to 55–60 degrees. From here it is a very short climb with some exposed bouldering moves to get to the top.

Descent: Retracing your route of ascent is a quick way to get back to your vehicle, but if it is too gripping or late in the day to return this way, descend the East Ridge to the large snow gully on the north side of the East Ridge. Goat trails can be found to assist in the descent.

52 MOUNT GOODE

(10,610 ft; 3233 m)

Route description ▲ East Ridge
Difficulty ▲ Alaska Grade 1
Elevation gain ▲ 2,600 ft
Average time ▲ 5–7 days, 1 day on route
Map ▲ Anchorage (B-3)
Resources ▲ *AAJ* 1959, p. 221; *AAJ* 1967, pp. 345–346; *Scree,* Nov 1965; *Scree,* Oct 1966

History: The name of this peak is pronounced "good." It was named for Richard Urquhart Goode, who was a geographer for the USGS. This peak was first climbed on

The route ascends the East Ridge of Mount Goode from the Knik Glacier (Photo: John Bauman)

April 24, 1966, by Helmut Tschaffert and Vin Hoeman.

Fly-in approach: This route can be most easily accessed by flying from the airstrip in Palmer onto the Knik Glacier at 8,000 feet.

Walk-in approach: To walk in, start on the north side of the Knik River from the Old Glenn Highway and travel up an off-road-vehicle trail to the base of the Knik Glacier. The travel up the glacier is difficult and broken, with quite a few river crossings. The other side of the river from the Knik River road is a reasonable access as well, but both routes require navigating through glaciated terrain.

Route description: The route from 8,000 feet on the Knik Glacier travels to the south, toward the East Ridge of Mount Goode. The routefinding is very straightforward, and skis were worn to within a few hundred feet of the summit on the first ascent. Just before the summit, however, skis must be replaced with crampons to safely navigate the summit ridge.

Descent: Just retrace your steps down to your skis. If the snow is good, enjoy yourself, but be careful of the crevasses on the way down.

 53 AWESOME PEAK

(8,645 ft; 2634 m)

Route ▲ South Face
Difficulty ▲ Alaska Grade 2, AI 3
Elevation gain ▲ 2,500 ft
Average time ▲ 1 week, 1 day on route
Maps ▲ Anchorage (C-3, C-4, D-3)
Resources ▲ *AAJ* 1999, p. 258; *AAJ* 2000, p. 216

History: Brian McCullough and Karl Swanson first climbed this route in the 1980s, and it didn't see another ascent until Willy Peabody and Mike Wood climbed it in April 1998. They took a couloir to the left in the main gully and were forced to traverse to the east to reach the summit. John Bauman and Leo Americus climbed the face in 1999. Most recently, Matt Porter completed a solo ascent of the North Face in 2000.

Fly-in approach: Meekin's Air Service can access the Spectrum Glacier, with the Super Cub plane landing at 6,000 feet.

Walk-in approach: From the Glenn Highway, follow the Monument Creek drainage to get to the Spectrum Glacier. This drainage can be pretty burly if you are not lucky enough to find the sporadic trails on the east side of the creek. Do not be fooled, though; the trails are not great, just less brushy than on the west side. Once above the 3,000-foot level, the brush thins

The South Face of Awesome Peak with the Spectrum Glacier below. Willy Peabody is on the North Ridge of Alabaster in the foreground. (Photo: Mike Wood)

and travel is easier. The last obstacle is negotiating the toe of the glacier. Travel up the right side (west) of the toe to reach the glacier. This approach is prone to avalanches, so be cautious in the winter months. Once on the glacier the travel is easy skiing to a base camp that provides easy access to Awesome and Alabaster (Route 54). The skiing up here is great, so bring the ol' boards!

Route description: The route can be seen quite clearly from a distance back in the cirque. It begins with a snow hike that narrows in the gully and looks like it dead-ends in the rocks. On a shallow snow year this is a small but awkward ice climb requiring screws and even some rock pro, but it may be snow-filled in heavy snow years.

Once this crux section is overcome, the main gully is about 40–50 degrees. Excellent rock pro and slinging horns can be found in the rock on the sides of the gully. The route keeps to the climber's right as you head up. A smaller gully goes up to the left, almost directly in front of you, but don't be fooled: it only leads to loose rock and ends far to the west of the summit; go right! This is a great gully, and it will bring you just to the east of the summit. A walk will put you right on the top.

Descent: Retrace the route of ascent. It may be necessary to rappel the first little crux.

54 ALABASTER PEAK
(8,065 ft; 2458 m)

Route ▲ North Ridge
Difficulty ▲ Alaska Grade 1
Elevation gain ▲ 1,500 ft
Average time ▲ 1 week, 1 day on route
Maps ▲ Anchorage (C-3, C-4, D-3)
Resources ▲ *AAJ* 1969, pp. 376–377; *AAJ* 1971, p. 335; *AAJ* 1975, pp. 119–120; *AAJ* 1999, p. 258

History: On July 2–6, 1971, Robert Spurr, Bob Pelz, and Royce Purinton approached the Spectrum Glacier

Alabaster Peak from the Spectrum Glacier. The route climbs the gendarme and then descends its backside to meet the North Ridge. See photo on page 133 for a view looking down the route. (Photo: Mike Wood)

from the Glenn Highway and endured the bushes up Monument Creek, finding sporadic game trails. They climbed the Northeast Chute to the North Ridge and on to the summit. This whole group of mountains is known as the "A" group, their names bestowed by Vin Hoeman, who gave all the peaks around the Spectrum Glacier names that begin with "A" and those around the Eklutna Glacier "B" names.

Approach: Follow the fly-in and walk-in directions given for Awesome Peak (Route 53).

Route description: The North Ridge of Alabaster, or Monument Peak, as it has been called, is an excellent place to do some great skiing! Ski up 500 feet until you hit the rocky ridge. Once you are done shredding, the route up the North Ridge is a great half-day trip. It weaves around and over several gendarmes, which require leaving the ridge to proceed, and regaining the ridge to continue. Toward the end of the route there is a traverse under crumby rock, primarily on the east side of the ridge. From the traverse, gain the upper slope to the summit.

Descent: If the avalanche conditions are safe, plunge-step down the left side of the North Face, staying close to the rocks. This puts you on the glacier below with a moderate walk back to your skis.

55 AMULET PEAK

(8,290 ft; 2526 m)

Route ▲ North Face
Difficulty ▲ Alaska Grade 2, AI 3
Elevation gain ▲ 3,300 ft
Average time ▲ 1 week, 1 day on route
Maps ▲ Anchorage (C-3, D-3)
Resources ▲ *AAJ* 1969, pp. 376–377; *AAJ* 2000, p. 216; *AAJ* 2001; *Scree* 10, no. 6, Apr 1968; *Scree* 42, no. 6, Jun 1999

History: Vin and Grace Hoeman, with Bill Babcock, returned on March 9, 1968, after attempting two other routes on this peak earlier that summer. They travelled up Gravel Creek to the South Ridge. Peter Sennhauser and Vaughn Hoeffler climbed the North Face route on August 19, 1979. In May 1999 Josh Sonkiss negotiated the river and hiked up Monument Creek to the base of the North Face to snag a solo ascent of this beautiful snow-and-ice couloir. This was followed by a March 2000 ascent by Matt Porter and Carl Oswald on the North Face.

Approach: Follow the fly-in and walk-in directions given for Awesome Peak (Route 53). In 1968 the approach for the South Ridge was up the Gravel Creek drainage from the Glenn Highway. It is pretty brushy, but it opens up onto tundra in the cirque. Alternate access is up the Monument Creek drainage (Route 53). At 2,500–3,000 feet the brush thins and eventually disappears as you reach the ice field that pours out of the North Face cirque. From here, non-threatening travel on moraine brings you to the base of the route.

Route description: The route up the North Face of Amulet is currently the most difficult climbing route on the mountain, and is objectively more dangerous than the South and East Ridges. However, it is a beautiful line and totally "in your face" from the Glenn Highway.

From the approach the angle of the North Face looks very intimidating, but as you get closer the angle backs off a bit, and it looks a little shorter. Once at the base, the initially wide couloir heads up toward the Northeast Ridge, but after about 800 feet it turns right (or west) and runs directly up the North Face. This gully defiantly funnels everything that falls from above down the center of the face, so sticking to either the right or left side is prudent.

In the middle of the route, the left side near the rocks is friendly, but begins to get a bit steeper. At this point you can aim for the two boulders hanging on the face to the left of the summit. Going between them and under the cornice works well, with only a short traverse to the left to circumvent the cornice. Once on the broad ridge, it is a short stroll to the summit.

Amulet Peak with Awesome Peak in the background. The route line ascends the North Face and the arrow indicates the descent down the East Ridge. (Photo: Mikey K)

Descent: The best route to descend depends on the conditions on the North Face in the winter. The route can be great plunge-stepping with only a short rappel from the cornice, or you may want to descend the East Ridge or the original ascent route down the South Ridge, into Gravel Creek, traversing the mountain. Be advised, though: going down this route will make returning to a camp on the Spectrum Glacier or recovering gear a total pain in the butt.

56 MOUNT MARCUS BAKER

(13,176 ft; 4016 m)

Route ▲ North Ridge
Difficulty ▲ Alaska Grade 2
Elevation gain ▲ 5,700 ft
Average time ▲ 10 days to 3 weeks, 3–5 days on route
Maps ▲ Anchorage (B-2, B-3, C-2)
Resources ▲ *AAJ* 1939, p. 255; *AAJ* 1959, pp. 225–226; *AAJ* 1976, pp. 437–438; *AAJ* 1977, pp. 166–167 (winter ascent); *AAJ* 1978, pp. 517–518; *AAJ* 1988, pp. 119–120; Sherwonit, *Alaska Ascents*

History: This highest peak in the Chugach mountains has a great history. Bradford Washburn, Peter Gabriel, Norman Bright, and Norman Dyhrenfurth first climbed this peak by flying in from the mud flats in Valdez with pilot Bob Reeve. The group spent a great amount of time (April 30 to May 30) just waiting to fly in to the peak and then waiting for all their members to get flown in. Finally everyone of the party was on the glacier and able to start the ascent of what was then called Mount Saint Agnes. This name, explained Bradford Washburn in the 1959 *American Alpine Journal* (p. 225), originated when "James W. Bagley of the USGS named this peak after his wife, but knowing that the name would not stick if the secret leaked out, he added 'St.' for concealment. The secret never did leak out until this moment, unless Brooks possibly got wind of it. At all events, Agnes, whether Saint or not, lost her peak to Mr. Baker [a cartographer and geologist]." Chief USGS Alaska geologist Alfred H. Brooks named Mount Marcus Baker and insisted that the name become official.

As epic as the naming of this peak sounds, the first ascent was by far more difficult. The Washburn party endured miserable weather on the ascent, but held tough for many weeks and made the summit after a very long summit day on June 19, 1938. The first winter ascent of the mountain was completed on February 6, 1976, by Brian Okonek, Robin Bowen, Charlie Hammond, and Greg Durocher.

Fly-in approach: Air support can be quite helpful, even on a walk-in approach. Two main sites exist for a ration resupply and fly-in approach on the glacier. The first is at the confluence of the Matanuska Glacier and Scandinavian Glacier, which flows in from the east at 4,500 feet. It is possible to land a Super Cub off the glacier in the warmer months, using a flower-covered gravel strip that offers a wonderful reprieve from the moraine and ice travel. In the more wintry months, a plane can land on skis at the same strip or on the Scandinavian Glacier between 5,100 and 5,200 feet near the Mountaineering Club of Alaska's Scandinavian Hut. Joining the club for a small fee can allow legal access to the inside. This membership is well worth the fee for the comfort and spectacular view from the hut. If you elect to stay at the hut, there is an outhouse that requires a plastic bag to line a bucket, which must be removed after use and flown out. Otherwise, dispose of feces as you would camping on the glacier. In the summer months use Leave No Trace protocols for proper disposal.

The second place to land, if your pilot chooses, can be at the 6,700–6,800-foot level on the west fork of the Matanuska Glacier. This spot puts supplies practically at the base of the route.

Walk-in approach: This is a large undertaking, beginning in the Matanuska Valley on the Glenn Highway and going up the Matanuska Glacier. Between the Glacier Park Resort parking lot at the toe of the glacier and the 7,500-foot level at the base of the climb lie 27 miles of moraine and crevasses. This route requires quite a bit of routefinding at the toe of the glacier. Recently, access has been gained most easily by staying on the north side of the glacier for the first 2 miles, and then working into the middle of the ice and threading your way up the medial moraine.

In the winter and early spring when the rivers are frozen, it is easy to access the Matanuska Glacier from Caribou Creek. Travel down the frozen creek to the

A member of the first winter ascent party approaches Mount Marcus Baker from the west fork of the Matanuska Glacier. (Photo: Brian Okonek)

toe of the Matanuska Glacier, then up onto the side of the glacier. On this approach the route is threatened by icefall on the west fork of the Matanuska Glacier from the south slopes between 6,200 and 6,500 feet.

Route description: The steep climbing on the North Ridge begins at 7,400 feet, at the head of the Matanuska Glacier. The terrain puts the climber in the position to seriously assess snow stability due to the prime angle of the slope. Expeditions have ascended along the south side of the ridge, rather than travelling the ridge crest. The ridge at 8,500 feet is not an obvious line, so traversing up and left will eventually deliver the climber to a faint rib above a rock band at 9,200 feet. The terrain here, as well as on the rest of the route, is littered with insidious crevasses.

From the little rib marked on the map at 9,200 feet, the route progresses to the left below Point 10,540,

keeping to the lowest-angle, least-crevassed line. Once the crevasses and bergschrund have been negotiated, head south into the small bowl, where a great camp can be established at 10,300 feet.

From this bowl the route heads straight up to the west and gains the ridge at 10,900 feet. Beyond here, the camping and climbing become very exposed to the weather. Remember you are on the highest point of the Chugach Mountains, right beside Prince William Sound, so the weather can be very inclement! The travel is on moderate- to low-angle slopes that are covered by brittle, ultra-thin, windswept bridges. From 11,000 to 12,000 feet the route stays on the west side of a bump/rib, keep this on your left side on the ascent.

The North Peak (12,360 ft) can be climbed any number of ways: up a trough or on the west side to a nice, narrow summit. From the north summit, you gain a commanding view of Mount Marcus Baker's higher south summit 2.5 miles away—if the day is clear. From the summit of the North Peak the route descends 700 feet to the south and travels 1.5 miles toward the west shoulder of Peak 12,800. Rappel or downclimb the 150–200 feet down the slope from the shoulder to the glacier below. This slope is very avalanche-prone and often has large cornices hanging from its edge. Fixed lines can be useful here to aid on the return trip and provide safety over the bergschrund, or in the event of an avalanche.

Once the 12,300-foot pass has been reached, the final slopes lie just ahead. The original route taken by the Washburn party was on the west side of the summit. The east side has also been ascended up a slope of 40–45 degrees to gain the ridge. The summit is hard-earned, but the panoramic views on a clear day are breathtaking. On a clear day a complete view of the Chugach, Aleutian, Alaska, Talkeetna, and Wrangell mountain ranges and Prince William Sound make the struggle worth every step.

Descent: Reverse the ascent route. Remember there is 900 feet of climbing and 3 miles to cover before re-turning to the high camp. Having many wands in place is strongly recommended. Once back at the base of the route, flying or walking out is your call; you may not have the option to fly out from 6,700–6,800 feet but may be able to get flown out from the Scandinavian Glacier at the lower elevation.

57 FINLAND PEAK

(9,405 ft; 2866 m)

Route ▲ North Ridge
Difficulty ▲ Alaska Grade 1
Elevation gain ▲ 1,000 ft once on the ridge
Average time ▲ 7–10 days, 1 day on route from hut
Maps ▲ Anchorage (C-2)
Resources ▲ There is a great, but unpublished guide in the Scandinavian Hut.

History: Unless recorded elsewhere the best first-ascent information to date is that the peak was first

Finland Peak from the Scandinavian Glacier (Photo: John Bauman)

climbed in 1960, with helicopter air support, by USGS employees. There is plenty of route information in the Scandinavian Hut guide and ascent log. It is worth being a member of the Mountaineering Club of Alaska just to have access to this resource inside the hut.

Fly-in approach: Fly in to the Scandinavian Glacier, which lies 16 miles up the Matanuska Glacier and flows in from the east. We recommend Meekin's Air Service, as Meekin's airstrip is a mere 20 minutes from the Scandinavian Glacier by air.

Walk-in approach: From the Glenn Highway, travel up the the Matanuska Glacier (see the walk-in approach for Route 56). Follow the Matanuska Glacier to the Scandinavian Glacier. Travel up the Scandinavian Glacier and head left (north) into the cirque.

This impressive little cirque holds quite a few awesome objectives, as well as comfortable accommodations at the Mountaineering Club of Alaska's Scandinavian Hut. The hike in can take a group with light packs 2–3 days. It is advisable to get your rations flown in if you are going to stay for any length of time.

Route description: From the hut, ski east to the base of the North Ridge of Finland Peak; the 1,000 feet of actual climbing starts there, requiring crampons and ice ax. The ridge climbing is moderate, but gaining the ridge requires negotiating some steep slopes capable of creating an avalanche. These slopes, though short, must be approached with caution. Once on the ridge a 30- to 40-foot step of about 50 degrees with a little rock at the top guards the last few steps to the summit. The view can be amazing, weather permitting, taunting the imagination with further climbing objectives.

Descent: Downclimbing may be necessary for that 30-foot section of 50-degree ice near the top. Continue the descent to your skis and enjoy the turns on the way down. Following some key wand markers will help ensure the correct route for your descent.

58 MOUNT THOR

(12,251 ft; 3734 m)

Route ▲ North Ridge
Difficulty ▲ Alaska Grade 1+
Elevation gain ▲ 3,750 ft
Average time ▲ 10–14 days, 1–2 days on route
Maps ▲ Anchorage (B-1, C-1)
Resources ▲ *AAJ* 1969, pp. 377–378 (Hoeman); *AAJ* 1992, p. 124 (Bauman); *Scree* 10, no. 9, Jul 1968 (Hoeman)

History: Mount Thor is the second-highest independent peak in the Chugach Mountains. The first ascent was on June 5, 1968, by Vin Hoeman, Winfred "Dub" Bludworth, and Harry Bludworth. The first ascent of the North Ridge and second ascent overall came on February 16, 1991, by John Bauman and Leo Americus.

Fly-in approach: This peak can be approached by airplane, but the plane should most likely be a Super Cub due to the limited landing area. It is also possible to fly to the toe of the Nelchina Glacier, if the glacier higher up offers no safe landing spot. Flying in to the toe of the glacier cuts the approach in half—to 16 miles—and eliminates many hateful alders and beaver swamps.

Walk-in approach: The hike in is one of the reasons this peak is so attractive. It lies up a very hidden glacial valley that travels through the forest along the west side of the Nelchina River. The approach is 32 miles from mile 118 on the Glenn Highway to the base of the mountain. In winter a snow trail exists from mile 118. This direct route crosses Goober Lake before descending the infamous "chute." In the summer months the trail begins at the radio tower as seen to the south of the Glenn Highway at mile 113, thus avoiding the bogs that the winter trail travels over. This trail also brings you to Goober Lake and the chute. The chute then brings you 1,200 feet down to the woods at the same level as the Nelchina River.

Once on the river the travel is pretty nice in the winter: just travelling over the ice to the toe of the Nelchina Glacier. In the summer, however, the Nelchina River is quite an obstacle. Travelling along the hillside on the west side of the river takes you through beaver ponds and along some old horse-packing trails. At the base of the Nelchina Glacier, meet the Sylvester Glacier (the Nelchina's east fork). Travel to the head of the Sylvester Glacier to meet Thor's North Ridge.

Route description: The climb begins under a steep knob that is circumvented to the right (east) side to gain the ridge proper. The route follows the well-defined ridge that falls to the east and west at 35–50 degrees for 1,000 feet on both sides. The first 1,500 feet of climbing can be well protected with ice screws and pickets. Allow plenty of time to soak in the views of the Chugach landscape.

The ridge gets broader when it meets the North Face at 10,000 feet. The next 250 yards cross crevassed ground to gain access to the upper slopes. The climbing continues on moderately angled slopes for the next 2,250 feet to the summit.

If the weather is in your favor, the view of the Chugach is incredible. It has been observed in the past that the entire river bar of the Nelchina River, although it is braided like most Alaskan rivers, has the potential of overflowing its banks when a natural dam

to lakes off the side of the glacier releases. The sight is amazing! A spout of water has been seen gushing *150 feet* into the air, carrying massive ice chunks the size of busses down the river and flooding the entire river bar.

Descent: Reverse the ascent route, following your wands as conditions dictate. To leave the base of the mountain, follow your steps out, or follow your own creative alternative to spend more time exploring the Chugach.

59 MOUNT VALHALLA

(12,135 ft; 3698 m)

Route ▲ Southern East Ridge
Difficulty ▲ Alaska Grade 1+
Elevation gain ▲ 4,700 ft
Average time ▲ 10–14 days, 1 day on route
Map ▲ Anchorage (B-1)
Resources ▲ *AAJ* 1956, pp. 40–45, *AAJ* 1958, pp. 92–93

History: The first ascent of Mount Valhalla was in June and July 1957. The party consisted of Lawrence E.

Mount Thor from the Sylvester Glacier (Photo: Raina Panarese)

Mount Valhalla from the Nelchina Glacier with Leo Americus in the foreground. The route ascends the ridge line. (Photo: John Bauman)

Nielsen, Arthur Maki, David Bohn, Martin Mushkin, and Don Mukski.

Fly-in approach: The flight in can come from any of the flight services operating in the Chugach Mountains. The closest strip is at Eureka Lodge on the Glenn Highway, or Mike Meekins's strip at Sheep Mountain. A landing can be made on the Nelchina Glacier at the pilot's discretion. It is also possible to land at the toe of the glacier in a Super Cub. Flying from the north side of the range is advantageous because weather observations can be made first-hand.

Walk-in approach: Follow the walk-in directions for Mount Thor (Route 58) to the toe of the Nelchina Glacier. It is necessary to cross the Nelchina River to reach the moraines at the toe of the glacier; the river can be difficult to cross in the summer. The route onto the Nelchina Glacier is straightforward by keeping low on the west side.

From here travel up the Nelchina is really dependent upon snow cover. This glacier is heavily crevassed all the way to the upper fork, which makes late-season travel pretty interesting on the "dry ice." The west fork of the Nelchina Glacier will bring you right to the base of the spectacular Mount Valhalla.

Route description: Mount Valhalla is a snow climb with fourth-class travel. The ridge begins as a broad slope that narrows down at about 8,117 feet. From here the ridge is a bit more defined, and the climbing is straightforward on the ridge top. The greatest hazard on this route occurs when moving across steeper slopes with some avalanche potential. Take care to avoid spots that are corniced. At about the 9,800-foot elevation the two ridges converge and continue for 2,335 vertical feet to the summit. The ridge is exposed, but the climbing is fantastic. Within 600 feet of the summit the ridge broadens a bit then steepens just before the summit.

Descent: To descend, reverse the route of ascent. It is also possible to continue down the Northern East Ridge to complete a traverse. The slopes on this ridge are avalanche-prone, however, plus there is a lot to be said for descending the known route, especially in the event of bad weather.

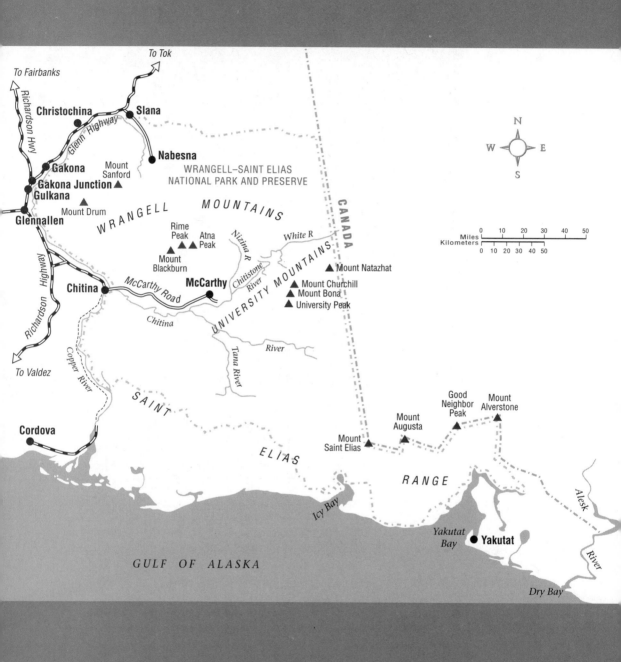

WRANGELL MOUNTAINS

The Wrangell Mountains are part of the Pacific Ring of Fire, a string of volcanoes that rims the Pacific Ocean from southern South America to Japan and continues southwest into the Philippines. The Wrangell Mountains arc across south-central Alaska from the Copper River near Glennallen in the west to their boundary with the Saint Elias Range in the east near the Chitistone River and Russell Glacier. Copper River, Jack Creek, and the Nutzotin Mountains form the northern boundary of the Wrangell Mountains. The Chitina and Nizina Rivers form the southern boundary of the range. At their western end, the Wrangells descend into the tundra and wetlands of the Alaskan Interior.

The Wrangell Mountains lie within Wrangell–Saint Elias National Park. The park is the largest in the United States, and in conjunction with Kluane National Park in Canada, it comprises the largest wilderness area in North America. The two parks form an international peace park that is the largest mountain wilderness area in the world.

The Wrangells contain eight peaks over 13,000 feet. The tallest is Mount Blackburn, at 16,390 feet. The Wrangells are characterized by their volcanic nature. Many peaks are dormant volcanoes or volcanic remains, and one volcano is still quite active: Mount Wrangell (14,163 ft). As early as 1924 Mount Wrangell experienced a "phreatic eruption," which is like a geyser, and steam can still be seen venting from near the summit on clear days. Mount Drum contains three active mud volcanoes on its western flank.

The weather in the Wrangells generally approaches from the south, with low-pressure systems originating off the coast. However, it is not uncommon for dryer, cold weather from the north to position itself over the mountains, especially in the winter months. The most popular time to visit the Wrangells is during the early spring and summer months (April–June).

The Wrangell Mountains are a dramatic view from the Glenn and Richardson Highways, which intersect at the town of Glennallen, and Mounts Drum, Sanford, Blackburn, and Wrangell Peak can be seen only 22 miles to the east. From this point, a combined Glenn/Richardson Highway leads north to Fairbanks, and the Richardson Highway leads south to Valdez. Travelling northward, the Glenn Highway eventually branches east at Gakona Junction, while the Richardson Highway continues north to Fairbanks. The Glenn Highway continues east to Tok, but at Slana a gravel road leads 43 miles to the community of Nabesna. Travelling south of Glennallen on the Richardson Highway, the Edgerton Highway cuts off to the east and leads to Chitina, and eventually to the community of McCarthy at the end of the McCarthy Road. There are a number of air taxis in the region that can fly you into the mountains.

Allow extra days for weather, especially if you fly into the mountains. It is difficult for the air services not located near Mounts Drum and Sanford to know what weather conditions are like on these mountains, so be aware that this can be a problem, and a potentially expensive one, for you.

There are airstrips at Gulkana, Chistochina, Nabesna, Chitina, and McCarthy. A partial listing of air taxis includes Ellis Air and Harley McMahan in Gulkana, Ultima Thule in Chitina, McCarthy Air and Wrangell Mountain Air in McCarthy, and K-Air in Nabesna.

60 MOUNT SANFORD

(16,237 ft; 4937 m)

Route ▲ North Ramp
Difficulty ▲ Alaska Grade 2
Elevation gain ▲ 7,000 ft
Average time ▲ 2–3 weeks, 1 day on route
Maps ▲ Gulkana (A-1, B-1)
Resources ▲ *AAJ* 1939, pp. 255–264; *AAJ* 1959, p. 230; *AAJ* 1960, pp. 110–112 (highest glacier landing); *AAJ* 1967, p. 347; *AAJ* 1969, p. 379; *AAJ* 1971, p. 333; *AAJ* 1976, p. 438; *AAJ* 1978, p. 518; *AAJ* 1980, p. 531; *AAJ* 1981, p. 168; *Descent* 5, no. 5, Sept/Oct 1973; *Scree* 21, no. 7, Jul 1978; *Climbing,* no. 64, 1981; *Climbing,* no. 104, 1987

History: On July 21,1938, Terris Moore and Bradford Washburn climbed the massive North Ramp. In his *American Alpine Journal* article, "Mount Sanford: An Alaskan Ski Climb," Terris Moore said, "Never has the writer visited the top of a high peak and found such a large, flat summit as that of Mount Sanford." In 1968 the famed Japanese mountaineer Naomi Uemura flew into Mount Sanford with food for 20 days and managed to reach the summit on September 19. This was the fourth ascent of the mountain and the first solo ascent. Unfortunately, Uemura, a two-time Everest summiter, later died while attempting a solo ascent and traverse of Denali.

Fly-in approach: This is a difficult place to fly into. It has a reputation for high, wind-scoured slopes too rough for landings. It can also be a pricey flight for you if the pilot can't land the first time and you have to return. The same circumstances on the return trip can make this a difficult nut to crack. It is commonly up to the pilot's discretion where to land. One common landing strip is Windy Ridge, located at 3,500 feet on the tundra. There is a steel cabin, which was built many years ago, and which can still be used for a brief respite from the elements. Harley McMahan in Gulkana, Wrangell Mountain Air in McCarthy, and Ultima Thule are the current air transport options.

From the hut and airstrip, travel southeast for 7 miles to Grizzly Pass and small Lake 5410, which is located on the pass. From here, drop 500 feet into the Sheep Creek drainage and onto the moraine about a mile from the toe of the Sheep Glacier. If it is early enough in the season to land on snow, the pilot may be able to land at about 6,000–6,500 feet on the west side and above the Sheep Glacier. This can eliminate quite a bit of walking, and the skiing down this face to the glacier can be a blast.

Walk-in approach: In winter and early spring it is quite easy to travel across the Copper River, beginning from the Glenn Highway at the Chistochina River. You can leave your car parked at the roadside pullouts, but leave a note with your itinerary. Another option is to ask a local business if you can park your car in their lot for the duration of your trip. Travel down to the Copper River and then upriver to Boulder Creek. Follow the creek all the way to Sheep Creek and the toe of Sheep Glacier at 6,000 feet.

Route description: This route offers little technical difficulty, but it will reinforce the basic skill requirements of Alaska mountaineering. This route is a glacier hike all the way to the summit. At 9,000 feet, you encounter more exposure on the mountain's flanks. Glacier travel and routefinding are fun, and being a strong winter camper is a must to safely endure a storm high on this mountain. This can be a great ski trip in with a lot of wildlife. Note that this is a multiuse area and there may be people who trap animals in this area. Respect their livelihood and do not disturb traps, an act that is considered a criminal offense. The benefit of multiuse areas is the possibility of packed snowmobile trails to make travel easier.

Route ascending the Sheep Glacier on Mount Sanford (Photo: Bradford Washburn, neg. no. 1529)

Once on the Sheep Glacier the travel is very straightforward up to about 7,500–8,000 feet, where there are a few crevasses. All this terrain can be easily navigated on skis, and camping can be found anywhere. The large nunatak, or glacial rock island, at 9,500 feet is a good goal for a first camp. Above this point the glacier can be travelled easily on skis to a high camp. It is easy to move quickly up this mountain. This could induce some high altitude illnesses if you are not cautious.

Dome 13,380 is a good landmark for a high camp around 13,000–13,500 feet. This is an important elevation at which to acclimatize prior to climbing higher. This snow dome is a good descent landmark as well.

The glacier at this elevation has a reputation for well-hidden crevasses. The reason for this condition is the extreme cold and wind. The combination creates very thin and brittle snow bridges. They give the appearance of solidity until they're stepped on. Using wands liberally from your first camp onward is a good idea. The lack of landmarks for orientation on the way down necessitates this precaution. Needless to say, the snow conditions up here can be quite wind-sculpted, so skiing may be very difficult. Sastrugi, wind-carved "snow dunes," 3 feet high and bulletproof are a common sight on this route.

From high camp, summit day is long, up moderate slopes to a high point. It is difficult to say exactly where the summit is, but your altimeter will indicate when you are close.

Descent: The descent can be a blast if the skiing is good and conditions permit; just follow your wands back down the mountain to your big fat cache.

61 MOUNT DRUM

(12,010 ft; 3660 m)

Route ▲ Southwest Ridge
Difficulty ▲ Alaska Grade 2+
Elevation gain ▲ 6,000 ft
Average time ▲ 2–3 weeks, 2–3 days on route
Map ▲ Gulkana (A-2)
Resources ▲ *AAJ* 1955, p. 160; *AAJ* 1959, p. 219; *AAJ* 1969, p. 379; *AAJ* 1975, p. 121; *AAJ* 1977, p. 167; *Descent* 9, no. 3, 1977; *Scree* 23, no. 10, 1980

History: Heinrich Harrer, Keith Hart, and George Schaller climbed the North Ridge route to the summit on June 4, 1954. On August 26,1967, Heinz Allemann and Niklaus Lötscher climbed the Southwest Ridge to claim the second ascent of the mountain.

Fly-in approach: This is a difficult place to fly in to. The wind blows the slopes clear of snow, making landings on skis difficult. Harley McMahan's air service in Gulkana has the best view of the area and so can tell what the weather is doing up on the mountain. Other services have to fly over first to check weather, increasing the cost to you if weather actually prohibits landing.

Fly in to Dry Lake and hike east through the tundra to the base of the Southwest Ridge.

Walk-in approach: The walk-in approach for the Southwest Ridge of Mount Drum follows one of two overland routes. Historically, the route that was used to access the southwest side of the peak was created by gold prospectors, and it departed from Copper Center on the Richardson Highway between Glenallen and Valdez. The Copper River could be crossed with a boat or on ice to its confluence with the Klawasi River. The Old Millard Trail, as it was called, was followed along the south side of the Klawasi River for about 6 miles.

Although the old timers used this route to reach the far-distant North Yukon River during the Klondike Gold Rush, travellers today find the route very hard to follow due to forest fires and overgrowth. Suffice it to say, once the upper headwaters of the Klawasi River are reached, the going becomes much easier as alluvial terraces and tundra offer unfettered access to the Southwest Ridge.

The other overland option is the Nadina River, beginning about 15 miles south of Copper Center and the Klawasi River. Again, the river must be followed, and, once at the confluence of the Copper and Nadina Rivers, you must flank the river using its frozen banks to access the tundra and alluvial benches above tree line. This route brings you to the Nadina Glacier, where more traversing northward on benches brings you to the base of the Southwest Ridge.

Mount Drum, with the Southwest Ridge forming the right skyline (Photo: Bradford Washburn, neg. no. 578)

Route description: The route up Mount Drum offers a modest technical challenge on a beautiful and exposed ridge. The Southwest Ridge begins on a relatively broad ridge of scree-laden slopes. At about the 6,500-foot level, the ridge acquires a permanent snowpack. The climbing up the ridge is straightforward and enjoyable, with good camping to be found most anywhere. The best camping can be found around 9,500–9,800 feet under a short, steep slope leading into a col. This camp is close enough to make for a great summit day. The ridge is crevassed, and care must be taken to get around these slots. There are also a few slopes that have avalanche potential. The wind formations on the top and along the ridge are remarkably cool.

Descent: Retrace your ascent route. It is very helpful to leave wands in places along the broad ridge, especially near the top. A traverse down the original ascent route on the North Face is also a good trip, but you would have to carry a lot of gear or go back around to your cache.

149

Mount Blackburn's North Ridge (Photo: John Bauman)

62 MOUNT BLACKBURN

(16,390 ft; 4995 m)

Route ▲ North Ridge
Difficulty ▲ Alaska Grade 2
Elevation gain ▲ 6,700 ft
Average time ▲ 2 weeks, 2–3 days on route
Maps ▲ McCarthy (C-7, D-7)
Resources ▲ *AAJ* 1959, pp. 237–242; *AAJ* 1965, pp. 406–407; *AAJ* 1968, pp. 127–128; *AAJ* 1973, p. 410; *AAJ* 1975, pp. 120–121 (winter ascent); *AAJ* 1976, p. 438; *AAJ* 1977, pp. 167–168; *AAJ* 1979, p. 175; *AAJ* 1983, pp. 98–101; *AAJ* 1988, pp. 121, 213; *AAJ* 1995, pp. 16–21, 146; *AAJ* 1996 pp. 185–188; *Scree*, May 1958; *Climbing*, no. 105, 1987; Sherwonit, *Alaska Ascents*, pp. 46–64

History: The first ascent was claimed on May 28, 1912, by Dora Keen, a tenacious woman from Philadelphia, who later married her summit partner G. W. Handy. In later years, however, it was discovered by USGS surveyors and cartographers that the higher summit was the Northwest Peak, not the 100-foot lower East Peak summited by the "first-ascent" party. Keen and Handy remained blissfully ignorant of this change in their achievement because they died before the error was discovered. The epic ascent of this mountain is well documented in Bill Sherwonit's book *Alaska Ascents*.

The second-ascent party, consisting of Bruce Gilbert, Dick Wahlstrom, Hans Gmoser, Adolf Bitterlich, and Leon Blumer, climbed the North Ridge and claimed the official first ascent on May 30, 1958. (Note that the North Ridge is often referred to as the Northwest Ridge, indicating a slight variation to the ridge's true aspect.) Mount Blackburn became the first peak in the Wrangell–Saint Elias region to get a winter ascent when, in 1974 Thomas Meachum, Paul Carnicelli, Art Ward, Gary Tandy, Steve Tandy,

The Nabesna Glacier is the landing spot for the routes described on Mount Blackburn and Rime and Atna Peaks. The route line descending Blackburn in this photo is the ski descent done by Ruedi Homberger, Ueli Bula, and Hans Peter in May 1993. (Photo: Ruedi Homberger)

John Pinamont, and Don Pahlke reached the top. This peak has been very attractive to many foreign climbers, especially the Japanese mountaineers.

There are a huge number of peaks to climb around the Nabesna Glacier at the base of Blackburn.

Fly-in approach: Fly in to the Nabesna Glacier from McCarthy. Most parties land at the 7,200-foot elevation and set up a base camp. This campsite is a good place to hang out and avoid uncomfortable weather higher up.

Walk-in approach: It is possible to do a long ski in from McCarthy, which would prove to be a true mountaineering undertaking. The best route up would be via the Kennicott Glacier and past Pack-saddle Island on its east side. From here, head for the pass at the head of the valley between Atna and Parka Peaks. There are quite a few crevasses in here, so take care. Once over the pass descend onto the Nabesna Glacier and head west through Mountaineers Pass to the base of the mountain. Once you look at the map, you'll understand why most people fly in.

Route description: The North Ridge is not the most technical route up Blackburn by a long shot, but it is great route for people who want to sharpen their teeth on large Alaskan mountains. It is also a great place to gain some altitude, plus it is a very good descent route for other routes on the mountain.

Set up base camp on the Nabesna Glacier. The main camps up higher are at elevations of 9,700,

11,300, and 13,300 feet. Stopping at these higher camps allows for a reasonable length of ascent, thus helping to avoid altitude-related illness. These camps also provide refuge from the storms that will rock your world for "a day or few." The climbing itself is nontechnical glacier travel with route-finding, with a maximum slope of 40 degrees. The greatest obstacle is the crevasses; be sure to bring 300+ wands to make sure you can get down in less than desirable conditions. Have fun on this route, and if you are so inclined, hang out to explore some of the other peaks in the area or ski back to McCarthy.

Descent: Reverse your route and follow the 300 wands that you left to securely find your way back to that cushy base camp.

63 RIME PEAK

(12,741 ft; 3883 m)

Route ▲ East Ridge
Difficulty ▲ Alaska Grade 1
Elevation gain ▲ 1,200 ft
Average time ▲ 2 weeks on glacier, 1 day on route
Maps ▲ McCarthy (C-7, D-7)
Resources ▲ *AAJ* 1966, pp. 121–122; *AAJ* 1980, p. 531; *AAJ* 1995, pp. 16–21

History: This peak was originally climbed from the Kennicott Glacier to the south. In July 1965 a party consisting of Vin Hoeman, Alex Bittenbinder, and Don Stockford ascended a ramp to the east of Atna Peak and traversed around the north side of Atna to gain the col where the camp is set up to climb both peaks. They could not retrace their route of ascent back around Atna Peak, so they had to descend to the Nabesna Glacier and travel east to a pass on the ridge to the south that they dubbed Mountaineers Pass.

Fly-in approach: Fly in to the Nabesna Glacier

from McCarthy. Most parties land at the 7,200-foot elevation and set up a base camp. From the Nabesna Glacier, travel south to the large saddle between Rime and Atna Peaks.

Skis might be a great mode of travel for ascending to this pass, affording you the option to ski back down effortlessly. The camp that is set up between the two peaks allows convenient access to the West Ridge of Atna Peak as well (Route 64).

Walk-in approach: Follow directions given for Mount Blackburn (Route 62). Once through Mountaineers Pass, head for the pass between Rime and Atna Peaks.

Route description: This route is a fine one for climbers looking for a mountaineering outing with few technical difficulties. The most demanding aspect of the route is the glacier travel and routefinding approach up to the pass.

From your base camp in the pass, the route is fourth-class snow climbing and ridge climbing. There is ample opportunity to build bomber camps on your way up the route, a good thing because you can be hit by serious weather on these slopes.

Descent: Follow your wands back down to the airstrip on the Nabesna Glacier.

64 ATNA PEAK

(13,860 ft; 4224 m)

Route ▲ West Ridge
Difficulty ▲ Alaska Grade 1
Elevation gain ▲ 2,500 ft
Average time ▲ 2 weeks on glacier, 1 day on route
Maps ▲ McCarthy (C-7, D-7)
Resources ▲ *AAJ* 1966, pp. 121–122; *AAJ* 1968, p. 127; *AAJ* 1980 p. 531; *AAJ* 1995, pp. 16–21

History: This peak was first climbed in 1955 by Keith Hart and party. Later, it was the scene of a traverse

Routes up Atna and Rime Peaks (Photo: Ruedi Homberger)

around the north side by Vin Hoeman and crew in an attempt to climb the full East Ridge to Mount Blackburn on July 16, 1965.

Approach: Follow the fly-in and walk-in approaches given for Rime Peak (Route 63).

Route description: This climb provides all the basic challenges of climbing in Alaska. The glacier travel is fantastic up to the pass. The camps that are built along the way must be ready to endure the strong winds that can nail this area, and the wanding of your ascent route is both easy and necessary for getting back safely in a whiteout. Do this route in conjunction with an ascent of Rime Peak (Route 63), as the pass between the two peaks is a very accessible place from which to climb both.

The climbing itself is snowy third- and fourth-class ridge climbing and no great technical challenge. But the ridge does become a steep snow slope and so be aware of avalanche potential. The use of running protection (pickets and deadmen) for security is very appropriate.

Descent: Follow your wands back down to that cache of groceries at the landing strip on the Nabesna Glacier.

Climber on Mount Saint Elias with Haydon Peak in the background (Photo: Joe Reichert)

SAINT ELIAS RANGE

The western boundary of this expansive group of mountains is the Copper River (see map on page 144). As the range curves to the northeast, it follows the southern edge of the Wrangell Mountains along the Chitina River to the Nizina River. From the Nizina River, the boundary extends through the Chitistone River valley to the White River. From here, the Alaska/Canada border forms the boundary. The mountains in Canada are called the Centennial Range, but geologically, they are part of the Saint Elias Range. The southern boundary of the Saint Elias Range ends at the Alsek/Tatshenshini River. This combination of the Wrangell and Saint Elias Mountains forms the Wrangell–Saint Elias National Park, the largest national park in the United States. The combination of Wrangell–Saint Elias National Park and Canada's Kluane National Park makes this mountain ecosystem the largest protected parkland in North America. When combined with the Chugach Range to the west, it makes the largest mountainous wilderness environment on earth.

Within the Wrangell–Saint Elias and Kluane National Parks is the greatest concentration of peaks over 14,500 feet in North America: nine of the sixteen highest peaks in North America tower in Wrangell–Saint Elias National Park. The second-highest peak in North America is Mount Logan (19,850 ft) in Canada's Kluane National Park, and the fourth-highest is Mount Saint Elias (18,008 ft), which is the second-highest in Alaska and the third-highest north of Mexico. All are located in the Saint Elias Range.

This range also contains the greatest number of glaciers in North America. At 1,500 square miles, the Malispina Glacier is larger in size than the state of Rhode Island. It is also the largest piedmont glacier in North America. The Hubbard Glacier, which flows out of the Saint Elias Range into Disenchantment Bay and the Russell Fjord, is the longest in North America, measuring 80 miles. This length varies with cyclical weather patterns, and the glacier has experienced radical fluctuations over the years. In 1986, the Hubbard Glacier surged forward and sealed off Russell Fjord. It broke two months after it had surged, but is still moving forward and is expected to eventually seal off all of Russell Fjord again.

The naming and designation of the boundary peaks that have "American" roots is historically interesting. At the time of the Klondike Gold Rush there came a need to delineate the border between America and Canada. The Russian–British Treaty of 1825 said only that the boundary was "the chain of mountains which follow at a very small distance the winding of the coast." This area had not been explored, and it remained essentially unknown to the treaty makers of the two countries. At the time, "a very small distance" was defined as being within 10 marine leagues. The border was estimated by plotting a line connecting the tops of the most prominent peaks in the area and creating a boundary no farther than 34.5 miles from the ocean, starting at the most southern tip of Alaska's panhandle (known to Alaskans as "Southeast") in the vicinity of Portland Canal and extending northwest to Mount Saint Elias at longitude 141 North.

There are many significant historic mountaineering events that have occurred in this range. The Duke of Abruzzi's amazing ascent of Mount Saint Elias started from the shore of Yakutat Bay. The Yukon-King expedition started by landing on the

Seward Glacier in a float plane. Andrew Politz and Walter Gove made a dramatic ascent of Saint Elias's South Face. There are many more enthralling stories of mountaineering feats in this vast mountain wilderness.

The weather in the Saint Elias Range is under a maritime regime. Big weather fronts coming in off the Gulf of Alaska can storm for several weeks at a time. Ten feet of snow fell during the first week of May on Bill Pilling and Carl Diedrich's trip to Good Neighbor Peak. On another attempt of Mount Saint Elias, John Bauman, David McGivern, and Leo Americus were nearly buried alive by a snowstorm; they were barely able to return to base camp and never recovered much valuable equipment.

When a big area of high pressure moves in, you may have weeks of sun, as in May 1990 and in 1993. The nearness of the relatively warm ocean means the peaks near the water will be warmer than their Alaska Range peers at similar altitudes. During clear weather, the moist maritime air creeping up the Seward and Hubbard Glaciers can form a thick fog overnight, requiring glacier traverses to follow compass bearings through whiteouts if they are to move at all. The wet snow avalanches and cornice collapses that occur during the warming trends have claimed lives. Climbing at night is necessary to take advantage of the colder-than-daytime temperatures that ensure firmer snow. Lastly, the Icefield Ranges are notable for impassable icefalls that stretch for miles along flat glaciers, so just because a glacier looks flat on the map, don't assume it is uncrevassed.

It is important to note that if you intend to do a route that lies more in Canada—even though it may begin in Alaska—you must contact Kluane National Park to get a permit. The positive aspect of this requirement is that the rangers have extensive knowledge of the mountaineering in their park and will be very helpful.

65 UNIVERSITY PEAK: NORTH RIDGE

(14,470 ft; 4410 m)

Route ▲ North Ridge
Difficulty ▲ Alaska Grade 2+
Elevation gain ▲ 4,000 ft
Average time ▲ 7–10 days, 1 day on route
Map ▲ McCarthy (B-3)
Resources ▲ *AAJ* 1955, pp. 84–87; *AAJ* 1956, p. 131; *Climbing*, no. 170, Aug 1997

History: Terris Moore first named this peak in 1950–51 during the first ascent of Mount Bona. The first-attempt party tried in earnest to access the 10,300-foot plateau, but the icefall and the crevasses severely hampered their progress later in the season (July). Two of the original members returned the next year a bit earlier in the season to forge a route up through this frozen mess. They succeeded after a 10-day push from the landing strip 20 miles down the Hawkins Glacier to the base of the route. The first-ascent party was composed of Keith Hart, Leon Blumer, Sheldon Brooks, Tim Kelly, Norman Sanders, Gibson Reynolds, and R. Houston. They climbed to the summit on June 19, 1955.

Approach: Fly in to the Hawkins Glacier. It is possible to land in the 10,000-foot basin above the former 6,000-foot landing spot in Fourth of July Cirque. Charlie Sassara informed me that this is referred to as "Beaver Basin." A walk-in may be possible, but it would be worth a look at the icefall before you entertain any such plans.

Route description: From the 10,000-foot basin the climbing is up steep snow slopes for 1,200 feet, interspersed with crevasses to the ridge. Above the slope the climbing is along a beautiful, broken, snow ridge. The climbing is mainly on the west side of the ridge. It is necessary to routefind up and along the ridge, sometimes dropping below the crest. Beware: these are typical lee-side conditions, so deposition is occurring. Cornicing and crevasses abound, but the

University Peak's North Ridge (Photo: Ruedi Homberger)

angle for the most part is relatively moderate. You may also observe a distinctive pair of cornices shaped like ears. The snow dome that tops this dramatic peak offers a great view of the Saint Elias Range.

Descent: Follow your wands back down the peak until you reach your base camp.

66 UNIVERSITY PEAK: EAST FACE

(14,470 ft; 4410 m)

Route ▲ East Face
Difficulty ▲ Alaska Grade 5, AI 4+
Elevation gain ▲ 8,500 ft
Average time ▲ 2–3 weeks, 3–5 days on route
Map ▲ McCarthy (B-3)
Resources ▲ *AAJ* 1955, pp.84–87 (first attempt); *AAJ* 1956 p. 131; *Climbing,* no. 170 Aug 1997

History: Carlos Buhler and Charlie Sassara climbed this route on May 3, 1997.

Approach: Contact Paul Claus of Ultima Thule Air Service. He will bring you to his lodge on the Chitina River. From there, fly in to the west fork of the Barnard Glacier and establish base camp about 2 miles south of the East Face. Ascend a low-angle glacier/snowfield to the base of the icefall just north of a large rock buttress at the base of the East Face.

Route description: Climb the couloir right of the buttress, then ascend steep snow and ice flutings that terminate in 80-degree ice just before returning to the crest of the buttress. (It is possible to chop a ledge for a tent on the largest fluting, about 600 feet below the ridge crest.) Climb three long pitches of ice, snow, and rock to the base of a rock cliff. Make a 40-meter rappel off the crest of the buttress to the south, then hug an overhanging rock wall while negotiating a series of crevasses, ice cliffs, and runnel between the rock on the right and the icefall on the left. A safe camp is possible here atop a snow dome under the rock wall.

Continue to climb ice runnels beneath the rock buttress, trending left for four or five pitches to meet

University Peak's East Face is the sunlit rib at right (Photo: Charlie Sassara)

an obvious, right-trending couloir that leads back to the crest of the buttress. Three difficult mixed pitches finish the rock buttress as it blends back into the ice rib that comprises the middle of the route. Ascend the crest of the ice rib, climbing short, vertical ice bands on rolling blue ice and snow to the base of a 50-degree ice sheet below the 300-foot ice cliff that guards the summit snowfields. Weave through the overhanging ice cliff, picking the line of least resistance on vertical ice. Once through the ice barrier, climb right to the broad slopes that lead to the summit.

Descent: Downclimb the North Ridge. Stay near the crest of the ridge, picking a line through the crevasses and ice cliffs. Beware of avalanche (slope) risk on western (lee) slopes. Climb across the col on the left side of the ear-shaped cornices. Trend left and traverse snow slopes back to the 10,000-foot col, dubbed "Beaver Basin," for pick up by aircraft.

67 MOUNT BONA AND MOUNT CHURCHILL

(16,421 ft; 5005 m), (15,638 ft; 4766 m)

Route ▲ East Ridge of Bona; South Ridge of Churchill
Difficulty ▲ Alaska Grade 2
Elevation gain ▲ 6,500 ft
Average time ▲ 2 weeks, 3–5 days on route
Maps ▲ McCarthy (B-2, B-3)
Resources ▲ *AAJ* 1931, pp. 245–254; *AAJ* 1952, pp. 241–249; *AAJ* 1959, p. 213; *AAJ* 1967, p. 347; *AAJ* 1969, p. 378; *AAJ* 1970, p. 114; *AAJ* 1978, p. 519; *AAJ* 1979, p. 176; *AAJ* 1986, p. 149 (first winter ascent); *AAJ* 1993, p. 143; *AAJ* 1995, p. 145; *AAJ* 1996, p. 188; *AAJ* 1997, pp. 188–189; *AAJ* 1999, p. 125

History: Allen Carpé, Terris Moore, and Andrew Taylor first climbed Mount Bona on July 2, 1930, from

Russell Glacier to the west of Mount Bona. Mount Churchill was first climbed by R. Gates and J. Lindberg from the south on August 20, 1951. The first winter ascent of Mount Bona was in February 1985 with Paul Denkelwalter, Earl Redman, Rich Burton, and Dave Pahlke.

Approach: Most air services land on the Klutlan Glacier to access the route to both peaks. The glacier landing usually is around 10,100 feet in elevation.

Route description: On this route, you are basically climbing both mountains at the same time with the exception of summit day. The first 4,300 feet up to the 14,500-foot saddle between Bona and Churchill is a routefinding challenge worthy of an Alaskan glacier.

The climb begins at the 10,100-foot airstrip on the Klutlan Glacier, east of Mounts Bona and Churchill. From the airstrip travel north toward a broad depression in the icefall west of unmarked Peak 12,400 and point 11,861. A camp can be installed around 11,600–11,700 feet, where the icefall backs off slightly. From this point travel up the path of least resistance to the broad, undefined east side of Mount Churchill. The

Mount Bona as seen from the summit of University Peak. The route ascends Bona's East Ridge from the saddle between Bona and Churchill. (Photo: Charlie Sassara)

altitude will start becoming very noticeable by this point, and it may be prudent to camp around the 13,500-foot elevation to acclimatize.

The next leg of the route toward the 14,500-foot saddle skirts the knob to the east (14,916 ft) and delivers climbers onto the saddle. This saddle can provide a good camp, but must be fortified to the max due to its exposed location. It is at this point that both the East Ridge of Mount Bona and the South Ridge of Mount Churchill can be climbed as one-day efforts from the same high camp. Both are snowy, moderate-angle ridge climbs.

Descent: It is wise to leave the ascent route well-wanded for the return trip to the airstrip. Similarly, on summit day the route to the tops should be well marked due to the broad, featureless nature of these peaks.

 68 MOUNT NATAZHAT

(13,435 ft; 4095 m)

Route ▲ Northeast Ridge
Difficulty ▲ Alaska Grade 3+, AI 3
Elevation gain ▲ 5,800 ft
Average time ▲ 2 weeks, 3–5 days on route
Maps ▲ McCarthy (C-1); McCarthy, Alaska 1:250,000
Resources ▲ Green, "The Boundary Hunters" *AAJ* 1997, p. 189; USGS Annual Report for 1909 (first attempt); USGS Annual Report for 1913; Herben, *Picture Journeys in Alaska's Wrangell–Saint Elias*

History: This peak was first summited from the south in June 1913 by a Canadian Boundary Survey party (this original route has changed and is now impossible). Barry, Hart, Hunt, and Lucey, made the first ascent of this route April 1997, following an earlier attempt by Hunt and Kost, who reached 9,800 feet in 1995.

Approach: Fly in to a small pocket glacier at the 7,600-foot level at the base of the ridge (just east of

Point 9,072 along the ridge). Use Ultima Thule or Wrangell Mountain Air.

Route description: Mount Natazhat rises more than 10,000 feet from the White River, which lies 14 miles to the north. From the landing site at 7,600 feet, moderate snow slopes lead to the ridge proper at 7,800 feet. From here, the ridge is a typical Alaskan ridge and involves cornices, crevasses, knife-edged ridge-walking, and some steep snow and ice slopes.

The ridge climbs up and down for 2 miles before reaching Point 9,753, at which point it narrows to a beautiful knife-edged ridge and requires an exposed traverse on steep ice to reach the main peak. After the traverse, and beyond 10,000 feet, the route is sustained 30–50-degree snow and ice with some knife-edged traversing. The Northeast Ridge is the dividing line between the steep North and East Faces of Mount Natazhat. This upper ridge is also broken by crevasses and seracs.

Descent: Descend the ascent route back to the landing site.

 69 MOUNT SAINT ELIAS

(18,008 ft; 5488 m)

Route ▲ Southwest Ridge (Harvard Route)
Difficulty ▲ Alaska Grade 4+, AI 3
Elevation gain ▲ 15,700 ft
Average time ▲ 3–4 weeks, 2–3 weeks on route
Maps ▲ Mt. Saint Elias (A-8, B-8)
Resources ▲ *AAJ* 1947, pp. 257–268; *AAJ* 1967, pp. 347–348; *AAJ* 1975 pp. 122–123; *AAJ* 1979, pp. 178–180; *AAJ* 1980, pp. 482–486, 531–532; *AAJ* 1985, pp. 182–183; *AAJ* 1987, p. 161; *AAJ* 1991, p. 162; *AAJ* 1995, pp. 16–21; *AAJ* 1997, pp. 49–52, 186 (winter ascent); *Climbing*, no. 165, Dec 1997; Waterman, *A Most Hostile Mountain*

History: This second highest peak in the United States was first sighted during the 1741 Bering Expe-

Mount Natazhat (Photo: Danny Kost)

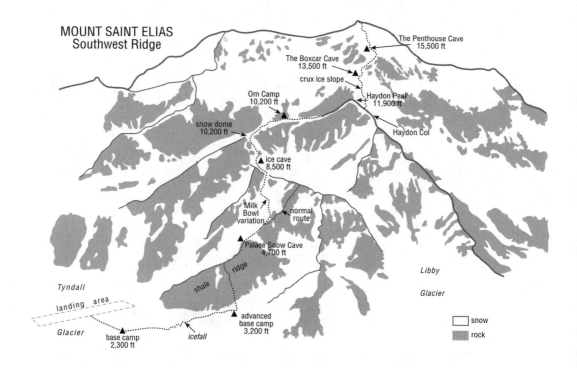

MOUNT SAINT ELIAS
Southwest Ridge

The Penthouse Cave
15,500 ft

The Boxcar Cave
13,500 ft

crux ice slope

Om Camp
10,200 ft

Haydon Peak
11,900 ft

snow dome
10,200 ft

Haydon Col

ice cave
8,500 ft

Milk
Bowl
variation

normal
route

Palace Snow Cave
4,700 ft

Libby

ridge

Glacier

Tyndall

shale

landing area

advanced
base camp
3,200 ft

Glacier

base camp
2,300 ft

icefall

snow

rock

dition along the Alaskan coast. Prince Luigi Amadeo di Salva, Duke of Abruzzi, first climbed it on July 31, 1897. This ascent came on the heels of many who had attempted this peak since 1886. In 1888 an English party made it to 11,600 feet. In 1890 and 1891 a team from the University of Michigan made it to 14,500 feet before being turned back by the weather. They were able to come very close to determining the height of the mountain, estimating it at 18,100 feet. The first ascent of the Southwest Ridge was in 1946 by the Harvard Mountaineering Club. The first winter ascent was on February 29, 1996. The climbers were Joe Reichert, Gardner Heaton, and Dave Briggs. Heaton's drawings of this route were featured in the 1997 *American Alpine Journal* and provide good, detailed information (the route map in this book is based on these drawings).

Approach: The most common approach currently

is to fly in from Yakutat onto the Tyndall Glacier, close to the base of the Southwest Ridge. Fly in to the "carrier strip" and establish base camp at 2,300 feet. Gulf Air in Yakutat offers the easiest access to this area. A walk-in from the ocean has huge potential, but would take an incredible amount of strength and determination.

Route description: The Southwest Ridge is an excellent climb that is comparable to, or a bit harder than, the West Rib on Denali (Route 30), or Mount Moffit's Western North Ridge (Route 44). The route is today the most-used line of ascent on the mountain, but to call it popular would not be fair. Mount Saint Elias in general is not a "popular" mountain, even though it is the second highest peak in the United States and North America's fourth-tallest peak. The atrocious weather is the greatest filter for parties interested in climbing this mountain. The views from

Mount Saint Elias showing the Southwest Face and the Harvard Route. Taan Fjord is visible in the foreground. (Photo: Joe Reichert)

this route are unbelievable if the weather permits, because you are looking directly out onto the Pacific Ocean—the Saint Elias summit is only 10 miles from the ocean's edge.

From your base camp at 2,300 feet on the Tyndall Glacier, travel through an icefall to access the base of the shale ridge at 3,200 feet. This is a common place for climbers to set up an advanced base camp to begin an expedition-style ascent of the route. Alpine style has only been employed twice on this route; expedition style has been used mainly to add

insurance up higher in case of bad weather.

The slope of the shale ridge is about 35–40 degrees, with steps disintegrating under foot the whole way, but this finally eases up at the 8,000-foot level and the going gets a bit easier. A camp can be put on the ridge at the 4,700-foot level before continuing up the ridge. You can make a variation from the ridge proper through the Milk Bowl, as the 1996 team called it, traversing northwest under a hanging glacier to a 2,000-foot couloir that ascends to the plateau at 7,800 feet. This helps avoid about 2,000 feet

Gardner Heaton and Dave Briggs on the flank of Mount Saint Elias during the first winter ascent (Photo: Joe Reichert)

of loose shale-climbing along the ridge.

A good camp can be installed at 8,000–8,500 feet, near the ice cave. This is usually Camp 2 on the route. The next obstacle is a 50-degree snow-and-ice dome. Once past the dome some crevassed terrain must be navigated to reach the next camp at 10,000–10,200 feet, below Haydon Peak (Om Camp).

From this point, Haydon Peak is traversed on the northwest side to reach the Haydon–Saint Elias col and another camp. This route works better than climbing Haydon Peak, only to lose a bunch of elevation on the other side. Just be careful to assess the avalanche risk carefully. The most difficult ice slope lies above the col camp. Climb 50-degree ice to reach a rock band and more mixed climbing, weaving through rock or ice and snow to reach a 60-degree ice slope. All of this terrain is avalanche-prone, so exercise due caution.

Once over this tricky and thought-provoking section, some crevassed terrain is in the way, but nice camping can be found at the 13,400–13,500-foot elevation at The Boxcar Cave. From here the ridge eases a little, and snow and névé are climbed to gain elevation and a campsite at 15,500 feet (The Penthouse Cave). This is your final camp on the ridge, and from here the summit is very attainable given good weather and snow conditions.

The ridge to the summit consists of steep snow and rock with some snow mushrooms on the ridge crest. One party traversed out onto the Southeast Face to circumvent these obstacles, but the cornice at the top appears unavoidable if you want to summit this way. Only this one group is known to have climbed this route, and a few members travelled down the opposite side to Russell Col. However, a traverse like this isn't done without effort of epic proportions. Helicopter support was employed to assist that party. The traverse still remains a challenging option to add to this already hard-won summit.

Descent: Return to your base camp via the route of ascent.

70 MOUNT AUGUSTA

(14,070 ft; 4288 m)

Route ▲ South Ridge

Difficulty ▲ Alaska Grade 5, 5.7, AI 4

Elevation gain ▲ 10,000 ft

Average time ▲ 3–4 weeks, 5–7 days on route

Maps ▲ Mount Saint Elias (B-7); Mount Saint Elias Alaska-Canada 1:250,000; Canadian map: 115 C/8

Resources ▲ *AAJ* 1959, p. 213; *AAJ* 1988, pp. 76–79; *AAJ* 1991, pp. 111–117; *AAJ* 1994, pp. 152–154; *Descent 9,* 1977

History: After the first ascent on July 4, 1952, by Peter Schoening, Victor Josendal, Bill Niendorf, Richard E.

McGowen, Bob Yeasting, Gibson Reynolds, Tom Morris, and Verl Rogers, the second ascent came in 1987 by a Canadian team consisting of Don Serl, Mike Carlson, Greg Foweraker, and Jeff Marshall. They climbed a route they called the North Rib, having been a bit confused by the first-ascent party's confusing directions. They did indeed climb a new route to gain the summit, and descended via the route described in the first-ascent account. On May 5–11, 1990, Bill Pilling and Carl Diedrich made the third ascent, using the route described below. The route originally required 5 days to climb, with another 2 for the descent. Ade Miller, Paul Mead, Rob Wilson, and Paul Knott made the fourth ascent in 1993 via the North Ridge.

Bill Pilling gives a little history in his description

Bill Pilling on the South Ridge of Mount Augusta (Photo: Mark Bebie)

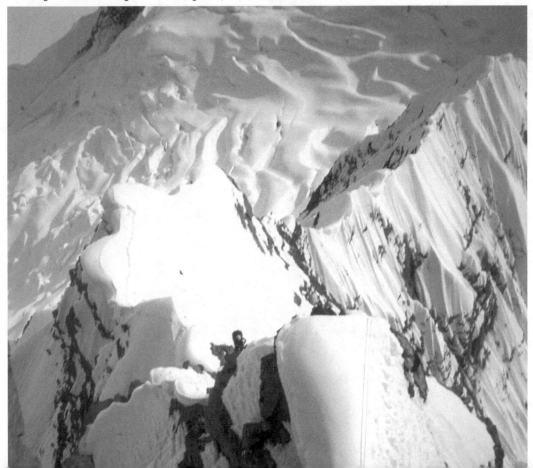

Mount Augusta's South Ridge with Bill Pilling in the foreground on the 8,200-foot snow dome (Photo: Mark Bebie)

of the third-ascent route: "I parked myself in the Mountaineers' clubhouse library [in Seattle] and read every *American* and *Canadian Alpine Journal* article on Alaska and Yukon mountaineering. An article from the fifties, describing a hike up the lower Seward Glacier, mentioned that finding a route up the 10,000-foot high South Face of Mount Augusta looked improbable. The lightbulb lit up: 10,000 feet! I went to buy the map.

"There were a lot of good alpinists in Seattle, but most of them didn't even know where the Saint Elias mountains were. I knew I'd need a climbing partner who was not only a good mountaineer, but a bold and independent spirit as well. I went right to Mark Bebie and badgered him to go, but he wouldn't commit until he'd seen a photograph. Finally, searching the old USGS photo archives in Tacoma, Mark found one. He walked over to the table where I was and sat down. This was it—was he going to go? He pointed to the photo and began 'first we'll go up to this saddle, next. . . . ' We were on our way.

"We had no idea what to expect in Yakutat; nobody we knew had ever been there. Camping next to the beach the night before flying in was a new way to start a climbing trip. Walking on the beach the next morning we were startled to see Mount Saint Elias showing above the trees: 60 miles away and 18,000 feet higher! From the sand pile north of the runway—one of Yakutat's great viewpoints—we could see Mount Vancouver standing above the horizon like a hallucination. The place is built on a titanic scale. The beauty and power of the land, sky, and sea, enchanted us again and again."

Approach: The flight in from Yakutat is the customary access for this peak. The landing area lies to the west of Dome Pass at 4,000 feet. From here you must drag everything up over the pass to the west side of the Seward Glacier near its confluence with the Augusta Glacier. If conditions permit, land near the base of the ridge at 3,600 feet, near the confluence of the Seward and Augusta Glaciers. Gulf Air in Yakutat most easily accesses this area.

Route description: This is an intricate route that provides quite a variety of climbing terrain and conditions, from glacier travel to corniced ridge climbing to pure rock and ice climbing on the route. Bill Pilling wrote a useful route description in the 1991 *American Alpine Journal* (see Resources above), but we will fill in some blanks from some more information he provided to us.

Leaving camp and approaching the 4,800-foot col on the South Ridge, ascend the snow gully until reaching the crest. The ridge is broad for about 2,000 feet, but it soon narrows until it is necessary to belay around some rock pinnacles in order to gain the 8,200-foot snow dome. From the snow dome, walk north down the glacial shelf to avoid the 9,047-foot peak. Descend onto the top of the large glacier and head for the bergschrund. Then ascend a snow ramp up and right to gain the small hanging glacier on the ridge flank above. Traverse this small hanging glacier and cross another bergschrund on the far north side. Once at the far side, keep your eyes peeled for twin snow gullies through a rock band beyond the glacier. Ascend ramps and gullies toward the ridge crest on mixed ground, and be on alert for rockfall if the day is warm. A difficult pitch leads to the crest. Once on the ridge crest a few pitches along the ridge will bring you over the first short rock band—all loose rock. This short section ends and a snow ridge will bring you to the base of the second rock band.

The base of the second rock band is a convenient spot for a bivi. The rock above is in the 5.7 range. Scramble up, and then climb on the left side of the ridge, mainly on moderately angled snow, until the ridge begins to get narrower and icy. Descend to a notch at the base of a tower along the ridge then head down a snow gully on the east side of the crest; traverse on snow below the towers and ascend back to the ridge. Follow the narrow and double corniced arête—a few obstacles are overcome by ascending and descending some vertical sections. More awkward rock sections at 5.7 and 5.8 are encountered along the ridge before the hanging glacier above is attained. Climb the left side of the glacier to the east ridge, and then follow the narrowing ridge to the top.

Descent: Head north from the summit, descending steep snow for hundreds of feet, until the ridge becomes defined. Walk down the ridge, curving left (west) and aiming ultimately for the col between Mount Augusta and a small, rocky, outlying peak to the north. Head down steepening slopes and serac cliffs toward the col, resorting to multiple rappels to reach the lobe of the Seward Glacier on the east side of the col. Follow the south side of the Seward Glacier east to Corwin Cliffs, then drop down snow and scree to follow the west edge of the lower Seward back to your base camp. There is some icefall danger on this descent route.

71 GOOD NEIGHBOR PEAK

(15,500 ft; 4724 m)

Route ▲ South Rib

Difficulty ▲ Alaska Grade 4+, 5.5, AI 3+

Elevation gain ▲ 7,000 ft

Average time ▲ 2–3 weeks, 3–5 days on route

Maps ▲ Mount Saint Elias B-5 or Mount Saint Elias Alaska-Canada 1:250,000 to get a view of Canada for the ski route out. Canadian map: Mount Vancouver 115 B/5 for the west, north, and northeast sides of the peak.

Resources ▲ *AAJ* 1950, pp. 368–378; *AAJ* 1959, p. 231; *AAJ* 1968, pp. 36–39; *AAJ* 1969, p. 382; *AAJ* 1979, p. 180 (correction); *AAJ* 1980, p. 532; *AAJ* 1994, pp. 87–89, 125; *AAJ* 1995, p. 145

History: Mount Vancouver's North Summit (15,700 ft; 4785 m) and what has become known as Good Neighbor Peak (South Summit) were first seen in 1874 by W. H Dall and Marcus Baker of the United States Coast Survey. From the ocean, these peaks looked impressive and were named in order of importance

by height. However, Mount Vancouver later proved to be higher. The reason for the boundary peaks importance and naming was to designate a line of delineation from the ocean that would separate Canada from the United States for the Klondike Gold Rush. The Russian-British Treaty of 1825 stated that the boundary was "the chain of mountains which follows at a very small distance, the winding of the coast." At any rate, that is how Mount Vancouver became known as Boundary Peak 181.

The North Summit (Mount Vancouver) was first climbed on July 5, 1949, by Alan Bruce Robertson, William Hainsworth, Robert McCarter, and Noel E. Odell via the Northwest Ridge. The South Summit (Good Neighbor Peak) was first climbed during the 1967 Centennial Climb of Mount Vancouver via the Southeast Ridge. The members of the Centennial Climb were from the Alpine Club of Canada: Monty Alford, Dr. Alan Bruce-Robertson, Glen Boles, and Les McDonald. The American Alpine Club members were Dan Davis, George Denton, Jed Williamson, and Vin Hoeman. They all climbed to the summit of Good Neighbor Peak, then divided to climb the central peak (Alford, Davis, Denton, Hoeman, and McDonald) and the Canadian summit peak of Mount Vancouver (Davis, Denton, Hoeman, and McDonald).

Bill Pilling and Carl Diedrich climbed the route described in this book in 1993. As Pilling recalls, "When [researching] . . . the South Ridge of Augusta, I also noticed that Mount Vancouver had an elegant and direct 7,000-foot ridge on its south side! When Mark Bebie and I climbed Augusta, we were amazed by the huge, isolated massif of Mount Vancouver. I knew I would have to come back.

"A couple years later I didn't even need a photograph to convince Carl Diedrich—a very determined climber and a great lover of the wilderness—to go to Mount Vancouver. Then the Canadian Alpine Club published a huge photo and we thought for sure someone else would climb it first. Someone almost did. One day I was in the Mountaineers' clubhouse library when Mark [Bebie] walked in to do some re-

Seth Shaw on the South Rib of Good Neighbor Peak (Photo: Kennan Harvey)

search. Mark and the ubiquitous Don Serl were going to the South Rib of Vancouver! Soon after, Serl decided he couldn't go, so we were spared their competition, or deprived of their collaboration."

Fly-in approach: Fly from Yakutat with Gulf Air to the very base of the South Rib at 7,500 feet on the north fork of the Valerie Glacier, south of Point 8,835. Base camp can be set up on the flats at 7,600 feet 2 miles south of the rib. Flying from the Canadian side is possible with Andy Williams out of Kluane Lake.

Walk-in approach: The walk in or out could be quite a wilderness experience, beginning on the Alcan Highway and ending on the Alsek River. Kennan Harvey and Seth Shaw did an awesome trip out of the range after completing the second ascent of this route.

Route description: The slender South Rib can be seen from the "sand pile" north of the Yakutat runway. The South Face of Good Neighbor Peak dominates the horizon to the north. A single rib rises directly up the face to the summit. The climbing route, with few variations, follows the crest of the rib to a hanging glacier beneath the summit, then ascends snow and ice to the top. Most of the belayed climbing on the route lies below 11,000 feet, while the upper section is (in May, at least) moderately difficult, unbelayed snow climbing. Since most of the climb is mixed ground on an uncorniced ridge crest, rock fall and avalanche hazard are minimal. The most dangerous section of the route is the corniced knife-edge ridge near the top, where the snow can be unstable. While

much of the rock on the rib is loose, the direct line to the summit of this enormous mountain places the climber in a striking situation, with views of the Hubbard, Valerie, and Seward Glaciers; Mounts Cook, Foresta, and Seattle; and the Pacific Ocean.

Once at the base of the rib, the west face of the lower ridge offers a snow gully that will access the crest. The ridge is a sharp arête, with a mixture of travelling through loose rock and snow with only small amounts of ice along the way. The climbing is fourth class and easy fifth class in sections, with the first bivi at 10,500 feet.

Follow the ridge up, and then veer west and climb an unmistakable couloir through a steep rock band. The elevation at the top of this couloir is 12,500 feet, and it marks the site of the first-ascent party's second bivi. Move left on snow to the terrain above this spot to avoid a steep section, then regain the ridge. Above the horizontal ridge section, the ridge becomes very sharp, and it may be corniced, as was the case for Pilling and Diedrich. They kept to the east side of the ridge and were forced to traverse the flank on steep and unstable snow.

At the top of the ridge on the west side, the last few pitches are ice that will bring you to a bivi spot at 14,300 feet on the highest hanging glacier. From this point up, the team of Pilling and Diedrich travelled on wind-sculpted snow through rime formations to the plateau of the South Summit: Good Neighbor Peak.

Descent: On the first ascent of this route Pilling and Diedrich opted to descend the original 1949 ascent route via the Northwest Ridge. The best option may be the Centennial Climb route on the South Spur of the Southeast Ridge. From the summit of Good Neighbor Peak, travel east down the ridge, avoiding steeper sections by routefinding on broad slopes along the ridge. At about 14,300 feet on the ridge, descend to the south on a broad snow face that may be avalanche prone.

Good Neighbor Peak (South Peak of Mount Vancouver). The South Rib route ascends the sun/shade line. (Photo: Bill Pilling)

Continue down, aiming for the western or right ridge, to reach the Valerie Glacier and your base camp.

72 MOUNT ALVERSTONE

(14,565 ft; 4439 m)

Route ▲ West Buttress
Difficulty ▲ Alaska Grade 5, 5.8, AI 4+
Elevation gain ▲ 6,000 ft
Average time ▲ 3 weeks, 5–7 days on route
Maps ▲ Mount Saint Elias (B-3, B-4); Canadian map: Mount Alverstone 115 B/6 (shows West Ridge and descent)
Resources ▲ *AAJ* 1952, pp. 227–236; *AAJ* 1996, p. 188; *AAJ* 1999, p. 265

History: The first expedition to the Mount Hubbard and Mount Alverstone Peaks area was in 1935 and was led by the indomitable Bradford Washburn on the National Geographic Society's Yukon Expedition to map the area. They discovered that the route chosen was too difficult, so they abandoned further attempts to climb the peak, but gathered valuable photographs that were later used by Walter Wood. Later the same year Wood returned for the American Geographic Society expedition and noticed the beautiful Mounts Hubbard and Alverstone during his ascent of Canada's Mount Steele.

Wood returned on July 28, 1958, with Robert H. Bates, Peter Wood, and Nicholas Clifford with the intention of climbing these peaks. Though the climbs were made successfully, the expedition ended tragically when the team learned that their pilot, along with Wood's wife Foresta and his daughter Valerie were lost—their remains were never recovered—from an apparent plane crash. An exhaustive search ensued with no results. A magnificent peak and glacier in the area are now named in their honor, near what is believed to be their final resting place.

In May 1995, Bill Pilling and Carl Diedrich climbed the West Buttress of Alverstone, taking 4 days for the ascent and 2 days for the return to their base camp.

Mount Alverstone's West Buttress with Mount Hubbard to the right (Photo: Bill Pilling)

Approach: Fly in from Yakutat to a landing at 7,800 feet on the Alverstone Glacier, near where the U.S.–Canada border crosses the glacier.

Route description: Begin the route on the north side of the West Buttress, in a snow bowl west of the hanging glacier low on the ridge. The snow climbing on the right side of the small hanging glacier is relatively straightforward.

From the highest point of the hanging glacier, traverse left on several pitches of ice and mixed ground to the base of a broad ice gully. The rock is granite, and though fractured, it is solid. Follow the gully upward, then move left to another 45–55-degree gully. Where the gully ends below a prominent, sharp tower that forms the ridge crest, traverse left on snow and ice into an embayment below and left of the tower. From the top of the embayment, ascend several mixed pitches, which reach 5.8 in difficulty, to the top of the ridge.

Continue up the crest on snow, ice, and mixed ground (fourth and fifth class) to reach the farthest right side of the prominent, rounded glacier lobe. Once at the top of the lobe, diagonal left up easy slopes to

the left and around a corner to an easy glacier that regains the ridge crest, which you follow to the summit.

Descent: Retrace your steps down the ridge of the upper West Buttress and down the easy glacier slope on the north side of the mountain, aiming for the flats at the head of the Great Shelf Glacier. Walk east down the north side of the glacier, then turn north to reach the broad saddle at 3520+ meters on the ridge dividing the Great Shelf Glacier from the southeast lobe of the Dusty Glacier.

Cut through the cornice overhanging the north side of the ridge. (A curious, upended rock obelisk used as a campsite by parties in 1965 and 1995 stands in a saddle near the smallest cornice.) Climb or rappel down to where snow walking is possible. Weave downward for 2,000 feet between serac cliffs, then cross the bergschrund to reach the Dusty Glacier (formerly known as the North Lowell Glacier). Walk west on the glacier until below the north side of Peak 3592 (meters), then ascend the face to its top. From the summit, descend easy snow and ice slopes on the Southwest Ridge and Face to the head of the Alverstone Glacier. It should take about 1.5 days to descend.

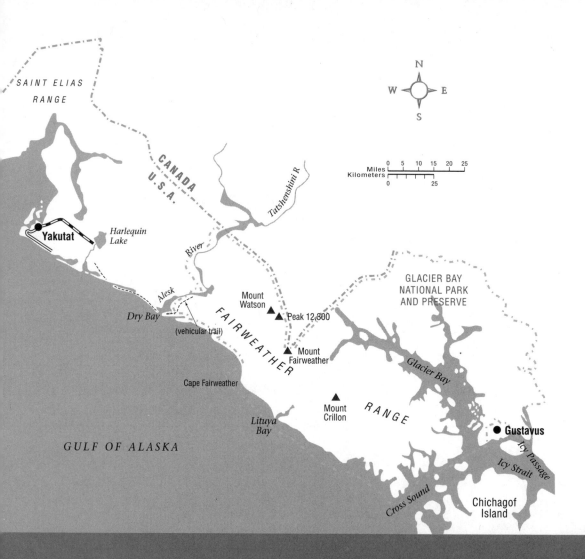

FAIRWEATHER RANGE

The Fairweather Range is located at the southern end of the Saint Elias mountains, along the coast of Southeast Alaska. The range's western boundary is the Alsek/Tatshenshini River. The northern boundary is the U.S.–Canada border, but the range actually extends into Canada all the way to the Melbern and Grand Pacific Glaciers flowing into Tarr Inlet. Glacier Bay comprises the rest of the northern border, as well as the eastern part of the range. The Gulf of Alaska flanks the entire southern edge. The summit of the largest peak in the range, Mount Fairweather, lies only 24 miles from the coast.

One of the most magnificent attractions in the area is the large number of tidewater glaciers. There are sixteen, twelve of which actively calve icebergs into the bay. The glaciers in this area are *very* active and have been witnessed retreating and advancing noticeably on four separate occasions. The mountains rise 3 vertical miles directly out of the sea.

Glacier Bay National Park and Preserve contains the vast majority of this entire range. Combined with the Wrangell–Saint Elias National Park and Preserve and the Tatshenshini–Alsek Provincial Park in British Columbia, Glacier Bay encompasses 24 million acres of wilderness. This entire area has been designated a World Heritage Site by the United Nations, and it contains the greatest amount of internationally protected land anywhere in the world. If you plan to attempt a route that is mostly in Canada, it is important to contact the Kluane National Park to get a permit. The Kluane rangers have extensive knowledge of the area and are very helpful.

The best time to attempt a climb in the Fairweather Range is May through June and early July. The weather is maritime, resulting in a healthy snowpack and warmer than average winter and early spring temperatures. Summer temperatures average 42–62 degrees Fahrenheit and winter temperatures range from 17–39 degrees Fahrenheit. In researching this area, Bill Pilling, who has extensive knowledge of the region, has observed that the southern Fairweather Range has a tendency to get worse weather than the northern mountains. He believes that the northern Fairweathers have less of a mountain barrier, thus allowing the pressure to more easily equalize. The National Weather Service provides separate forecasts for the areas north and south of Cape Fairweather; there is often a big difference between conditions in Yakutat and Lituya Bay.

The northern Fairweathers get bigger high-pressure systems and there is often such a short period of time between storms that just about the time a route could be considered safe another storm rolls in to pin you down. This weather pattern may urge mountaineers to adopt a style of travelling into the mountains that relies less on air support, a course strongly advocated in many articles written by Walter Gove in the *American Alpine Journal*. This style also allows a greater amount of flexibility in your schedule and turns the entire experience into a truly well-rounded wilderness adventure.

Consider including a cheap FM weather radio in your gear. This allows you to tune into National Weather Service broadcasts, thus saving the batteries of your communication radio. A marine VHF can contact Yakutat from high on Mount Fairweather or the Grand Plateau Glacier.

The major settlement in the area is the town of Gustavus, located at the mouth of the Salmon River on the north shore of Icy Passage, off the Icy Strait.

The other major town, where climbers most commonly embark on their expeditions, is Yakutat, located north of Gustavus. Yakutat is located on the Gulf of Alaska, where the panhandle of Southeast Alaska joins the rest of the state. Both towns have daily jet service and can be accessed from Anchorage, Juneau, and Seattle. Both towns also have full services for an extended stay if the weather is too unsettled for flying, which can happen often.

The major air taxi service to access the Fairweather Range is Gulf Air out of Yakutat. Gulf Air has accommodated climbers faithfully for years now. The air service's extensive knowledge of the region can be very helpful in filling in the intricate details of where to land and in advising parties as to which radio communication will work best.

Another form of transportation that can work well in this area is the sea kayak, especially in accessing the peaks within Glacier Bay itself. Those weighing the merits of this form of access should keep in mind the comparative freight capacity of kayaks and plan accordingly.

73 PEAK 12,300

(12,300 ft; 3749 m)

Route ▲ West Face
Difficulty ▲ Alaska Grade 2, AI 3
Elevation gain ▲ 2,800 ft
Average time ▲ 2 weeks, 1 day on route
Maps ▲ Skagway (A-7, A-8), Mount Fairweather (D-6)
Resources ▲ *AAJ* 1975, pp. 43–46; *AAJ* 1978, pp. 397–402; *AAJ* 1993, pp. 85–90; *Alaska Geographic* 9, no. 1, 1993, p. 7 (Alaska's Glaciers Revised Edition; photo of route from lower (3,000 ft) to upper (7,000 ft) Grande Plateau Glacier)

History: The history of climbing this peak is best summed up in the article written by Walter Gove and Bill Pilling for the 1993 *American Alpine Journal*. Gove is a true explorer of this region and has done an incredible job of recording his ascents and adventures in the journal throughout his climbing career in Alaska. He has made first or second ascents of all but one of the peaks bordering the Grand Plateau Glacier. He gives detailed information and route descriptions, along with a true sense of reverence for the country.

In his article on Peak 12,300 he explains his different ways of approaching the upper Grand Plateau Glacier area. Bill Pilling and Walter Gove climbed this beautiful peak on June 4, 1992, after a difficult approach.

Fly-in approach: It is possible to totally skip the grueling walk-in to the upper Grand Plateau Glacier. You can fly from Yakutat directly to the 10,500-foot plateau at the base of this climb.

Walk-in approach: Fly from Yakutat to the beach along the last sandy section north of the outlet that drains from the large lake at the toe of the Grand Plateau Glacier. Land below the low-tide mark. It is possible to travel around the lake or take a collapsible boat to negotiate the lake directly.

From the lake, head east-northeast into the middle of the glacier. It will become necessary to travel to the north to circumvent the initial icefall lower on the glacier (1,000–1,500 feet). The fork that circles the low nunatak to the north is constantly changing character, so the travel conditions are very unpredictable here. It is about 20 miles from the lake, travelling north around the icefalls, to get to the north fork of the Grand Plateau Glacier at 2,950 feet, where the massive icefall drains the upper Grand Plateau Glacier.

This is where the major decision making on routefinding comes into play. The following information is based on the route description from Walter Gove's 1975 *American Alpine Journal* article combined with other short descriptions on approaching this area.

Attempts were made to go up the rock rib that

Walter Gove, with the West Face of Peak 12,300 in the background (Photo: Bill Pilling)

splits the two major north and south icefalls, but the base of the rib was blocked by too many crevasses and so this approach was abandoned. The next plan was to travel back downglacier about a mile and follow a chute on the north side of the glacier's north fork, passing below a large rock buttress between 3,000 and 4,000 feet. This buttress extends about one-third of the way up the side of the glacier's slope.

From the top at 4,000 feet, there is a mild trough for about 2 miles that cuts across the icefall at a southeast heading and reaches an obvious open area at 5,400–5,500 feet. From here, travel up another chute, which tops out at 6,500 feet, heading directly east to what looks like an open plateau. One mile north of Point 8,800 is the 7,000-foot contour. In the 1993 *American Alpine Journal* account, Bill Pilling mentioned that there was a large chute to follow at the 7,000-foot level. They may have taken a route different from past climbs, or perhaps the terrain has changed. From this spot, heading southeast to the pass will only lead to major crevasses that could not be bypassed in 1974.

The key to accessing the plateau is to go around the north side of the 8,680-foot nunatak travelling between it and the West Ridge of Mount Watson. From this gap the travel into the plateau is relatively easy. Another 2–3 miles bring you to the 9,000-foot contour in the cirque at the base of the East Ridge of Mount Watson, Peak 12,300, and Mount Root. A huge word of caution: The *only* person who truly knows this area, having done four trips into the basin, is Walter Gove. His accounts appear to show varying degrees of difficulty travelling through the icefall to reach the upper basin every time. This book's description should be treated as a rough sketch and is no substitute for good and skillful routefinding. It appears that this approach could take 1–2 weeks just to reach the upper basin. The treasures that exist above this glacial puzzle appear fully worth the effort.

Route description: Congratulations on making it to the base of the climb! Once you are on the upper glacier, the climbing it is very straightforward. Beginning at the base of the West Face travel upward, crossing the bergschrund and up the 50–55-degree snow slopes. These eventually give way to ice and get a bit steeper. The climb follows a shallow rib up the face. The top of the climb is along the corniced ridge to the right of the summit. The view is absolutely spectacular from this position: on a clear day you can see from south of Glacier Bay to Mounts Saint Elias and Logan.

Descent: Rappel and downclimb the route.

 ## 74 MOUNT WATSON

(12,516 ft; 3814 m)

Route ▲ East Ridge
Difficulty ▲ Alaska Grade 2
Elevation gain ▲ 3,000 ft
Average time ▲ 2 weeks, 1 day on route
Maps ▲ Skagway (A-7), Mount Fairweather (D-5)
Resources ▲ *AAJ* 1975, pp. 43–46; *AAJ* 1978, pp. 397–402; *AAJ* 1993, pp. 85–90

History: On June 5, 1974, Walter Gove, Lawrence Dauelsberg, Donald Liska, Alice Liska, and Michael Allen landed on the lake at the base of the Grand Plateau Glacier. They managed to find their way up into the upper basin surrounded by awesome peaks. The approach was fraught with anxiety about the weather and wondering if the pilot would be able to drop their rations. The weather finally broke, their rations arrived, and they were able to successfully ascend Mount Watson on June 18. The party climbed many peaks in the area during their stay.

Fly-in approach: Fly from Yakutat to the 10,500-foot plateau, high on the upper Grand Plateau Glacier at the base of this climb.

Walk-in approach: Follow the directions to the upper Grand Plateau Glacier given for Peak 12,300 (Route 73).

Route description: The route starts at the head of the Grand Plateau Glacier's north fork and looks much easier on the map than it is in reality. From the airstrip, go north to intersect the East Ridge. Aim for

Route ascending Mount Watson's East Ridge as seen from the summit of Peak 12,300 (Photo: Bill Pilling)

the saddle between Mount Watson and Peak 12,300. The first 1,000 feet to gain the saddle is via the northern couloir, which leads at a 45-degree angle from the base of the climb over the bergschrund. Near the top of the couloir, a bit of rock must be climbed, creating a rock-fall hazard to those below. Once you reach the saddle, the beginning of the ridge consists of moderately-angled snow slopes, but this soon turns into some deceptively steeper and more exposed terrain. A rock step is encountered along the way, and shortly afterward, some down-sloping traverses. The difficulty of these sections depends on the amount of snow on the route. It could be good walking, or it could be lightly dusted ice or rock at a 70-degree angle with cornicing along this ridge to the summit.

Descent: From the top of the peak retrace your steps back down to the saddle, carefully downclimbing or rappelling the steeper or less secure ice slope sections. From the saddle rappel the upper part of the gully, then continue downclimbing to the base of the route and back to camp.

75 MOUNT FAIRWEATHER

(15,300 ft; 4663 m)

Route ▲ South Ridge (Carpé Ridge)
Difficulty ▲ Alaska Grade 3+, 5.6, AI 3
Elevation gain ▲ 10,700 ft
Average time ▲ 2 weeks, 3–5 days on route
Map ▲ Mount Fairweather (D-5)
Resources ▲ *AAJ* 1931, p. 221; *AAJ* 1932, pp. 429–444; *AAJ* 1981, pp. 29–35; *AAJ* 1982, pp. 139, 141; *AAJ* 1983, pp. 150–151; *AAJ* 1984, p. 159; *AAJ* 1985, p. 183 (winter ascent); *AAJ* 1991, p. 162; *AAJ* 1994, pp. 126–127; *AAJ* 1995, pp. 147–148; *AAJ* 1997, pp. 186–187 (ski descent); *AAJ* 1999, p. 258; *Climbing,* no. 105, 1987; Roper and Steck, *Fifty Classic Climbs*

History: Since the earliest expeditions to this area, navigators remarked on this beautiful landmark. In 1778 the famous explorer and navigator Captain James Cook used the mountain and the point of land below the mountain, the "Cape of Fairweather" as a bearing.

The first two expeditions to the area were made in 1926. The expedition from the west was recounted by W. S. Ladd; the expedition from the east was written by Allen Carpé. Another attempt on the mountain was made prior to the first ascent. Bradford Washburn attempted the approach from Lituya Bay, but was bogged down by major routefinding obstacles.

The first ascent of this peak was completed in 1930 on an expedition led by Dr. William Sargent Ladd, accompanied by Allen Carpé, Terris Moore, and Andrew Taylor. Using the valuable information shared by Bradford Washburn, the party was able to navigate around the obstacles that prevented Washburn from reaching the mountain.

Perhaps one of the most noteworthy experiences that has occurred while attempting to climb Mount Fairweather was a very near miss in Lituya Bay by a 1958 Canadian party. Upon their arrival to Lituya Bay for a scheduled pickup, they were able to radio out to Juneau, only to learn that deteriorating weather would delay their pickup if they didn't leave that afternoon. Just hours after their departure, a massive earthquake created a tsunami that swept the hillsides up to 1,700 feet and created large-scale devastation. This event would have undoubtedly killed the whole party.

Fly-in approach: Fly-in with Gulf Air from Haines or Yakutat to 5,500 feet on the Fairweather Glacier, directly at the base of the South Ridge. You stand a good chance of waiting in town for quite a while to get into the mountains, and you could spend a fair bit of time waiting for pickup to return to civilization.

Walk-in approach: If you want an intense, life-transforming experience, walk in from the coast of Cape Fairweather or Lituya Bay up Desolation Valley and the Fairweather Glacier.

Route description: The route that rises above you for the next 10,700 feet was once described as a snow climb, but in the years following the first ascent, the ridge has undergone many changes. Climbers who have climbed the ridge have returned with a variety of different experiences.

The landing area and base camp are at the base of the ridge (4,700 ft). The climbing begins by weaving upward through the icefall for about 1,200 feet. Once past these wild ice formations, traverse left (west) across 40-degree snow slopes. Depending on how much the icefall has changed, it has also been reported that you may need to skirt it by climbing three crumbly rock pitches to reach the snowfield above. A camp can be established at 5,900 feet, but beware of a potential rock-fall hazard here.

From this point it is possible to find a couloir that

An overland approach to Mount Fairweather from Cape Fairweather (Photo: Joe Reichert)

climbs to the upper slopes on the Carpé Ridge. This couloir is about 40–50 degrees and is very narrow near the top. Others have climbed 1,100 feet of low-angle ice and rock to get to the main ridge. Once on the upper ridge, "Camp 2" can be placed at around 7,400 feet. Another option exists: Traverse the slopes farther to the west and put a camp at 7,400 feet at the base of a couloir. (The 2,300-foot-long couloir is a great ski and tops out between 9,700 and 10,000 feet on the ridge.)

The climbing between 7,400 and 9,400 feet is broad ridge climbing on a 20- to 30-degree slope and remains moderate to 10,300 feet. A great camp can be placed at 10,300. Moderate-angle slopes leading east arrive just below the ice ridge at approximately 11,500–12,000 feet. For the next 2,200 feet the climb-ing is about 40 degrees and runs into a steeper ice face. The climbing on the ridge above this point is relatively knife-edged in places and is spectacular. There are quite a few large crevasses intersecting the ridge and two seracs that must be negotiated at around 13,500–14,000 feet.

There is a false summit (13,800 ft) that must be passed before accessing the upper part of the mountain. In places it may be necessary to belay ice pitches at about 14,300 feet. After the Ice Nose, or serac, is climbed or passed, the slope eases a little and the summit is well within reach. Hopefully you will have good weather to take in the amazing view of the ocean and surrounding mountains.

Descent: Reverse your line of ascent, following all those wands you left on the way up.

Mount Crillon. The West Ridge ascends the right skyline. (Photo: Bradford Washburn)

76 MOUNT CRILLON

(12,726 ft; 3878 m)

Route ▲ West Ridge

Difficulty ▲ Alaska Grade 4, 5.5, AI 4

Elevation gain ▲ 8,500 ft

Average time ▲ 2 weeks, 5–7 days on route

Map ▲ Mount Fairweather (C-4)

Resources ▲ *AAJ* 1934; *AAJ* 1935, p. 382; *AAJ* 1959, pp. 215–217; *AAJ* 1973, p. 307; *AAJ* 1978, pp. 520–521; *AAJ* 1995, pp. 22–29, 148; *National Geographic,* 1935, pp. 361–400

History: Bradford Washburn and H. Adams Carter first climbed Mount Crillon via the South Face on July 19, 1934. Loren and Marsha Adkins, Richard Benedict, Jerry Buckley, and Bruce Tickell first climbed the West Ridge on June 9, 1972. This route received a second ascent in July 20, 1977.

Fly-in approach: From Yakutat, fly in to 4,000 feet on the North Crillon Glacier with Gulf Air. From the drop-off point, travel up the glacier for 9 miles to arrive in the cirque below the Northwest Face of Mount Crillon at between 4,500 and 5,000 feet.

Walk-in approach: Gulf Air uses lands on the west side of Lituya Bay, but reaching the North Crillon Gla-

cier from here could be logistically difficult. Getting onto the toe of the glacier is said to be very hazardous; it can be quite overhanging right into the bay, and there is loose rock on the ice, melting loose and falling, or precariously anchored to the ice.

Route description: From base camp, travel due south up the slope to the notch on the West Ridge at 6,000 feet. Climb the ridge from the 6,000-foot col, traversing the rock ridge leading to the 6,944-foot subpeak along the ridge to the south. Eventually you regain the ridge and find a decent place to camp at 6,500 feet. The most difficult climbing begins from this camp. The ridge is steep and exposed, with cornicing along a vast majority of its length. There is another good place to bivi at the 8,000-foot elevation, just below a large gray tower. This gray tower can be climbed head-on with some 5.5 crack climbing directly over the south shoulder. Traversing the south flank is time-consuming and is the greatest obstacle on the ridge. At 9,000 feet there is a large gash across the ridge, which the 1972 expedition rappelled down. A line was left fixed so they could ascend without difficulty on the return. This strategy can be a real time-saver. From 9,500 feet on the ridge the terrain gets broader, and the climbing to the top relatively easy.

Descent: Retrace your ascent route, rapelling as necessary.

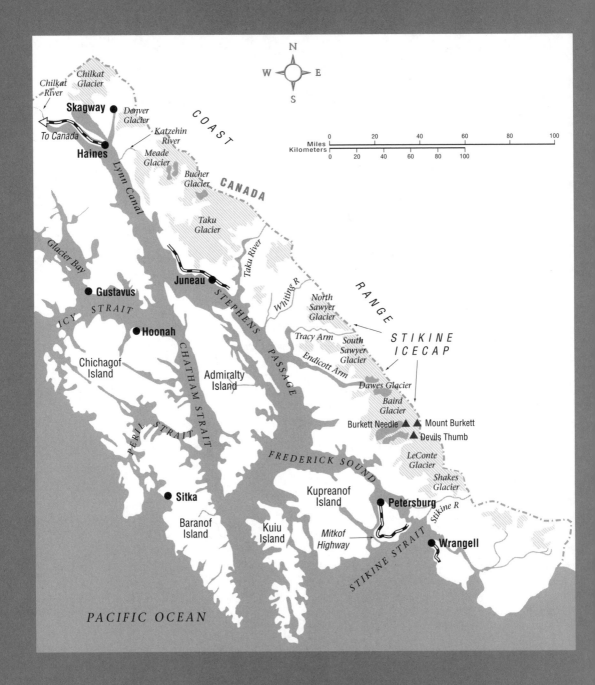

COAST RANGE/ STIKINE ICECAP

Introduction by Dieter Klose

This is one wet, sodden place. Petersburg, a quaint Norwegian fishing town in the heart of the Alexander Archipelago, receives roughly 105 inches of rain annually. In the lowlands where trees grow that's called a "rain forest," but in the mountains just to the east lies a magnificent "rain-icecap."

Located between the Stikine River and the coastal waters of Frederick Sound, the Stikine Icecap straddles the U.S.–Canada border. To the north the Whiting River draws a line between the Stikine Icecap and the Juneau Icefields. A vast, underlying granite batholith provides good rock and mountains that are compelling by design.

The southern portion of the range lies mostly within the Stikine–LeConte Wilderness Area. The LeConte Glacier is the southernmost tidewater glacier in the Northern Hemisphere, calving tons of ice into LeConte Bay daily. The resultant icebergs appealed to a clutch of adventurous Norwegian fisherman at the turn of the century, who would use the ice to keep their salmon and halibut fresh. It is said that the Norwegians only dallied here in order to ice their fish and wait for the rain to stop. They are still here, waiting.

An almost endless soaking from the prevailing southerly winds out of the Gulf of Alaska batters the Coast Range. The weather, though not often violent, is basically atrocious. However, for the climber perched and ready to go during a clear and lasting northerly, this area provides a spectacular alpine wilderness bordering on the heavenly.

The Witches Cauldron is a unique spot in the region, and well worth a visit. It is a deep, four-armed canyon surrounded by walls and peaks of Himalayan-style splendor, including Devils Thumb. Though pummeled by magnificent avalanches from its many surrounding icefalls and serac walls, the relatively high summer temperatures annually melt the glaciers' winter snows and avalanche debris. It has become a dead glacier, lying well below the firn line. There are no crevasses; rather, it is riddled with azure melt-water ponds. In springtime the ski touring is superb, but in summer the bare ice is covered by scree and talus, making for miserable walking. During foul weather the itinerant witches boil up a dense cloud-soup, and avalanches roar unseen down the hillsides.

The Northwest Face of the Devils Thumb deserves mention, as it rises at an average angle of 67 degrees for its entire 6,700-foot height. Such immense scale is anomalous to the region, and it may well be the steepest big wall of that size in North America. It remains unclimbed. The bordering Northeast Face and the North Pillar have each had one ascent, and the West Buttress has been ascended almost to the summit, but the Northwest Face remains elusive. A hidden gem and horror combined, this wall might require new rules. Rising out of the Witches Cauldron from a mere 2,400 feet elevation, it transits three climatic zones. Willows would grow at its base if not for the continual barrage of avalanches, yet the summit seldom wearies of snow.

Attempted now a dozen times, this face has seen the only climbing fatality in the region. Only two attempts have reached the halfway point (barely). The great Northwest Face of the Devils Thumb is a wall to be respected—and perhaps ignored.

Background left to right: Burkett Needle and Mount Burkett. Foreground left to right: Witches Tits, Cats Ear Spire, and Devils Thumb (South Pillar, in the right skyline). (Photo: Dieter Klose)

Elsewhere on the icecap, the plateaus and glacial valleys are generally broad and only occasionally interrupted by crevasse fields and icefalls. Ski travel is generally straightforward. Many of the mountain-side glaciers, however, have a confusing jumble of transverse crevasses, the negotiation of which can be quite tricky, if not absurd.

Fred Beckey and crew upgraded the state of the art in North American alpinism here in 1946 with their audacious ascent of Devils Thumb. These mountains continue to be climbed by only the most intrepid and determined alpinists, and for good reason: the commitment factor is high. The odds of a decent weather window for success are slim, and the chances of rescue are slim-to-none. There is no road or village one can walk to, although flagging down a boat running the Stikine River is a possibility. The skies can turn from placid to vicious in a matter of hours, and then

they can stay that way for weeks—yes, weeks! Kind of a little Patagonia: heaven when the sun shines; hell when it doesn't.

To date Devils Thumb has had about thirty-seven attempts; of those, only fourteen parties have actually stood on the summit. The other mountains in the region have each had four ascents or fewer. Due in great part to the notorious weather, fewer than three parties tend to visit the entire icecap per year. When there, you are almost assuredly alone.

The climbing season is basically May through August, although ski travel in all but the upper elevations is best completed by late June. Below the firn line the glaciers become bare yet walkable ice. Snow slopes and couloirs tend to be at their mushiest in July and early August; this coincides with the driest time for pure rock routes, but only when it's not raining! Throughout the summer the summits can have anything from rain to rapid icing conditions. Heavy rime forms on the higher peaks during a good, wet blow.

Firn line is between 3,000 and 4,000 feet, but water trickles can often be found as high as 6,000 feet. Being a maritime climate, the temperatures are never extremely low.

In the off-season, the storms are at their worst during the six weeks involving each equinox. The dead of winter has occasional stretches of clear skies, but there is no discernable pattern. The best clear spell I've seen in the mountains has been in May and June, which lasted almost three weeks; but usually clearings last from only 1 to 5 days.

Getting a good stretch of weather boils down to plain old luck. Allowing a month for a climbing trip in this area is prudent; most of that time may well be spent waiting.

Generally speaking, there are two recommended ways to approach the icecap, both originating in Petersburg. Each requires air or watercraft support, for there is no place to walk or drive from. The island town of Petersburg is accessed by either the Alaska Marine Highway ferry or by Alaska Airlines. Petersburg has no climber-specific goods or services, although food and white gas are readily available.

The pure, on-foot approach originates at tidewater in Thomas Bay, where the Baird Glacier comes to a screeching halt on a gravelly outwash plain. A hired boat or floatplane can get to the beach in Thomas Bay in almost any weather. Incorporating an airdrop into the flight allows for a lightweight 2- to 5-day approach to the various peaks. The numerous arms of the Baird Glacier give broad access to the myriad playgrounds. Skis are the preferred means of transport, and a light sled is often handy. The Baird Glacier is a virtual all-weather cruise for the experienced glacier traveller, with only the occasional call for a rope. The opportunity to climb a mountain from sea level makes this straightforward approach well worth consideration.

Another option is the helicopter. Just wait (and wait!) in Petersburg for flying weather. Be prepared to wait for weeks, even during the summer season. Pure luck with weather is key. The local populace may offer some good advice on dealing with waiting in the rain. Go to either the Harbor Bar or Kito's Kave to get the advice.

After the trip, wait for helicopter-friendly weather again or ski and hike down to Thomas Bay for a pre-arranged boat or floatplane pick up. Most of the icecap just south of Devils Thumb is off-limits to helicopter landings, as it lies within the Stikine–LeConte Wilderness.

VHF radios will often reach Petersburg from the upper elevations, but don't count on it. Ski-equipped airplanes are not available. Considering the price of admission, the Stikine region requires the three Ps: payment, patience, and persistence.

77 BURKETT NEEDLE

(8,500 ft; 2590 m)

Route ▲ South Face (Reichert/Heaton route)
Difficulty ▲ V, 5.9 A3
Elevation gain ▲ 2,000 ft (4,700 ft from base camp)
Average time ▲ 2–3 weeks, 2–3 days on route
Map ▲ Sumdum (A-2)
Resources ▲ *AAJ* 1965; *AAJ* 1966, pp. 125–126; *AAJ* 1980, p. 535; *AAJ* 1995, p. 148; *AAJ* 1996, pp. 181–184; *Rock and Ice,* no. 68, 1995; *Climbing,* no. 168, Jun 1997

History: Layton Kor and Dan Davis first climbed Burkett Needle in August 1964 via the North Buttress. In March 16, 1995, Joe Reichert and Gardner Heaton turned up to attempt the main line through the Emerald Eye. They made it up a total of eleven pitches before they were forced to retreat due to wind and poor weather. A month later the team of Greg Foweraker, Dan Cauthorn, and Dan Collum arrived at the base of the South Face and began a line to the west of the Reichert/Heaton attempt. This three-man team reached the summit on this new route for the second ascent of the peak. Gardner Heaton is quite sure that the route he and Reichert were not able to finish could link up with the Foweraker/

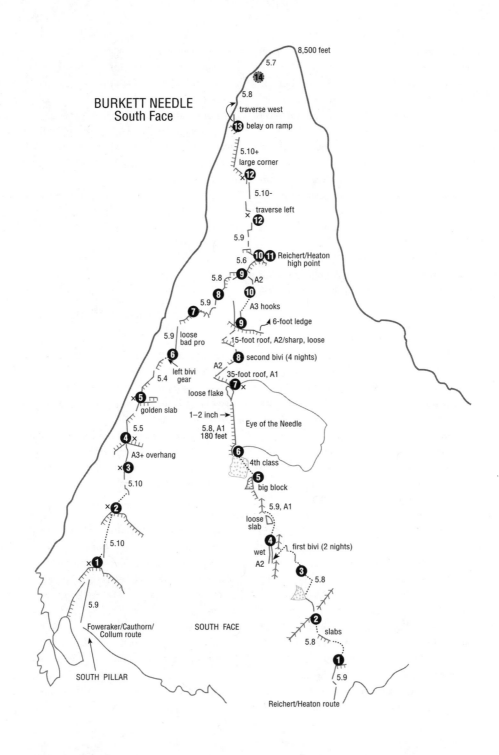

BURKETT NEEDLE
South Face

8,500 feet

5.7

⓮

5.8
traverse west

⓭ belay on ramp

5.10+
large corner

⓬
✕

5.10−

traverse left
✕
⓬

5.9

⓾ ⑪ Reichert/Heaton
high point

5.6

5.8
⑨ A2

⑩

⑧ A3 hooks

5.9

⑦ ⑨ 6-foot ledge

5.9 loose
bad pro
15-foot roof, A2/sharp, loose

⑥ ⑧ second bivi (4 nights)

A2
left bivi
gear
35-foot roof, A1

5.4
⑦ ✕

loose flake

⑤
golden slab
1−2 inch

5.8, A1
180 feet
Eye of the Needle

5.5

④ ✕

A3+ overhang

⑥

✕ ③
4th class

5.10
⑤ big block

② ✕
5.9, A1

5.10
loose
slab

④ first bivi (2 nights)

① ✕
wet
A2

③ 5.8

5.9

② slabs

Foweraker/Cauthorn/
Collum route
5.8

SOUTH FACE
①

SOUTH PILLAR
5.9

Reichert/Heaton route

The South Face of Burkett Needle, with the Foweraker/Cauthorn/Collum route on the left and the Reichert/Heaton route intersecting it on the right (Photo: Joe Reichert)

Cauthorn/Collum route to finish the climb to the summit, and the two routes may at present have a one-pitch overlap.

In the spring of 1999 Lionel Daudet and Sebastian Foissac completed the third ascent of Burkett Needle via a new route on the Southwest Buttress/South Face. Their route was sixteen pitches long, with the climbing difficulty to grade V, 5.12, A3+.

Fly-in approach: Fly from Petersburg to the Baird Glacier. Follow the south, or right, fork of the Baird Glacier and reach the base of the wall via one of the two small glaciers draining the cirque.

Walk-in approach: From Petersburg, fly in or take a boat to Thomas Bay in Frederick Sound. Walk and ski up the Baird Glacier to the base of the route.

Route description: Following the Reichert/Heaton route, diagonal up crack systems to the first bivi under a large roof called Eye of the Needle. Start aid climbing out roof. Climb over roof to diagonal crack that gains the Foweraker/Cauthorn/Collum route. Climbing is free and mostly 5.8–5.9. See the topo that accompanies this description (based upon an original drawing by Gardner Heaton).

Descent: Rappel your route of ascent, or rappel the

Foweraker/Cauthorn/Collum route, which has fixed rappel stations.

78   MOUNT BURKETT

(9,730 ft; 2965 m)

Route ▲ Golden Gully (South Face Couloir to Northwest Ridge)
Difficulty ▲ Alaska Grade 4, 5.8, AI 4
Elevation gain ▲ 2,800 ft (5,800 ft from base camp)
Average time ▲ 2–3 weeks, 2–3 days on route
Maps ▲ Sumdum (A-1, A-2)
Resources ▲ *AAJ* 1965; *AAJ* 1966, pp. 125–126; *AAJ* 1980, p. 535; *AAJ* 1981, pp. 169–170; *AAJ* 1995, p. 148

History: Norman Harthill, John Denton, David Wessel, Kenneth Bryan, George Liddle, Edward Thompson, and (Leader) Derek Fabian climbed the Southeast Ridge on July 25, 1965. The second ascent of the mountain was made in 1979 via the Northeast Ridge. The 1980 ascent route described here was climbed by Dieter Klose and Michael Bearzi. The most recent ascent was by Greg Col-

South Face of Burkett Needle (left) and Mount Burkett (right), with the prominent Golden Gully on its left side (Photo: Dieter Klose)

lum and Dan Cauthorn in 1994 via the Southeast Face.

Fly-in approach: Fly from Petersburg. With the use of the helicopter, it is likely that you can touch down just about anywhere you want near the base of the climb.

Walk-in approach: From Petersburg, fly in or take a boat to Thomas Bay in Frederick Sound. Walk and ski up the Baird Glacier. Take the right-hand fork of the glacier to reach the south face base camp for Mount Burkett.

Route description: The first part of the route up to the base of the Golden Gully is straightforward, except for the large crevasses. Once at the base of the 2,000-foot couloir, a comfortable and safe bivi can be made. The gully increases in steepness until within the last 250 meters from the top of the gully, which may have 60-degree ice and some very loose rock for about 60 feet before reaching the top. From this point on, the climbing is mainly mixed or on straight rock that is a bit shattered. The difficulty of the rock climbing on the ridge is 5.8.

Descent: Rappel and downclimb your route of ascent.

79 DEVILS THUMB: EAST RIDGE

(9,077 ft; 2766 m)

Route ▲ East Ridge
Difficulty ▲ IV, 5.8, AI 4
Elevation gain ▲ 2,300 ft
Average time ▲ 2–3 weeks, 2–3 days on route
Maps ▲ Sumdum (A-1, A-2)
Resources ▲ *AAJ* 1947, pp. 268–277; *AAJ* 1971, pp. 339–340; *AAJ* 1972, pp. 112–113; *AAJ* 1980, p. 535; *AAJ* 1992, pp. 74–80, 128; *AAJ* 1996, pp. 181–184; *AAJ* 1997, pp. 184–185; *Descent* 2, no. 4, 1970; *Descent* 3, no. 3, 1971; *Mountain,* no. 59, Jan 1978; *Rock and Ice,* no. 2, 1984; *Rock and Ice,* no. 68, 1995; *Climbing,* no. 79, 1993

History: The first ascent of Devils Thumb was a mountaineering feat unprecedented in the United States in 1946. The tenacity that was demonstrated by Fred Beckey and his companions is amazing. The first attempt in July of that year took Beckey, with Fritz Wiessner and Donald Brown, 70 miles up the Stikine River, where they were dropped off at the headwaters of the Flood Glacier. From here they packed their supplies onto the glacier, but Fritz sprained his knee, so the party was forced to turn around. This was Fritz Wiessner's second time into the Stikine area. From Wrangell the tenacious Beckey got on the horn and recruited Clifford Schmidtke and Bob Craig from Seattle, who were on the boat and in Wrangell within a week.

They returned to the cache site on the Flood Glacier to find that mountain goats had raided their cache. From here they travelled upglacier to climb Kate's Needle, then turned their focus to the South Face and East Ridge of Devils Thumb. They endured miserable weather to the base and on the route as well. They climbed the Southeast Face up to the East Ridge. Wearing tennis shoes, they negotiated difficult rock pitches over cold, icy rock. They retreated in the face of an oncoming storm, only to get hammered by rain. The Stikine River rose 3 feet, and the boys soaked up and ladled 14 gallons of water out of their tent during this storm. They awoke to beautiful weather and, 3 days before they needed to meet the boat, climbed to their previous high point, finally summiting on August 24, 1946. An experienced party nowadays may climb the route in a long day.

Fly-in approach: From Petersburg, fly in via helicopter to the Witches Cauldron and the Southeast Face of the East Ridge. Note that the icecap just south of Devils Thumb is off-limits to helicopter landings, because it lies in the Stikine–LeConte Wilderness Area.

Walk-in approach: From Petersburg, fly or take a boat to Thomas Bay in Frederick Sound. Travel 3 to 4 days from sea level up the Baird Glacier to Witches Cauldron.

Route description: From a base camp at 6,500 feet, the 1946 route heads up a snow slope to a prominent

Devils Thumb from the east, showing the East Ridge (Beckey) route with the Klose/Bearzi variation (left line). The South Pillar forms the left skyline. (Photo: Joe Reichert)

saddle, and then continues up snow and mixed terrain to a low notch in the East Ridge. Once on the ridge there is fifth-class climbing and a gendarme stands in the middle of the ridge. This can be traversed on the right side. When it was done by Beckey in 1946 in wet tennis shoes, it was indeed a feat! This is the crux of the Beckey route, as well as negotiating some mixed terrain getting onto the ridge. More mixed climbing past the gendarme brings you back to the ridge.

A variation to the Beckey route is to go up the same snow face and saddle, but rather than heading right toward the ridge, climb straight up to a notch west of a small, yet prominent pinnacle on the ridge. Dieter Klose and Michael Bearzi climbed this variation in 1980. It involves some mixed pitches before the ridge, and a wandering 5.8 lead. Once on the ridge, the north side drops dramatically to the Witch's Cauldron 6,700 feet below on your right. The Bearzi/Klose variation intersects the East Ridge above the gendarme crux. Near the top of the ridge is a prominent notch that separates you from the horizontal summit ridge. Once past this notch, the fourth- and easy fifth-class climbing continues to the summit, the farthest west of a series of three gendarmes.

Descent: When looking at the summit ridge from base camp, the summit is the left (west) end of the horizontal ridge. A key landmark for the descent is the notch at the far right (east) end of the horizontal ridge. From the top, climb back along the East Ridge to the notch and begin rappelling down the southeast face. A fixed anchor can be found on a small ledge above and west of the notch. Two 60-meter rappels will bring you to lower-angle slopes. Then there are one or two more rappels down a little rock buttress below. Be sure to diagonal east from the bottom of the buttress, across the mixed ground to the highest snow rib coming up from the snow saddle on the Beckey route. Downclimb the Beckey route from here back to camp.

80 DEVILS THUMB: SOUTH PILLAR

(9,077 ft; 2767 m)

Route ▲ South Pillar
Difficulty ▲ V, 5.10, A2
Elevation gain ▲ 3,200 ft
Average time ▲ 2–3 weeks, 2–3 days on route
Maps ▲ Sumdum (A-1, A-2)
Resources ▲ *AAJ* 1992, pp. 74–80; *Climbing*, no. 128, Oct/Nov 1991; *Mountain*, no. 33, 1999, p. 15 (photos and diagram)

History: Seattle climbers Bill Pilling and Mark Bebie made the first ascent of this route May 22–24, 1991. Prior to this ascent they had climbed another new line on the Northeast Face. Pilling and Bebie made one earlier attempt up to the start of the South Pillar, but decided to head back because the weather was closing in. The storm lasted 2 days before they returned to the route. Pilling and Bebie's South Pillar route came very close to the 1973 Lowe/Jones/Flores route to the left on the South Face. At one point near the top the routes almost converge.

Approach: Follow the approaches given for the East Ridge (Route 79). To reach the base of this route from the base camp below the East Ridge, travel west and descend the snow slopes on the north side of the icefall, perhaps travelling through the rocks as you hug the side of the glacier. Move smartly to minimize the risk of icefall. Continue down the north edge of the glacier to the bottom of its low-angle spur, then turn right and head up onto the easy western flank of the spur.

Route description: Scrambling and a few easy fifth-class pitches up the spur below the pillar lead to a good bivi on snow at the base of the main pillar. The route above primarily follows cracks just right of the pillar crest on the incredibly solid, course-grained, featured granite that offers many fractures for protection placement. There is very little loose rock on this route.

From the toe of the pillar, step right on snow to climb a short moderate rock pitch up the right side of an alcove to a ledge. From the left end of the ledge follow cracks and flakes for four to five pitches, just right of the crest to the base of an angular pillar (5.8–5.9). A pitch up the right side of this pillar (with a few aid placements) ends on a ledge on the crest. This was the second bivi on the first ascent and the ledge is not too big or comfy.

Step right around the crest to reach a right-slanting ramp—the key "Quartz Pitch"—and climb to its top. Above, ascend a left-facing flake to reach the conspicuous black band that crosses the face. Traverse the band straight left to a belay on the very spine of the pillar (5.10 A2; tiny nuts and thin blades useful). Several

Mark Bebie on the South Pillar of Devils Thumb (Photo: Bill Pilling)

pitches up cracks, a V-trough, and around a ceiling lead to slabs and the top of the pillar. Low-angle non-technical snow and rock lead to the summit. Good bivi sites on snow will be found in the area.

Descent: Follow the descent route described for the East Ridge (Route 79).

APPENDIX A: ALASKAN MOUNTAIN GRADES

The Alaska Grade System can be confusing. In order to help readers better assess the difficulty of climbs in this book, we have compiled the following table of climbs grouped according to grade. Rock routes with no Alaska Grade are grouped separately. We have also included ratings for other well-known Alaska climbs and for Mount Rainier in Washington State, giving them an Alaska Grade. This should help readers to better understand what the Alaska Grade ratings mean.

Mountain	Route	Elevation Gain (ft)	Technical Difficulty	Grade
Ariel	S Ridge	1,100	Class 3	AK 1
Tugak	N Ridge	1,000	Class 3	AK 1
Finland	N Ridge	1,000	Class 3–4	AK 1
Alabaster	N Ridge	1,500	Class 3–4	AK 1
Whiteout Spire	W Face to N Ridge	1,500	Class 3–4	AK 1
Michelson	S Face to E Ridge	1,500	Class 3–4	AK 1
Yukla	E Face to NE Ridge	2,000	Class 3–4	AK 1
Goode	E Ridge	2,600	Class 3–4	AK 1
Chamberlin	W Ridge	3,200	Class 3–4	AK 1
Rime	E Ridge	1,200	Class 3–4	AK 1
Atna	W Ridge	2,500	Class 3–4	AK 1
Dickey	W Face	2,500	Class 3–4	AK 1
White Princess	W Ridge	4,000	Class 3	AK 1
Pavlof	NW Face	4,000	Class 3	AK 1
Redoubt	N Face	5,500	Class 3	AK 1
Shishaldin	E Face	6,000	Class 3	AK 1
Iliamna	NW Ridge	6,500	Class 3	AK 1
Brooks	N Ridge	6,500	Class 3–4	AK 1+
Valhalla	Southern E Ridge	4,700	Class 3–4	AK 1+
Pioneer	N Face	4,500	Class 3–4, AI 2	AK 1+
Silverthrone	N Ridge	4,700	Class 3–4	AK 1+
Rainier	Disappointment Clever	4,000	Class 3–4	AK 1+
Thor	N Ridge	3,750	Class 3–4	AK 1+
Doonerak	SE Ridge	4,200	Class 3–4	AK 1+
Polar Bear	NW Face	2,600	Class 3–4	AK 1+
Sunrise Spire	NW Couloir	2,000	5.6, A1, AI 4	AK 2

Mountain	Route	Elevation Gain (ft)	Technical Difficulty	Grade
Peak 12,300	W Face	2,800	AI 3	AK 2
Four Horsemen	W Couloir to S Ridge	3,100	5.6, AI 4	AK 2
Neacola	W Face Couloir	4,600	AI 4	AK 2
Watson	E Ridge	3,000	Class 4–easy Class 5	AK 2
North Triple	NW Couloir to W Ridge	1,900	5.6, AI 4	AK 2
Arthur Emmons	W Ridge	1,500	5.5, AI 3	AK 2
Amulet	N Face	3,300	AI 3	AK 2
Awesome	S Face	2,500	AI 3	AK 2
Sanford	N Ramp	7,000	Class 3	AK 2
Blackburn	N Ridge	6,700	Class 3–4 Class	AK 2
Bona/Churchill	E Ridge/S Ridge	6,500	Class 3–4	AK 2
Marcus Baker	N Ridge	5,700	Class 3–4	AK 2
Denali	W Buttress	9,000	Class 3–4	AK 2+
Hayes	E Ridge	6,400	Class 3–4	AK 2+
Drum	SW ridge	6,000	Class 3–4	AK 2+
University	N Ridge	4,000	Class 3–4	AK 2+
Russell	N Ridge	3,500	Class 3–4	AK 2+
Kimball	SW Ridge	3,300	Class 3–4	AK 2+
Denali	Muldrow/ Harper	9,000	Class 3–4	AK 3
Foraker	NE Ridge (Sultana Ridge)	10,500	Class 3–4	AK 3
Mather	N Ridge	6,500	Class 3–4 (cornicing)	AK 3
Fairweather	S Ridge (Carpé Ridge)	10,700	5.6, AI 3	AK 3+
McGinnis	NE Ridge	6,000	AI 3	AK 3+
Natazhat	NE Ridge	5,800	AI 3 (cornicing)	AK 3+
Deborah	NW Ridge	5,600	AI 3 (cornicing)	AK 3+
Huntington	W Face Couloir	3,000	AI 4	AK 3+
Mooses Tooth	Ham and Eggs Couloir	2,800	5.9, AI 4	AK 3+
Denali	W Rib	9,000	AI 3	AK 4
Crillon	W Ridge	8,500	5.5, AI 4	AK 4
Moffit	Western N Ridge	8,000	AI 3	AK 4
Peak 11,300	SW Ridge	4,100	5.9, AI 3	AK 4
Thorn	E Face	3,000	5.5, WI 5 (mixed)	AK 4
Burkett	Golden Gully	2,800	5.8, AI 4	AK 4
Saint Elias	SW Ridge (Harvard Route)	15,700	AI 3	AK 4+
Hunter	W Ridge	7,600	5.8, AI 3 (cornicing)	AK 4+
Good Neighbor	S Rib	7,000	5.5, AI 3+	AK 4+
Augusta	S Ridge	10,000	5.7, AI 4	AK 5
Denali	Cassin Ridge	9,000	5.8, AI 4	AK 5
University	E Face	8,500	AI 4+	AK 5
Alverstone	W Buttress	6,000	5.8, AI 4+	AK 5

Mountain	Route	Elevation Gain (ft)	Technical Difficulty	Grade
Hunter	Moonflower	6,100	5.8, A3, AI 6	AK 6
Foraker	Infinite Spur	9,000	5.9, AI 4	AK 6

Rock Routes	Route	Elevation Gain (ft)	Technical Difficulty	Grade
Xanadu	W Face to S Arête	1,500	5.7	III
Middle Troll	S Face	1,500	5.9	III
Throne	S Face	1,500	5.9+	III
Devils Thumb	E Ridge	2,300	5.8, AI 4	IV
Serenity Spire	SE Face	1,200	5.10	IV
Trinity Spire	SE Face	1,500	5.10, A0	IV
Royal Tower	E Buttress	2,300	5.10	IV
Shot Tower	W Ridge	1,500	5.8, A2	IV
Middle Triple	E Buttress (Gargoyle Buttress)	3,600	5.10, A2	V
Devils Thumb	S Pillar	3,200	5.10, A2	V
Eye Tooth	W Face	2,800	5.10	V
Sugar Tooth	W Face	2,000	5.10+, A2	V
Burkett Needle	S Face	2,000	5.9, A3	V
Flattop Spire	SE Pillar	2,300	5.10, A3	VI
Barrill	E Face (Cobra Pillar)	2,650	5.10+, A3	VI

APPENDIX B: CONTACT INFORMATION

PARKS

Chugach State Park; 550 W 7th Ave, Suite 1260, Anchorage, AK 99501-3557; 907-269-8400; fax, 907-269-8901; email, pic@dnr.state.ak.us; *www.dnr.state.ak.us/parks/units/chugach/index.htm*

Denali National Park and Preserve Mountaineering Rangers; Talkeetna Ranger Station, PO Box 588, Talkeetna, AK 99676; 907-733-2231; fax, 907-733-1465; email, DENA_Talkeetna_Office@nps.gov; *www.nps.gov/dena*

Gates of the Arctic National Park and Preserve; 201 First Ave, Fairbanks, AK 99701; 907-456-0281

Glacier Bay National Park and Preserve; 1 Park Rd, PO Box 140, Gustavus, AK 99826; 907-697-2230; fax, 907-697-2654; email,GLBA_Administration@nps.gov; *www.nps.gov/glba/*

Kluane National Park and Reserve; PO Box 5495, Haines Junction, Yukon, Canada Y0B 1L0; 867-634- 7250; fax, 867-634 7208; email, kluane_info@pch.gc.ca; *http:// parkscan.harbour.com/kluane/*

Lake Clark National Park and Preserve; Field Headquarters, 1 Park Place, Port Alsworth, AK 99653; 907-781-2218; fax, 907-781-2119; email, dennis_knuckles@nps.gov; *www.nps.gov/lacl/*

Tatshenshini–Alsek Provincial Park; BC Parks, Skeena District; 3790 Alfred Ave, Bag 5000; Smithers, BC, Canada V0J 2N0; 250-847-7320; fax 250-847-7659; email, SKDinfo@Victoria1.gov.bc.ca; *www.elp.gov.bc.ca/bcparks/explore/parkpgs/tatshen*

Wrangell–Saint Elias National Park and Preserve; 105.5 Old Richardson Hwy, PO Box 439, Copper Center, AK 99573; 907-822-5234; fax, 907-822-7216 email, wrst_interpretation@nps.gov; *www.nps.gov/wrst/*

ORGANIZATIONS

Alaska Alpine Club; PO Box 81174, Fairbanks, AK 99708; 907-479-2149; email, climb@alaskanalpineclub.org; *www.uuaf.edu/aac/*

Mountaineering Club of Alaska; PO Box 102037; Anchorage, AK 99510

National Weather Service, Alaska Region Headquarters; 222 West 7th Ave #23, Anchorage, AK 99513-7575; Fairbanks phone, 907-456-0372 or 907-456-0373; *www.alaska.net/~nwsar/*

AIR SERVICES

Alaska Backcountry Adventure (Tom Thibodeau); Anchorage; 888-283-9354

Alaska Flyers (Walter Audi); Kaktovic; 907-640-6324

Alaska West Air, Inc.; PO Box 8553, Nikiski, AK 99635; 907-776-5147

Alpine Air Service; Girdwood; 907-783-2360

Bettles Air Service; PO Box 27, Bettles, AK 99726; 800-770-5111 or 907-692-5111

Brooks Range Aviation, Inc. (Jay and Judy Jespersen); PO Box 10, Bettles, AK 99762; 907-692-5444

Doug Geeting Aviation; PO Box 42, Talkeetna, AK 99676; 907-733-2366; fax, 907-733-1000; email, airtours@alaska.net

Ellis Air Taxi; Mile 118 Richardson Highway, PO Box 106, Glennallen, AK 99588; 800-478-3368 or 907-822-3368; email, ellis@alaska.net

Frontier Air; 5245 Airport Industrial Road, Fairbanks, AK 99709; 800-478-6779 or 907-474-0014; email, info@frontierflying.com

Gulf Air; Yakutat; 907-784-3240; *www.gulfairtaxi.com*

Harley McMahan; PO Box 284, Gakona, AK 99586; email, mcmahanflying@cvinternet.net

Hudson Air Service; PO Box 648, Talkeetna, AK 99676; 907-733-2321; fax, 907-733-2333

K2 Aviation; PO Box 545, Talkeetna, AK 99676; 907-733-2291; fax, 907-733-1221; email, explore@alaska.net; *www.flyk2.com*

K-Air Service; HC 63 Box 1415, Gakona, AK, 99586

Meekin's Air Service (Mike Meekin); Palmer; 907-746-1626

McKinley Air Service; Talkeetna; 800-564-1765 or 907-733-1765

Penn Air; Anchorage; 800-448-4226 or 907-243-2323

Reeve Air; 4700 West International Airport Road, Anchorage, AK 99501; 800-544-2248 or 907-243-4700

Steve Hakala; Sand Point; 907-383-6324

Talkeetna Air Taxi; Talkeetna, AK 99676; 907-733-2218; email, flytat@alaska.net

Ultima Thule Air Service (Paul Claus); Anchorage Office, 1010 H Street, Anchorage, AK 99501; 907-258-0636

Wrangell Mountain Air (Kelly Bay); #25 PO Box MXY, McCarthy, AK 99588; 800-478-1160 or 907-554-4411; *www.wrangellmtnair.com*

Wright Air Service, Inc. (Robert Bursiel); PO Box 60142, Fairbanks, AK 99706; 907-474-0502

SURFACE TRANSPORTATION

Alaska Marine Highway System; PO Box 25535, Juneau, AK 99802-5535; 800-642-0066

Alaska Railroad Corporation, Passenger Service Department; PO Box 107500, Anchorage, AK 99510-7500; 800-544-0552 or 907-265-2494

Alaska Shuttle; Anchorage; 907-274-2222

Alaska Travel Shuttle; Anchorage; 907-248-3566

Alaska Backpackers Shuttle; Anchorage; 800-266-8625 or 907-344-8775

Denali Overland Transportation; PO Box 330, Talkeetna, AK 99676; 907-733-2384

Parks Highway Express Inc.; Fairbanks; 888-600-6001

Talkeetna Shuttle Service; PO Box 468, Talkeetna, AK 99676; 888-288-6008 or 907-733-1725; fax, 907-733-2222

Talkeetna Taxi and Tours, Talkeetna, AK; 907-733-8294

Valley Airport Shuttle; Wasilla; 907-373-7933

APPENDIX C: SELECTED RESOURCES AND REFERENCES

MAPS

Alaska Atlas and Gazetteer published by DeLorme gives an overview of the state.

The United States Geological Survey (USGS) provides standard topographical maps of Alaska. They can be purchased at climbing stores in Anchorage or directly from the USGS (907-786-7000).

"Mount McKinley, Alaska," 1:50,000, edited by Bradford Washburn is available at climbing stores or by contacting Alaska and Polar Region Department, University of Alaska, Fairbanks, Fairbanks, AK 99775-1005; 907-474-6773.

BRADFORD WASHBURN PHOTO-GRAPHS

Photographs can be obtained through the Boston Museum of Science and the University of Alaska, Fairbanks. 8 x 10 contact prints cost $25 plus $10 for research, postage, and handling. Use the negative number of the print when making an order. Contact one of the following:

Dr. Bradford Washburn, Museum of Science, Science Park, Boston, MA 02114-1099; 617-589-0228; fax, 617-589-0363

University of Alaska, Fairbanks, attn.: Marge Heath, 201 Rasmussen Library, Fairbanks, AK 99775-1005; 907-474-6773

EQUIPMENT SOURCES

Alaska Mountaineering and Hiking; Anchorage; 907-272-1811

Costco; Anchorage; 907-344-6436

Brown Jug; Anchorage; 907-563-3008

REI; Anchorage; 907-272-4565

Skinny Raven Sports; Anchorage; 907-274-7222

Windy Corner; Talkeetna; 907-733-1600

Windy Corner; Wasilla; 907-373-6117

METRIC CONVERSIONS

Feet into meters: Multiply by 0.3048

Meters into feet: Multiply by 3.2818

Miles into kilometers: Multiply by 1.609
Degrees Fahrenheit into degrees Centigrade: Subtract
　32, multiply by 5, and divide by 9

PERIODICALS AND BOOKS

American Alpine Club. *Accidents in North American Mountaineering.* New York: American Alpine Club Press, 1977 to present.

Beckey, Fred. *Mount McKinley, The Icy Crown of North America.* Seattle: The Mountaineers Books, 1993.

Brease, P., and A. Till. *The Geology and Glacial History of Denali National Park and Vicinity, Geologic Society of America Field Trip #9 Guidebook and Roadlog.* Cordillera Section Meeting, Fairbanks, AK, May, 1995.

Brown, Belmore. *The Conquest of Mount McKinley.* 1913. Reprint, Boston: Houghton-Mifflin, 1956.

Brown, W. E. *Denali, Symbol of the Alaska Wild.* Talkeetna, AK: Alaska Natural History Association, 1993.

Cassin, Ricardo. *Fifty Years of Alpinism.* Seattle: The Mountaineers Books, 1981.

Collier, M. *The Geology of Denali National Park.* Talkeetna, AK: Alaska Natural History Association, 1989.

Coombs, Colby. *Denali's West Buttress.* Seattle: The Mountaineers Books, 1997.

Davidson, A. *Minus 148°.* New York: W. W. Norton and Co., 1969.

DuFresne, J., *Alaska: A Travel Survival Kit.* Victoria, Australia: Lonely Planet, 1994.

Fredston, J., and D. Fesler. *Snow Sense: A Guide to Evaluating Snow Avalanche Hazard.* Anchorage: Alaska Mountain Safety Center, 1994.

Green, Lewis. "The Boundary Hunters." *American Alpine Journal* (1997).

Greiner, James. *Wager with the Wind.* 1974. Reprint, New York: St. Martin Press, 1982.

Hackett, P. *Mountain Sickness.* New York: American Alpine Club Press, 1980.

Herben, George. *Picture Journeys in Alaska's Wrangell–Saint Elias.* Alaska Northwest Books, 1997.

Herrero, S. *Bear Attacks: Their Causes and Avoidance.* Guilford, CT: Globe Pequot Press, 1988 (reprint).

Houston, C. *Going Higher.* Boston: Little, Brown and Co., 1987.

Hubbard, Bernard. *Alaskan Odyssey.* London: R. Hale, 1952.

———. *Cradle of the Storms.* New York: Dodd, Mead and Co, 1935.

Krakauer, Jonathan. *Eiger Dreams.* New York: Bantam, Doubleday, Dell Publishing Group, 1990.

Marshall, Robert. *Arctic Wilderness.* Berkeley: University of California Press, 1956.

Miller, T. P. "Geothermal Resources of Alaska," in *The Geology of Alaska*, The Geology of North America series, v. G1, edited by George Plafker and H. C. Berg, pp. 979–987. Boulder, CO: Geological Society of America, 1994. '

Moore, Terris. *McKinley: The Pioneer Climbs.* 1967. Reprint, Seattle: The Mountaineers Books, 1981.

Mountaineering Rangers of Denali National Park and Preserve. *Mountaineering: Denali National Park and Preserve.* Talkeetna: Alaska Natural History Association, 1987.

Murie A. *Birds of Mt. McKinley.* McKinley Park, AK: Mount McKinley Natural History Association, 1963.

Murie, A. *Mammals of Denali.* Talkeetna, AK: Alaska Natural History Association, 1962.

Powers, P. *NOLS Wilderness Mountaineering.* Mechanicsburg, PA: Stackpole Books, 1993.

Pratt, V. E. and F. G. Pratt. *Wildflowers of Denali National Park.* Anchorage: Alaskakrafts, Inc., 1993.

Randall, G. *Mount McKinley Climber's Handbook.* Evergreen, CO: Chockstone Press, 1992.

Roberts, David. *The Mountain of My Fear* and *Deborah: A Wilderness Narrative.* Seattle: The Mountaineers Books, 1999.

Roper, Steve, and Allen Steck. *Fifty Classic Climbs.*

San Francisco: Sierra Club Books, 1979.

Selters, Andy. *Glacier Travel and Crevasse Rescue.* Seattle: The Mountaineers Books, 1999.

Sherwonit, Bill. *Alaska Ascents.* Anchorage: Alaska Northwest Books, 1996.

———.*To the Top of Denali.* Anchorage: Alaska Northwest Books, 1990.

Snyder, H. *Hall of the Mountain King.* New York: Charles Scribner's Sons, 1973.

Stuck, H. *The Ascent of Denali.* Prescott, AZ: Wolfe Publishing Company, 1988.

Tilton, B., and F. Hubbell. *Medicine for the Backcountry.* Merrillville, IN: ICS Books, 1995.

Tremper, Bruce. *Staying Alive in Avalanche Terrain.* Seattle: The Mountaineers Books, 2001.

Twight, Mark and James F. Martin. *Extreme Alpinism.* Seattle: The Mountaineers Books, 1999.

United States Geological Survey. 1909 and 1913 Annual Reports.

Walker, T. *Denali Journal.* Mechanicsburg, PA: Stackpole Books, 1992.

Washburn, Bradford. *Mount McKinley, Conquest of Denali.* New York: Harry N. Abrams, 1991.

———. "Mount McKinley from the North and West." *American Alpine Journal* (1947): 282–293.

———. "Mount McKinley: The West Buttress." *American Alpine Journal* (1952): 213–226.

———. "The Ascent of Mount St. Agnes," in *Alaska Ascents* edited by Bill Sherwonit. Anchorage: Alaska Northwest Books, 1996.

———. "The Conquest of Mount Crillon." *National Geographic* (1935): 361–400.

Waterman, Jonathan. *A Most Hostile Mountain: Recreating the Duke of Abruzzi's Historic Ascent of Mount Saint Elias.* New York: Henry Holt Publishing, 1997.

Waterman, Jonathan. *High Alaska: A Historical Guide to Denali, Mt. Foraker, and Mt. Hunter.* New York: American Alpine Club Press, 1988.

———. *Surviving Denali: A Study of Accidents on Mount McKinley, 1903-1990.* New York: American Alpine Club Press, 1991.

Werner, A. "Glacial Geology of the McKinley River Area." Master's thesis, Southern Illinois University, 1982.

Wilkerson, J., B. Cameron, and J. Hayward. *Hypothermia, Frostbite, and Other Cold Injuries.* Seattle: The Mountaineers Books, 1986.

Wilcox, J. *White Winds.* Los Alamitos, CA: Hwong Publishing Company, 1981.

Wilson, Rodman and Paul Crews Sr. *Todrillo: Pioneer Climbs and Flights in the Tordrillo Mountains of Alaska.* Anchorage: Todd Communications, 2000.

INDEX

ABOUT THE AUTHORS

MIKE WOOD began climbing in Alaska in 1991. He now lives in Talkeetna, Alaska, where he is a climber and carpenter. He also instructs and guides for the Alaska Mountaineering School and Alaska Denali Guiding.

COLBY COOMBS and his wife, Caitlin Palmer, live in Talkeetna, Alaska, and direct the Alaska Mountaineering School and Alaska Denali Guiding (*www.climbalaska.org*). Coombs's first climb in Alaska was Denali's West Buttress in 1985, and he has been climbing and instructing in Alaska ever since. He is also the author of *Denali's West Buttress: A Climber's Guide to Mount McKinley's Classic Route,* published by The Mountaineers Books.

THE MOUNTAINEERS, founded in 1906, is a nonprofit outdoor activity and conservation club, whose mission is "to explore, study, preserve, and enjoy the natural beauty of the outdoors. . . . " Based in Seattle, Washington, the club is now the third-largest such organization in the United States, with 15,000 members and five branches throughout Washington State.

The Mountaineers sponsors both classes and year-round outdoor activities in the Pacific Northwest, which include hiking, mountain climbing, ski-touring, snowshoeing, bicycling, camping, kayaking and canoeing, nature study, sailing, and adventure travel. The club's conservation division supports environmental causes through educational activities, sponsoring legislation, and presenting informational programs. All club activities are led by skilled, experienced volunteers, who are dedicated to promoting safe and responsible enjoyment and preservation of the outdoors.

If you would like to participate in these organized outdoor activities or the club's programs, consider a membership in The Mountaineers. For information and an application, write or call The Mountaineers, Club Headquarters, 300 Third Avenue West, Seattle, WA 98119; 206-284-6310.

The Mountaineers Books, an active, nonprofit publishing program of the club, produces guidebooks, instructional texts, historical works, natural history guides, and works on environmental conservation. All books produced by The Mountaineers Books fulfill the club's mission.

Send or call for our catalog of more than 500 outdoor titles:

The Mountaineers Books
1001 SW Klickitat Way, Suite 201
Seattle, WA 98134
800-553-4453
mbooks@mountaineersbooks.org
www.mountaineersbooks.org

 The Mountaineers Books is proud to be a corporate sponsor of Leave No Trace, whose mission is to promote and inspire responsible outdoor recreation through education, research, and partnerships. The Leave No Trace program is focused specifically on human-powered (nonmotorized) recreation.

Leave No Trace strives to educate visitors about the nature of their recreational impacts, as well as offer techniques to prevent and minimize such impacts. Leave No Trace is best understood as an educational and ethical program, not as a set of rules and regulations.

For more information, visit *www.LNT.org*, or call 800-332-4100.